Citrix XenApp® 7.5 Desktop Virtualization Solutions

Plan, design, optimize, and implement your XenApp® solution to mobilize your business

Andy Paul

BIRMINGHAM - MUMBAI

Citrix XenApp® 7.5 Desktop Virtualization Solutions

First published: October 2014

Production reference: 1141014

Published by Packt Publishing Ltd.
Livery Place
35 Livery Street
Birmingham B3 2PB, UK.

ISBN 978-1-84968-968-7

www.packtpub.com

Cover image by Shivani (shivani6@gmail.com)

Credits

Author
Andy Paul

Reviewers
Markus Darda

Ben Piper

Neil Spellings

Acquisition Editors
Pramila Balan

Meeta Rajani

Content Development Editor
Shubhangi Dhamgaye

Technical Editor
Shruti Rawool

Copy Editors
Insiya Morbiwala

Sayanee Mukherjee

Aditya Nair

Stuti Srivastava

Project Coordinator
Venitha Cutinho

Proofreaders
Simran Bhogal

Ameesha Green

Paul Hindle

Indexers
Hemangini Bari

Mariammal Chettiyar

Rekha Nair

Production Coordinator
Conidon Miranda

Cover Work
Conidon Miranda

Notice

About the Author

Andy Paul is an accomplished virtualization architect, instructor, and speaker. He has designed and delivered virtualization projects for Fortune 500 companies, public and private health care organizations, and higher education institutions. He has also served as a lead technical trainer, adjunct professor, and guest speaker for multiple organizations.

He is a leading industry consultant. He currently manages multiple delivery teams, oversees project architecture, assists large enterprise customers across various industries, and is a global VDI subject matter expert.

Visit his blog at www.paultechnologies.com/blog.

My wife, Mandy; our three beautiful children; and my parents, Steve and Vicki—thank you for always encouraging and supporting me.

To my mentors, Steve Bone and David Lennox, for helping me stretch and reach further than I ever expected. For all of your guidance and friendship over the years, thank you.

About the Reviewers

Markus Darda is the owner of MD Consultancy (Germany) and DaComp GmbH (Switzerland). As a senior Citrix engineer and architect, he works for enterprise customers across Europe to design and implement Citrix (XenApp and XenDesktop) environments. As a Citrix trainer, he teaches all the Citrix products to customers and works for Citrix as a subject matter expert in different courseware and exams.

He has worked for Lanxess, Germany; T-Systems, Germany; Koenen en Co, the Netherlands; and for companies in Switzerland, Sweden, and Norway.

He has worked on different courseware from Citrix.

Ben Piper is a hands-on IT consultant, network and systems engineer, developer, and author specializing in advanced enterprise networking and virtualization technologies, including Cisco, Citrix, Microsoft, RedHat Enterprise Linux, and VMware. He has over 10 years of experience designing and implementing technology and consulting for organizations such as McKesson, the National Science Center, the Department of Veterans Affairs, as well as dozens of hospitals, health care organizations, and small businesses. He has numerous Cisco, Citrix, and Microsoft certifications. He has authored technology content for ExecSense and Corp! Magazine, and his technology advice has been featured on news media outlets, including CNBC, Investor's Business Daily, NASDAQ, and Monster.com. His consulting website, `http://benpiper.com`, provides a variety of free resources for Citrix, Cisco, Linux, VMware, scripting, coding, and more.

Neil Spellings is an independent virtualization and cloud infrastructure consultant who has been working with Citrix products since the early days of WinFrame and MetaFrame, and he was instrumental in the initial deployments of server-based computing technologies for a number of large financial institutions in the UK and Europe.

He is a Citrix Certified Expert - Virtualization and is certified across numerous other Citrix and Microsoft products to give a balanced view of the virtualization marketplace. He is a recognized subject matter expert by Citrix Education and has contributed questions to numerous XenApp 6, 6.5 CCA, CCAA, and CCEE exams, and he has also helped write the recent XenDesktop 7 Design exam.

He is an active member of the Citrix community in the UK. He usually travels around Europe to both present and attend E2E/PubForum events, such as Synergy; he is one of the founding members of the UK Citrix user group and remains on its steering group. He blogs at `http://neil.spellings.net` and frequently shares his opinions on Twitter via `@neilspellings`.

He was awarded the Citrix Technology Professional (CTP) status in 2013 for his contributions to the community.

He is a STEM ambassador and runs a Code Club in a local primary school with the ambition to inspire and encourage children to take up a career in ICT and learn to code.

He lives in Surrey, England with his wife, Ina, and 6-year-old daughter, Zoë.

www.PacktPub.com

Support files, eBooks, discount offers, and more

You might want to visit www.PacktPub.com for support files and downloads related to your book.

Did you know that Packt offers eBook versions of every book published, with PDF and ePub files available? You can upgrade to the eBook version at www.PacktPub.com and as a print book customer, you are entitled to a discount on the eBook copy. Get in touch with us at service@packtpub.com for more details.

At www.PacktPub.com, you can also read a collection of free technical articles, sign up for a range of free newsletters and receive exclusive discounts and offers on Packt books and eBooks.

http://PacktLib.PacktPub.com

Do you need instant solutions to your IT questions? PacktLib is Packt's online digital book library. Here, you can access, read and search across Packt's entire library of books.

Why subscribe?

- Fully searchable across every book published by Packt
- Copy and paste, print and bookmark content
- On demand and accessible via web browser

Free access for Packt account holders

If you have an account with Packt at www.PacktPub.com, you can use this to access PacktLib today and view nine entirely free books. Simply use your login credentials for immediate access.

Instant updates on new Packt books

Get notified! Find out when new books are published by following @PacktEnterprise on Twitter, or the *Packt Enterprise* Facebook page.

Table of Contents

Preface

Designing Citrix XenApp 7.5 as the basis for a desktop virtualization solution requires extensive planning. There are numerous options and scenarios to consider. Taking the time to properly plan and then execute is key to any successful deployment.

This book covers how to use Citrix XenApp 7.5 for desktop virtualization solutions. XenApp can be classified as both application virtualization as well as desktop virtualization. When using XenApp, you can provide end user access to select applications or an entire virtual desktop. Providing a virtual desktop with XenApp is also known as using the Hosted Shared Desktop (HSD) model. This means that multiple users can share the same desktop with common resources as opposed to a dedicated desktop.

What this book covers

Chapter 1, *Planning Desktop Virtualization*, provides an overview of desktop virtualization and the associated components. This includes an overview of the building blocks of VDI and determining the right fit for your environment.

Chapter 2, *Defining Your Desktop Virtualization Environment*, focuses on understanding the business requirements and driving factors of your virtual desktop strategy, including creating use cases by understanding your users and applications as well as planning your overall VDI strategy.

Chapter 3, *Designing Your Infrastructure*, explains how to design and scale the core infrastructure to host your XenApp solution. This involves creating high-level reference architectures and planning the virtual, physical, networking, and storage infrastructures.

Chapter 4, *Designing Your Access Layer*, explains how to design the Access layer components, including NetScaler and StoreFront, delving into the design specifics and identifying any constraints.

Chapter 5, *Designing Your Application Delivery Layer*, explains how to design the Application Delivery layer components, including all of the XenApp site design elements such as controllers, session hosts, Delivery Groups, and application publishing models.

Chapter 6, *Designing Your Virtual Image Delivery*, focuses on workload imaging services and delivery. This includes an overview of Provisioning Services and Machine Creation Services as well as best practices and recommendations.

Chapter 7, *Designing Your Supporting Infrastructure Components*, focuses on the remaining supporting components for the XenApp solution, including licensing, database requirements, monitoring services, and print services.

Chapter 8, *Optimizing Your XenApp® Solution*, focuses on the auxiliary components that can be used to further optimize and customize the XenApp environment. This includes profile management, Citrix policies, Active Directory policies, and printing considerations.

Chapter 9, *Implementing Your XenApp® Solution*, covers the final steps to implement a XenApp solution. It focuses on building the desktop and applications for delivery, capacity planning, load testing, user acceptance testing, and production rollout planning.

What you need for this book

This is based on Citrix XenApp 7.5 Platinum Edition and all its associated components, including StoreFront 2.5, License Server 11.11, and Provisioning Services 7.1. We will also take a look at XenServer 6.0.2, Citrix NetScaler 10.1, Microsoft SQL Server 2012, and Microsoft File Services.

In order to recreate the steps in this manual, you will need a minimum of two Windows Server 2008 R2 or Windows Server 2012 systems, preferably more. You will also need the downloadable Citrix XenApp 7.5 media from www.citrix.com.

Who this book is for

This book is written for Citrix engineers, Citrix architects, virtualization consultants, and IT project managers. It is assumed that the reader has some prior experience with Citrix XenApp and related technologies or with desktop virtualization. However, prior experience is not required to understand the main concepts and flow of the material presented.

This book attempts to balance technical detail and business logic. Each topic is written using an easy-to-follow guide based on real-world experience and explains the reasoning behind the recommended design decisions.

Introduction to the XenApp® 7.5 platform

Before we delve too deep into desktop virtualization solutions, you need to first understand more about Citrix XenApp. Citrix XenApp was previously known as Citrix Presentation Server. Prior to that, it was also known as Citrix MetaFrame Server and Citrix WinFrame Server. You may hear some of these other terms or see them mentioned in other articles or legacy documentation. With the introduction of Citrix XenDesktop 7, XenApp and XenDesktop were merged into a common code base. The material presented in this book for XenApp 7.5 applies to XenDesktop 7.5 environments as well.

Citrix XenApp operates on top of Microsoft Remote Desktop Services, also known as Terminal Services or Remote Desktop Session Host. XenApp contains its own management suite (called Studio) as well as its own transportation protocol (ICA, short for Independent Computing Architecture). The combination of management and streamlined protocol has allowed Citrix to maintain status as the industry leader in application and desktop virtualization. Combining this with other products of Citrix allows enterprises to create secure and scalable virtualization solutions.

In its most simplistic form, Citrix virtualization is about enabling users to use their applications from any device anywhere. If a user is not able to use his/her applications effectively, then there is little point to virtualization. Even in a traditional desktop environment, Citrix can be leveraged to deliver applications to users in a secure and scalable fashion.

In most environments, XenApp can deliver the entire desktop and application set. In other environments, you may see a mix of XenApp and XenDesktop, as shown in the following figure:

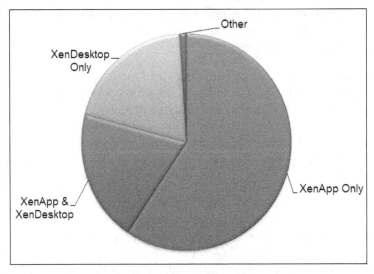

The distribution of XenApp and XenDesktop in VDI consulting engagements

Benefits of using Citrix XenApp®

The key objective in all of this is to allow users to remotely interact with applications. If a user is not able to use their application effectively, then there is no reason for businesses to invest in virtualization. Using remote applications with Citrix XenApp offers numerous benefits; they are outlined in the following table.

The following benefits illustrate why organizations, large and small, see the value of using Citrix XenApp for their virtualization solution. There may be additional benefits for your organization as well, such as:

Benefit	Description
Accessibility	Using the latest Citrix Receiver allows users to access their Citrix XenApp applications and desktops from virtually any device and any location in the world.
Compliance	Many industries, including health care and finance, have strict regulations governing computer systems. These regulations could include software applications, versioning control, and data security. By using XenApp, you centrally control the applications and the data.

Consistency	Since the applications and data are managed within the data center, users have a common and consistent experience regardless of their client device. A user who is accessing applications from home has the same experience as those accessing their applications from their office PC.
Convenience	Administrators can manage applications from a single console. Users can access all applications from a single portal. This provides convenience and ease of use for everyone.
Management	The central management of applications and desktops and their maintenance allows ease of administration.
Monitoring	By keeping all operations in the data center, you can effectively monitor the XenApp environment to ensure optimal performance. This also allows the effective auditing of users and application access, where required.
Portability	Citrix XenApp enables a flexible workforce, including BYOD users, work-at-home users, office employees, and road warriors.
Reliability	The ICA protocol, used by Citrix XenApp, is built to create a reliable and stable remote connection.
Scalability	Citrix XenApp can rapidly scale both up and out to support a growing number of applications or users, or both.
Security	Keeping all data and data operations within the data center ensures that there is no sensitive information leaving the secure zone. Since none of the data resides on the client device, there is limited risk of data loss.
Stability	Citrix XenApp can be built on robust hardware configured for fault tolerance and High Availability. This ensures a level of stability and minimal downtime, thus ensuring a production environment.

Citrix XenApp® 7.5 feature comparison

This book is written about XenApp 7.5 Platinum Edition. This feature set was chosen because it is the most current XenApp release at the time of writing, as well as the most feature rich one. The following table shows the feature comparison between the different XenApp licensing levels. Note that while Platinum Edition is the most expensive, it is also the most common in enterprise environments. Also, since XenApp 7.5 and XenDesktop 7.5 use the same code base, many of the features overlap.

	Advanced	Enterprise	Platinum
Application access			
Enterprise App Store	X	X	X
Microsoft App-V Integration	X	X	X
Offline applications		X	X
Server-hosted applications	X	X	X
Session virtualization	X	X	X
VM-hosted applications		X	X
Supported devices			
Browser-based access	X	X	X
Linux	X	X	X
Mac	X	X	X
Smartphone	X	X	X
Tablet	X	X	X
Thin client	X	X	X
Windows	X	X	X
User experience			
HDX 3D Pro		X	X
HDX mobile	X	X	X
HDX seamless local applications			X
HDX user experience optimization	X	X	X
HDX vGPU sharing		X	X
Unified communications optimization		X	X
WAN optimization	X	X	X
Image management			
Amazon AWS integration		X	X
Delivery Group assignment	X	X	X
Hybrid cloud provisioning		X	X
Machine Creation Services	X	X	X
Profile Management	X	X	X
Provisioning Services		Limited	X

	Advanced	Enterprise	Platinum
Scalability			
Centralized management	X	X	X
Enterprise scalability	X	X	X
High Availability and failover	X	X	X
Hypervisor agnostic	X	X	X
SCCM integration		X	X
Security			
Two-factor authentication support	X	X	X
Centrally secured applications	X	X	X
Centrally secured desktops	X	X	X
Encrypted application access	X	X	X
File and data containment	X	X	X
NetScaler Gateway universal license			X
SmartAccess			X
SSL VPN			X
Manageability			
AppDNA			X
Configuration logging		X	X
Delegated administration		X	X
Enhanced monitoring		X	X
Historical performance trending			X
Simple to deploy	X	X	X
User experience network analysis			X

For a comparison of XenApp features across different product versions as well as licensing levels, visit `http://www.citrix.com/go/products/xendesktop/feature-matrix.html`.

Comparing Citrix XenApp® 7.5 with previous versions

The following table compares terms and concepts previously used in earlier versions of XenApp with the equivalent or replacement terms and concepts in XenApp 7.5:

Previous XenApp versions	New XenApp 7.5 nomenclature
Independent Management Architecture (IMA)	FlexCast Management Architecture (FMA)
Farm	Delivery Site
Worker Group	Session Machine Catalog
	Delivery Group
Worker	Virtual Delivery Agent (VDA)
	Server OS machine
	Desktop OS machine
Zone and data collector	Delivery Controller
Delivery Services Console	Citrix Studio and Citrix Director
Publishing applications	Delivering applications
Data store	Database
Load evaluator	Load management policy
Administrator	Delegated Administrator
	Role
	Scope

What's new in Citrix XenApp® 7.5

The following features are new in XenApp 7.5 / XenDesktop 7.5:

- XenApp built on FlexCast management
- A single management console (Citrix Studio)
- A monitoring and troubleshooting console (Citrix Director) with integrated EdgeSight features
- Cloud deployments
- Full AppDNA support

- StoreFront 2.5
- Extended support for Web Interface 5.4
- Remote power control for physical PCs

The following features are added as part of XenDesktop 7.1:

- GPU integration
- vGPU sharing
- Windows Server 2012 R2 and Windows 8.1 support

The following features are added as part of XenDesktop 7:

- A machine catalog for server OS and desktop OS machines
- A machine catalog for applications
- Windows Server 2012 and Windows 8 support
- Desktop composition redirection
- Windows Media client-side content fetching
- Multicast support
- Real-time multimedia transcoding
- User Datagram Protocol (UDP) audio for server OS machines
- Webcam video compression
- HDX 3D Pro
- Server-rendered rich graphics and video
- Improved Flash Redirection
- Streamlined installer
- Profile management
- Configuration logging
- Desktop Director with EdgeSight features
- Delegated administration
- Personal vDisk
- Machine Creation Services (MCS) support for Microsoft Key Management System (KMS) activation
- Multitouch support
- Remote PC access
- Universal Print Server

Conventions

In this book, you will find a number of styles of text that distinguish between different kinds of information. Here are some examples of these styles and an explanation of their meaning.

Code words in text, database table names, folder names, filenames, file extensions, pathnames, dummy URLs, user input, and Twitter handles are shown as follows: "This was accomplished by placing the application in a folder called VDIOnly and hiding this folder."

A block of code is set as follows:

```
select UserID, StartDate, MachineID from [MonitorData].[Session]
where userID = 2
order by StartDate DESC
```

Any command-line input or output is written as follows:

```
# cp /usr/src/asterisk-addons/configs/cdr_mysql.conf.sample
    /etc/asterisk/cdr_mysql.conf
```

New terms and **important words** are shown in bold. Words that you see on the screen, in menus or dialog boxes for example, appear in the text like this: "Click on **Retrieve Attributes to verify**."

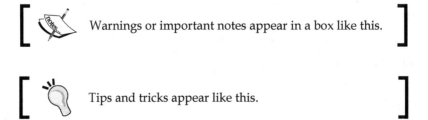

Warnings or important notes appear in a box like this.

Tips and tricks appear like this.

Reader feedback

Feedback from our readers is always welcome. Let us know what you think about this book—what you liked or may have disliked. Reader feedback is important for us to develop titles that you really get the most out of.

To send us general feedback, simply send an e-mail to feedback@packtpub.com, and mention the book title via the subject of your message.

If there is a topic that you have expertise in and you are interested in either writing or contributing to a book, see our author guide on www.packtpub.com/authors.

Customer support

Now that you are the proud owner of a Packt book, we have a number of things to help you to get the most from your purchase.

Downloading the color images of this book

We also provide you a PDF file that has color images of the screenshots/diagrams used in this book. The color images will help you better understand the changes in the output. You can download this file from: `https://www.packtpub.com/sites/default/files/downloads/9687EN_ColoredImages.pdf`.

Errata

Although we have taken every care to ensure the accuracy of our content, mistakes do happen. If you find a mistake in one of our books—maybe a mistake in the text or the code—we would be grateful if you would report this to us. By doing so, you can save other readers from frustration and help us improve subsequent versions of this book. If you find any errata, please report them by visiting `http://www.packtpub.com/submit-errata`, selecting your book, clicking on the **erratasubmissionform** link, and entering the details of your errata. Once your errata are verified, your submission will be accepted and the errata will be uploaded on our website, or added to any list of existing errata, under the Errata section of that title. Any existing errata can be viewed by selecting your title from `http://www.packtpub.com/support`.

Piracy

Piracy of copyright material on the Internet is an ongoing problem across all media. At Packt, we take the protection of our copyright and licenses very seriously. If you come across any illegal copies of our works, in any form, on the Internet, please provide us with the location address or website name immediately so that we can pursue a remedy.

Please contact us at `copyright@packtpub.com` with a link to the suspected pirated material.

We appreciate your help in protecting our authors, and our ability to bring you valuable content.

Questions

You can contact us at `questions@packtpub.com` if you are having a problem with any aspect of the book, and we will do our best to address it.

1
Planning Desktop Virtualization

Planning for desktop virtualization requires understanding the building blocks of Virtual Desktop Infrastructure, commonly referred to as VDI. This entails not only understanding the technical components of VDI, but also the business drivers and how VDI fits into your overall environment. Mapping your business objectives with the proper technology should be the ultimate goal of any VDI project.

In this chapter, you will learn about the following:

- The building blocks of VDI
- VDI layers
- How to determine the right fit for your environment
- The road map to success
- Managing your project

The building blocks of VDI

The first step in understanding **Virtual Desktop Infrastructure (VDI)** is to identify what VDI means to your environment. VDI is an all-encompassing term for most virtual infrastructure projects. For this book, we will use the definitions cited in the following sections for clarity.

Hosted Virtual Desktop (HVD)

Hosted Virtual Desktop is a machine running a single-user operating system such as Windows 7 or Windows 8, sometimes called a **desktop OS**, which is hosted on a virtual platform within the data center. Users remotely access a desktop that may or may not be dedicated but runs with isolated resources. This is typically a Citrix XenDesktop virtual desktop, as shown in the following figure:

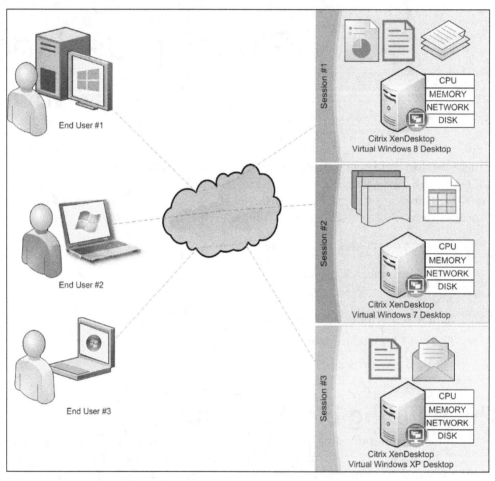

Hosted Virtual Desktop model; each user has dedicated resources

Hosted Shared Desktop (HSD)

Hosted Shared Desktop is a machine running a multiuser operating system such as Windows 2008 Server or Windows 2012 Server, sometimes called a **server OS**, possibly hosted on a virtual platform within the data center. Users remotely access a desktop that may be using shared resources among multiple users. This will historically be a Citrix XenApp published desktop, as demonstrated in the following figure:

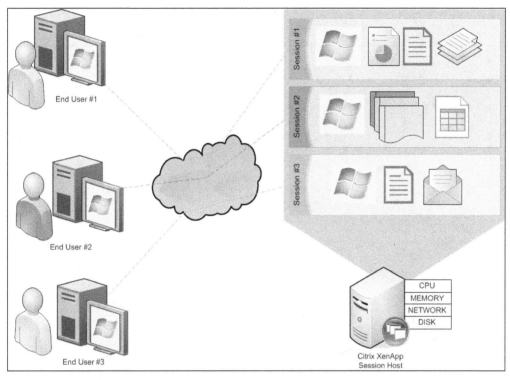

Hosted Shared Desktop model; each user shares the desktop server resources

Session-based Computing (SBC)

With Session-based Computing, users remotely access applications or other resources on a server running in the data center. These are typically client/server applications. This server may or may not be virtualized. This is a multiuser environment, but the users do not access the underlying operating system directly. This will typically be a Citrix XenApp hosted application, as shown in the following figure:

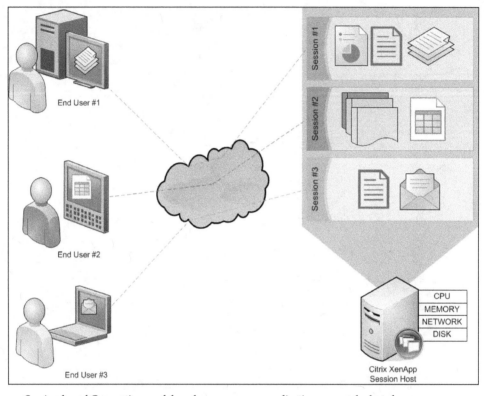

Session-based Computing model; each user accesses applications remotely, but shares resources

Application virtualization

In application virtualization, applications are centrally managed and distributed, but they are locally executed. This may be in conjunction with, or separate from, the other options mentioned previously. Application virtualization typically involves application isolation, allowing the applications to operate independently of any other software. This will be an example of Citrix XenApp offline applications as well as Citrix profiled applications, Microsoft App-V application packages, and VMware ThinApp solutions. Have a look at the following figure:

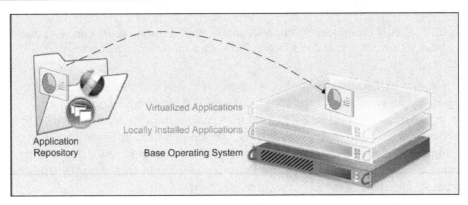

Application virtualization model; the application packages execute locally

The preceding list is not a definitive list of options, but it serves to highlight the most commonly used elements of VDI. Other options include client-side hypervisors for local execution of a virtual desktop, hosted physical desktops, and cloud-based applications. Depending on the environment, all of these components can be relevant.

Understanding VDI layers

Before engaging in a virtual desktop solution, the key question is, "What do you need?" As a virtualization architect, I have been involved in countless design and implementation projects. These range from simple proof-of-concept projects for 200 users to migrations for global implementations of 30,000 users. I have seen too many projects fail simply because the right questions were never asked.

One of the first items to determine is which flavor or flavors of VDI to use. Will traditional session-based computing (for example, hosted applications only) suffice or do you need to provide a full desktop? Will users need dedicated resources or can they share resources? Which applications will be available within the VDI space; all or just the most critical? How tightly controlled or locked down will you want this new environment to be? As you can imagine, there is no right and simple answer. In most environments, the answer is a mixed-bag solution.

When considering VDI, there are many factors to choose from, all of which will impact the design decisions. These factors include application compatibility (first and foremost), performance, manageability, scalability, storage, upfront capital costs, and long-term operating costs. Additional factors are reliability, ease of use, mobility, flexibility, recoverability, fault tolerance, and security. In the end, a technology solution should be there to support the business; the business should not be there to support the chosen technology. This means that IT departments cannot work in a vacuum. The driving forces must be what is good for the business and what empowers the application users.

Any technology solution should be there to support the business; the business should not be there to support the chosen technology.

Your choice of VDI solution should be based on your business needs. To fully understand your needs and how they relate to VDI, your entire computing environment must be analyzed. The factors to understand when preparing for a virtual desktop solution include user data, personalization, application management, image management, and device management. These are business drivers that illustrate how users work in the current environment, and they must be understood for successful adaptation in any new environment.

Analyzing your user data

User data includes personal documents, application data, and shared corporate data, all of which must be identified and managed. Home drive assignment, folder redirection, profile management, exclusions, and file synchronization are all viable methods to manage user data in a VDI environment. In order to gain the full benefits of mobility and flexibility within VDI, user data should be managed as its own layer to keep it separate from the operating system, as shown in the following figure:

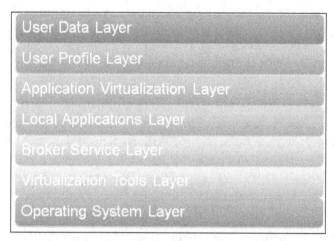

Virtual machine layers

Planning your personalization layer

User personalization settings are commonly known as profiles. Profiles typically include mission-critical elements such as core application settings and non-critical items such as favorites, backgrounds, and pictures. Although the non-critical elements may seem mundane, they are often necessary to ensure end-user satisfaction and acceptance. Profile management (or lack thereof) can greatly impede performance metrics measured around logon and logoff times when profiles are loaded or unloaded. Profile management is also essential to enable smooth roaming capabilities. Organizations will differ on how much personalization is allowed (none to virtually everything); it is important to identify what to allow and then optimize its management. We'll cover this in more detail in *Chapter 2, Defining Your Desktop Virtualization Environment.*

 User data and personalization impact the end users' perception of the environment. A negative perception by users can cause virtual desktop environments to fail through lack of acceptance.

Understanding your applications

Application management involves understanding not only which applications are installed, but also what and how they are used. Usage includes data requirements, compute resource consumption, companion applications, network bandwidth utilization, and access patterns (for example, are there midmorning or afternoon spikes, is the application only used at certain times such as during month-end batch processing, do users run the application consistently all day long, and so on). All of these considerations are used to build an application profile. Properly gauging application profiles is important to scale your environment with the proper amount of resources. Underpowered systems will become sluggish and hamper implementation, while overpowered solutions might unnecessarily consume resources, driving up the project costs.

Application delivery identifies how applications are delivered to the end user. This may primarily be dependent on application compatibility and interoperability. Some applications may need to be locally installed as part of the base image, others may be streamed as part of virtualization, and some may be hosted on application servers. Other determining factors include maintenance schedules such as update and patch frequency. Determining how and where applications are delivered may impact the overall solution. This will be covered in more detail in *Chapter 5, Designing Your Application Delivery Layer.*

Planning for operating system delivery

Image management is used to control the delivery and changes to base operating system images. This includes the initial base image design (operating system, core applications, and common utilities), patch management, antivirus configurations, application delivery, and version controls. Factors to consider are provisioning methods and finding a balance between common and unique elements. *Chapter 6, Designing Your Virtual Image Delivery*, deals with image management in more detail.

Anticipating device management

Device management is often an afterthought in many virtualization projects, but it should be considered upfront. It is not enough to consider whether you will use mobile devices; you should also identify which mobile platforms you will support. Other considerations are thin clients, laptops, repurposed desktops, kiosks, multimedia stations, and so on. Along with the device type, peripherals must be understood. Is there any specialty equipment or add-ons that are required for your environment, such as scanners, badge readers, or custom printers? Determine which types of endpoint devices might impact functional requirements.

 Understanding application workloads and user requirements is the biggest piece of the VDI puzzle. Choosing the right VDI technology is reliant upon completely understanding your environment and business objectives.

Defining your business use cases helps map users, devices, and requirements into a usable format. Business cases will vary in scope and detail; each case has its own usage and delivery requirements that might be unique. VDI does not include a one-size-fits-all solution; it should be designed with as much flexibility as possible. We will examine use cases more in *Chapter 2, Defining Your Desktop Virtualization Environment*.

Infrastructure planning

The entire virtual desktop solution will still need physical infrastructure to support operations. This infrastructure will need to be designed for cost, scalability, and reliability. This includes analyzing your current capabilities to determine whether you can grow your current infrastructure or if you need to create a brand new design. Some organizations will choose new environments as part of a capital project budget. This aids in design and deployment since it becomes a parallel effort to existing operations. *Chapter 3, Designing Your Infrastructure*, will explore infrastructure design in detail. Have a look at the following figure:

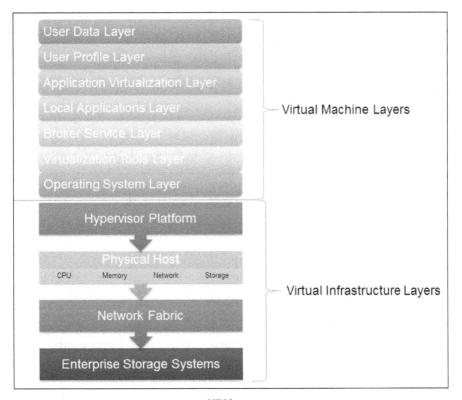

VDI layers

Determining the right fit

With so many layers and so many options from Citrix (as well as other vendors), the challenge becomes determining the right fit for your environment. There is no easy answer to this conundrum since each organization is different, with diverse goals and objectives.

The following are multiple real-world examples from consulting engagements. These may help you decide which types of VDI are the right fit for you:

- **XenApp for scalability**: A Fortune 500 insurance company was designing a new **Bring Your Own Device (BYOD)** initiative. This organization had well-defined use cases and a strong team providing central management. Hence, they decided everything can run on a hosted, shared desktop model on physical servers. This allowed them the greatest possible user density by leveraging shared resources among all users, thus reducing the total cost of ownership.

- **XenApp as a proven technology**: A global food-services organization was considering a secure computing environment for offshore contractors. When looking at VDI options, they felt many vendors and products were capable of delivering the necessary applications and performance. This company ultimately decided to focus on server-hosted applications to provide utmost flexibility with the lowest overhead. They went with XenApp because this was a proven technology and the market leader, with strong support both internally and externally.

- **XenDesktop for application compatibility**: A leading personal credit lending organization was migrating to a centralized data center model with the added goal of using lightweight thin clients for data entry. This initiative was started in order to better manage secure access to their data and provide workforce flexibility for their call centers. A major concern was that their primary line of business application was only supported on Windows desktop operating systems. In order to meet all requirements, a XenDesktop solution was deemed necessary. Since all their users used the same applications, with no variance, they were able to achieve a company-wide solution with limited design constraints.

- **XenApp for application hosting**: A healthcare software development firm needed a mature product to deliver their custom application suite to subscribers in the home-health field. The platform required secure remote access to the patients' data applications within a centralized database. Their business model required a scalable and mature product set using session-based computing for the hosted application, with high levels of fault tolerance.

- **XenDesktop for peripheral support**: A medical school was already using thin clients to deliver hosted XenApp applications from within their data center. Through a green initiative, they needed to deploy digital radiology and eliminate X-rays developed on film. This would speed the X-ray viewing process, and it would also reduce the cost and chemicals associated with film development. The new equipment required enhanced USB support and 32-bit graphics to achieve the proper resolution.

- **XenApp as a desktop replacement**: A regional university needed to have a highly scalable and secure desktop replacement for all classrooms and student labs. They needed a solution to replace managing high-risk workstations containing local applications. The solution was a two-tiered XenApp environment: one collection of session hosts provided a published desktop with primary applications locally installed and the second collection of session hosts provided specialty applications on demand.

- **XenDesktop for resource isolation**: A major landscape management company was facing resource issues with their primary route planning and mapping software. They were leveraging XenApp for all applications in a hosted shared environment. When the route planners used the geographical information software to plan the drivers' routes, the intense calculation consumed the bulk of the server's shared CPU and memory resources. This degraded the performance for other users. Moving the geographical and routing software packages into a desktop image, the customer was able to dedicate and isolate resources, so other users were not affected by the processes.

- **XenDesktop for enhanced graphics**: A global manufacturing client needed to provide detailed 3D graphics for its computer-aided design systems supporting engineers working remotely. Instead of investing in expensive laptops, the client chose blade PCs for XenDesktop with advanced graphics cards. This allowed the facility to centrally control the images and data, while still meeting the performance and graphical requirements of the design engineers.

- **XenApp for consolidation**: A national food services company was in the process of acquiring additional companies and consolidating disperse operations. As part of this initiative, they needed to move over 100 different lines of business applications spread across five different data centers. To accomplish this, a new XenApp environment was designed and deployed based on a new consolidated server image.

"There is no right or wrong answer when deciding between a XenDesktop or XenApp solution as either one works in most use-case scenarios. In evaluating the technical criteria and value of each option, the final decision often comes down to comfort and familiarity." – Dan Feller, Lead Architect, Citrix Systems

The road map to success

Just like there is no one solution to VDI, there is no magic bullet when it comes to a successful deployment. However, there are some tried and true elements, demonstrated in the following figure, which will help you succeed:

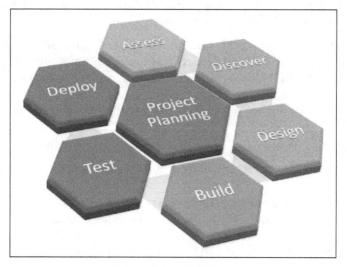

Basic project methodology

The basic methodology of any IT project should follow something like this:

- **Assess**: Assess your environment to determine what you currently have and what you need. This is one of the most critical elements since it includes your business case development and established criteria for success.

- **Discover**: Discover your existing infrastructure. This is ultimately an extension of the assessment phase, but it is focused more on technical capabilities.

- **Design**: Design a new environment or enhance an existing environment. This design should be a comprehensive architectural plan and should take numerous iterations to finalize. This design plan can be used as a build guide and should be revised as changes are implemented. All design plans should include items such as system architecture, scalability, risk identification, and disaster recovery planning.

- **Build**: Build the environment. Most environments start with a proof-of-concept build to validate the design and technological components. The build phase may induce changes to the overall design, so all baselines should be updated. The build process should include iterative testing as components are brought online.

- **Test**: Test the environment to ensure functionality. This includes unit-level testing to ensure the components operate as designed, which is generally included as part of the build process. This also includes user acceptance testing. This will be discussed in more detail in *Chapter 9, Implementing Your XenApp® Solution*

- **Deploy**: Deploy the environment to end users. Start with a small pilot deployment with a limited number of power users. Once the pilot is complete, assuming success, a phased deployment approach for production should be planned. This will ensure full acceptance by users and limit the impact of any previously unknown issues. Monitoring is a continuation of deployment, helping validate that the environment reaches a steady state of operations.

A good friend of mine once said, "Users don't remember WHEN you go live, they remember HOW you go live." It is more important, in the long term, to ensure everything is right and functional rather than delivered on an arbitrary delivery date.

Project management in the real world

I use a slightly different model when deploying virtual desktop solutions. The first and foremost phase is assessment and discovery. The focus should be on high-level strategy and business drivers during this phase. This is the most critical element since all future decisions will hinge on this analysis. Once all the requirements and expectations are defined, determining the best solution for your environment can proceed.

Once the base analysis is complete, the project moves to a design phase. During design, the results of analysis and business requirements are translated into a high-level technical architecture. This includes determining the hardware, software, and all infrastructure components. Once approved, this high-level architecture becomes the design plan.

During the build phase, all of the technology and infrastructure is put in place. This might include building out the data center presence or simply creating the VDI components on top of the existing infrastructure. Once a base build is complete, the environment is ready to test and validate.

The testing phase should include base functionality testing, capacity testing, application integration testing, and user acceptance testing. Testing results are used not only to validate functionality and performance, but also to validate scalability and design decisions. If testing reveals a change in the baseline, the design should be modified as well. Testing is an iterative process that must be repeated with each change to ensure optimal quality and project success.

In smaller environments, or when time is sensitive, the design, build, and testing phases can be consolidated into a single effort (building and testing while designing). However, this is risky and can sometimes lead to delays or overruns.

[Pick any two: Good, fast, and cheap.]

The pilot phase should be integrated as part of the overall project plan. This may be part of the testing and validation phase, or it may occur once the initial testing is complete. Successful pilot programs are phased in to increase server loads and user counts, and they should encompass multiple use case scenarios. A pilot should mimic production just on a smaller scale. Pilot testing results may lead to baseline or design changes, and subsequent testing cycles may be necessary. However, note that an extensive pilot program is critical to organizational acceptance and project success. You are better off identifying critical issues during a small pilot phase than during a major production rollout.

The last step, of course, is production rollout. Production rollout should be established in phases to keep support manageable as well as to monitor impact on the infrastructure and the overall system performance. An often overlooked key component to production rollout is communication. This includes setting management and end user expectations properly and user training. Open communication will also ease concerns users may have over the state of their desktop. The time spent properly communicating, or over communicating, is quickly recouped through reduced help desk calls.

The following diagram represents the iterative process of IT project management. Notice the weight on analysis as well as the iterative processes, check points, and the phased rollout:

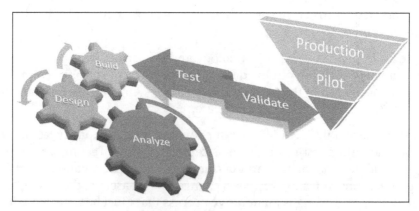

Enhanced project methodology

Managing your project

Communication is critical not just for customer satisfaction, but also to manage the project as a whole, including identifying any changes in scope, timelines, and budget. There are six key factors to ensure your project is successful, which are:

- Managing the scope (what is being done)
- Managing the schedule (timelines)
- Managing the budget (avoiding cost overruns)
- Ensuring quality (everything works as planned)
- Managing risk factors (avoiding the big pitfalls)
- Ensuring customer satisfaction (did you meet the project goals)

The following figure represents the six components for successful project management:

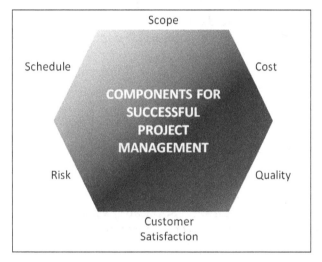

Project management components

Customer satisfaction is critical. This is often overlooked in the IT world as our customers are commonly our coworkers. I was involved in one project that was on time, on budget, and worked. However, the project was a failure because the end users were never properly assessed and what was delivered was not what was needed or wanted.

According to a 2012 survey by McKinsey & Company of large IT projects:

- 45 percent go over budget
- 7 percent go over time
- 56 percent deliver less value
- 17 percent fail so miserably that they threaten the company's existence

 My good friend from the Marines likes to remind me of their saying, "Slow is fast." This means that slow is smooth, smooth is fast, therefore slow is fast. In other words, you can't rush quality.

Summary

In this chapter, we explored the building blocks of a virtual desktop infrastructure. We looked at different models to deliver virtual desktops, including hosted virtual desktops, hosted shared desktops, session-based computing, and application virtualization. We also discussed the various layers of desktop virtualization and we looked at scenarios to help determine the right fit for your environment. You may find that you will need a mix of models and solutions, which is not uncommon.

In addition to looking at the various virtual desktop components, we also discussed building a road map to success. It is not good enough to have a proper design; you must be able to deliver the design successfully. To do so requires some project planning and project management skills, the most notable of which is communication.

In the next chapter, we will look at further defining our virtual desktop environment, including understanding our users and applications in order to build our use cases. We will also look at assessing our current environment and fine tuning our strategy for our new environment.

2
Defining Your Desktop Virtualization Environment

In the previous chapter, we explored the building blocks of a virtual desktop infrastructure. We looked at different VDI components and models, including desktop- and server-based solutions. We also discussed the various layers of a VDI model.

Now that we understand the basic layers, we can begin defining our business requirements and driving factors for our solution. This strategy is a critical factor to successful deployment. Although this is a non-technical element, it will drive our technical discussions and decisions.

In this chapter, you will:

- Understand your end users
- Understand your applications
- Define your use cases
- Plan your strategy

Understanding your end users

Understanding the end users of a target environment is the first major step in a successful virtual desktop design. Who are the users? What do they use? How do they use it? A successful desktop solution must meet the needs of the users and be useful. It does no good to design a solution that goes unused or does not fit the needs of the target audience.

When understanding users, it is best to start with basic classifications. In most organizations, this is done by worker-type or department members. In the graph presented in the following diagram, you can see that our fictional organization has six different classifications of users: **Customer Support**, **Case Managers**, **Finance**, **Legal**, **IT**, and **HR**. Using a simple pie chart to represent our user populations helps us see that **Customer Support** and **Case Managers** make up the vast majority of our user population. When designing our environment, they will be the most likely candidates to target for analysis and design. Remember, however, it is possible that not every user or use case will be a candidate for VDI.

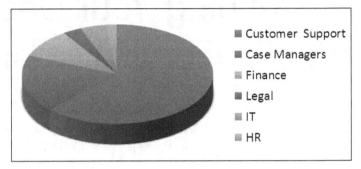

A breakdown of the user population by department

Users can also be classified by location (Texas, California, and so on) or by access types (local, remote, domestic, international, work at home, and so on). Some organizations classify users by permission levels such as standard user, power user, and developer. Other organizations might classify users as internal and external or full-time and part-time, or they might have no set classifications at all. Regardless of exactly how users are defined, creating the logical groups is the first step.

Along with defining users, it is important to understand how many users will be supported. This should include the total number of users, calculated by taking into consideration both total users and concurrency (how many users are online at any given time.) This will impact licensing, scalability, and performance of the final design. We will discuss scalability in detail in *Chapter 3, Designing Your Infrastructure*.

The next step is to define the user requirements for each classification of user. These requirements should include the elements listed. These elements might vary from organization to organization, so, what one company defines as supporting, another may call primary. The critical takeaway is to provide some form of structure for classifications that makes sense for your environment. The classification elements are:

- **Primary applications**: These include line-of-business applications, productivity software, specialty software, and custom applications

- **Supporting applications**: These are common or standard applications across the organization, typically including core productivity suites (such as Microsoft Office), PDF readers, communication software, and so on

- **Device types**: These include desktop, thin client, laptop, tablet, and so on

- **Required peripherals**: These include printers, badge readers, signature pads, and so on

- **Access patterns**: These include hours of operations, locality, remote connectivity, and so on

- **User issues**: These are concerns or pain points to be addressed, which might also include special requirements around business processes, workflows, data access, and so on

As part of the gathering of the user requirements, it is helpful to document user workflows. Workflows help illustrate the usage process and ensure all stakeholders in a solution design are in agreement. Understanding the user workflows will drive the environmental design elements to ensure all requirements can be met. The following are some sample workflows and user requirements based on real-world examples across different industries.

Use case – clinical physicians

Doctors require access to a hospital's medical record systems while roaming between patient rooms. Doctors use their RFID badges for quick connect login and require smooth roaming, so their applications remain open and essentially follow them.

Decision element	Decision point
Primary applications	Hospital electronic medical records system and patient monitoring software
Supporting applications	Web browser, e-mail, and Word processor
Devices	Thin clients on mobile carts and patient room computers
Peripherals	Smartcard badge reader and unit printer
Access patterns	12-hour shifts, 24/7 access required
User issues	Requires tap-and-go badge access for login and smooth roaming; requires extended time-out periods
User workflow	• Physician accesses a computer in the patient's room • Physician taps an RFID badge on a reader for rapid touchless login • Medical record application should sign in automatically

The physician's workflow detailed in the preceding table is illustrated in the following figure:

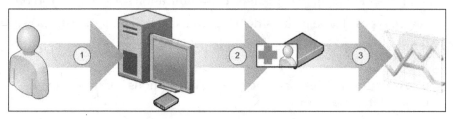

Clinical physician's user workflow

Use case – data entry clerks

Data entry clerks are required to process data into a terminal emulator program as well as transpose data into spreadsheets and e-mails when necessary. Management requests a full *Windows* experience to minimize training costs:

Decision element	Decision point
Primary applications	Emulator screen for data processing
Supporting applications	Web browser, e-mail, Word processor, and spreadsheet applications
Devices	Thin clients in pod work centers
Peripherals	Central departmental printers and multiple monitors
Access patterns	3 shifts per day, 8 hours per shift, Monday to Friday only; the shifts start at 8 A.M., 4 P.M., and 12 A.M.
User issues	Requires a full Windows desktop look and feel and support for multiple monitors
User workflow	• Clerks sign in on the first available workstation • Full Windows desktop experience is launched • Clerks perform data entry through emulator applications

The data entry clerk's workflow detailed in the preceding table is illustrated in the following figure:

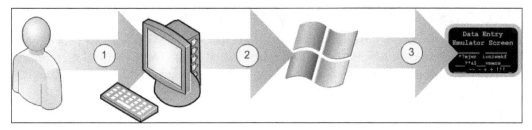

Data entry clerk's user workflow

Use case – office workers

The branch office workers for a financial services company need to access their applications across the corporate wide area network. These users might be uploading documents provided by customers as part of the financial application:

Decision element	Decision point
Primary applications	Microsoft Office, e-mail, and financial service applications
Supporting applications	Internet Explorer, Google Chrome, and Cisco Unity
Devices	Assigned laptop and desktop workstations across multiple field offices
Peripherals	Local printers, some scanners, and USB drives
Access patterns	Typical business hours are between 8 A.M. and 6 P.M. from Monday to Friday
User issues	All applications and data are hosted in a secured data center; seamless application appearance required
User workflow	• Users sign in to the StoreFront website • Users can launch any application from the receiver

The office worker's workflow detailed in the preceding table is illustrated in the following figure:

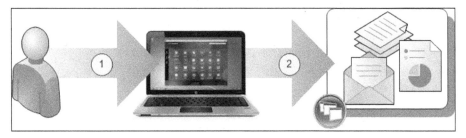

Office user's workflow

Use case – hospital administration clerks

In this sample use case, hospital administration clerks are responsible for processing incoming patients. This includes entering data into the electronic medical records systems, scanning insurance cards, capturing patient's images, and printing patient ID labels:

Decision element	Decision point
Primary applications	Hospital electronic medical records systems
Supporting applications	Web browser and Word processor
Devices	Admission computers (full PC)
Peripherals	Digital camera, printer, and scanner
Access patterns	Primary admissions are from Monday to Friday from 6 A.M. to 9 P.M. in two shifts Emergency departments operate from 9 P.M. to 6 A.M. every day, including Saturdays and Sundays
User issues	Requires access to scan patient information (photo identification and insurance information), print to admissions printers (including barcode labels), and use a digital camera to create a visitor badge
User workflow	• Admission clerks sign in to local desktop with devices attached • Launch virtual desktops • Launch medical records systems • Scan and input data into medical records systems; generate and print reports from medical records systems

The hospital administrator's workflow detailed in the preceding table is illustrated in the following figure:

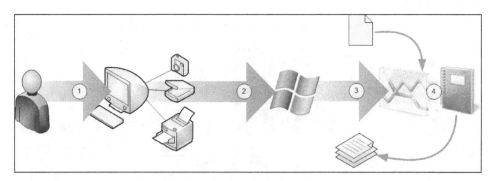

Hospital admissions' user workflow

Use case – call center customer service representatives

In this sample use case, call center customer service representatives are responsible for handling inbound customer calls in the company support hotline. As part of customer services, the representatives need to record all customer information as well as look up product data and knowledge base articles. As an added service, video chat is enabled for a more personal touch:

Decision element	Decision point
Primary applications	Data entry emulator, telephony software, and customer relationship management software
Supporting applications	Web browser, video chat, and e-mail
Devices	Call center PC
Peripherals	Audio headset, video camera, and voice-over-IP phone
Access patterns	Three shifts per day, 8 hours per shift, Monday to Friday; shifts start at 7 A.M., 3 P.M., and 11 P.M.; one shift per day, 10 hours per shift on Saturdays and Sundays; the shift starts at 7 A.M.
User issues	Requires Windows 7 OS (due to software compatibility); requires telephony integration with voice-over-IP phone system; requires webcam for optional customer video chat
User workflow	• Call center service representative signs into their call center PC with webcam and phone attached; users must enter ID into phone system to complete the login process • User connects to hosted Windows 7 desktop with locally installed software • Inbound calls are mapped to customer accounts and displayed on the screen

The call center customer service representative's workflow detailed in the preceding table is illustrated in the following figure:

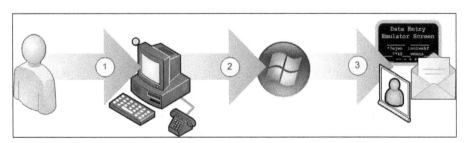

Call center user's workflow

Use case – business executives

The senior management team wants to empower all corporate executives with the ability to maintain secure e-mail communication and access to productivity reports regardless of location. These executives primarily work from their desks, but they might use their tablets from various conference rooms while on-premise. Remote access for tablet usage is also necessary for traveling executives:

Decision element	Decision point
Primary applications	E-mail and productivity reporting
Supporting applications	Web browser, Microsoft Lync, and Microsoft Office Suite
Devices	Assigned laptop and desktop workstations and Apple iPads
Peripherals	None defined at this time
Access patterns	Atypical access patterns that must be available all the time
User issues	Required support for wireless tablet devices
User workflow	<ul><li>Executive signs into Citrix Receiver on a tablet device</li><li>Executive can launch any published application from a receiver</li></ul>

The business executive's workflow detailed in the preceding table is illustrated in the following figure:

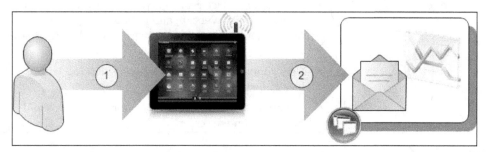

Business executive user's workflow

Translating the user workflow

The preceding sample use cases are used to simplify what the users need in order to perform their jobs. They are not intended to be fully comprehensive. For example, an office user may use more applications than Microsoft Office, e-mail, a web browser, and an instant messaging chat utility. However, the vast majority of their daily activities will focus on the activities mentioned previously. We will discuss the outliers later, but for now, understand that the focus of use case definition is to define what the majority of use cases will need.

It is also important to understand that a use case workflow is a simplified version of what happens behind the scenes. In the previous diagrams, we focused on what the user sees. In the *Clinical physician user workflow* figure shown previously, we see the three steps a clinical physician takes to access their patient system. The following table shows the full workflow of what is happening behind the scenes in order to meet the user workflow requirements.

This detailed technical workflow is based on the assumption that the medical records application is hosted on a XenApp environment to provide centralized version control and security. Since the application suite is hosted, users can access the application from any location and receive the same basic functionality. This allows the doctors to move from room to room and still maintain their application access:

Workflow steps	Activities
1	Physician approaches in-room computer (or mobile cart).
2	Physician taps the RFID badge to the reader for rapid touchless login.
3	Badge reader system validates the physician's credentials and triggers a sign on into Windows running on the workstation.
4	Windows passes credentials to the Citrix Receiver running on the workstation using the Single sign-on functionality.
5	Citrix Receiver passes the user credentials through Citrix StoreFront.
6	Citrix StoreFront uses XML to check with Citrix XenApp Controllers to determine which session host can support this physician's session or whether an existing session already exists.
7	If no session exists, a new instance of the medical records application is opened; if a session exists for this user, this session is reconnected.
8	The electronic medical records application is presented to the physician for use; with single sign-on, the physician's user ID and password are passed for automatic sign in.

The entire step-by-step workflow detailed in the preceding table is illustrated in the following diagram. While the users only see three unique steps, the actual process takes eight technical steps.

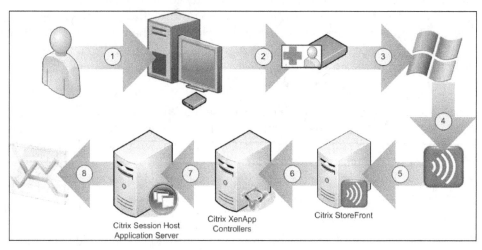

Clinical physician's expanded workflow

Understanding applications

Understanding your applications is the next step in a virtual desktop design. Which applications are installed? Which applications are actually in use? Which applications are critical to core business operations? Which applications require backend data? Virtualization design is all about the applications. If a user cannot use the applications they need, they will not be able to do their job successfully.

The first step is to create a comprehensive list of applications currently in use. This will create the basis to determine which applications should be included in the virtual desktop solution. Once the application list is compiled, you will need to verify application compatibility and interoperability. There might be certain applications that require other supporting applications, specific resources, or are only licensed for certain operating systems. Understanding these constraints will come into play when developing your final use cases.

There are multiple ways to collect this data, as highlighted in the following table:

Collection method	Pros	Cons
User survey	Input directly from users Low-cost solution	Prone to errors and omissions Might not be comprehensive Might not be detailed enough
User workflow analysis	Input directly from users Should identify the most commonly used applications and processes	Time-consuming process to generate detailed workflows Might be incomplete
Business unit owner listing	Liaison for each business unit identifies what this unit uses or needs Low-cost solution	Prone to error Might not be detailed enough
Automated collection	Empirical data Full details, including different versions of the same software	Can be expensive Can be overly detailed, requiring in depth analysis
Existing catalog	Review of existing offerings Low-cost solution	Will not see out-of-band software

As you can see, no single method is perfect for identifying applications. Using multiple methods, such as a user server and an automated collection to create a list of software packages, is preferred. Business unit owners should be engaged to help identify the key packages from the listings. As with use case definitions, this is simply a starting point. Building a list of applications and requirements feeds into image creations, but once the user testing phase begins, changes might be required.

Making a questionnaire for an application

Application questionnaires help define the application specifics. These specifics help administrators define technical requirements, including interoperability and compatibility. For example, one application suite might require Java 6 Update 16 while another package requires Java 7 Update 13.

Along with knowing which applications are required, a final application list should include relevant details such as:

- Application version (if there are multiple versions, can they be streamlined to a single version?)
- Supporting requirements (for example, Java, Word, and so on)
- Operating system compatibility (32-bit or 64-bit capable)
- Resource overhead (is it processor, memory, or disk intensive?)
- Special licensing requirements (limited number of concurrent or named users, host-based licensing)
- Interoperability requirements (must it be isolated from or co-exist with certain packages?)

The following table represents a sample application qualification questionnaire and illustrates the pertinent information that should be collected. This is typically given to an application or business unit owner. All applications should be tested in an isolated test environment before being placed in a production environment.

Base application information
Application name.
Application vendor.
Application version.
Installation media source location.
Which users or locations will need access to this application?
Estimated number of concurrent users.
Who is the application owner, subject matter expert, or primary contact?
Who is responsible for testing the application functionality?
When does the application need to be ready for production?
Criticality factor (rank 1-5, 1 = optional, and 5 = mission critical).

Application functionality		
Are there any backend data requirements, such as file share, database, and so on? If there are, please list them.		
Are there any specific hardware or software prerequisites? If there are, please list them.		
Is there any special licensing required for this application?		
Are there any additional custom configurations required?		
Are there any other special considerations, such as 3D graphics, intense processor utilization, or heavy resource consumption?		
Compatibility information		
Is the application supported on Windows Server 2008 R2?	Yes Yes with issues No Unknown	
Is the application supported on Windows Server 2012?	Yes Yes with issues No Unknown	
Is the application supported on Windows 7?	Yes Yes with issues No Unknown	
Is the application supported on Windows 8?	Yes Yes with issues No Unknown	
Is the application supported on Citrix XenApp or Microsoft Terminal Server / Remote Desktop Services?	Yes Yes with issues No Unknown	
Additional comments or requirements		

Automated application data collection

Application auditing tools provide a great resource to collect empirical data on which applications are installed and are actually in use. This is useful for environments starting from scratch, which may not know what they have or what they need. These tools are also helpful to review an environment and see what is actually used by the users to determine whether changes are necessary.

There are numerous products on the market to assist you with application data collection. Some organizations may already have products in use that can assist with this; others may require third-party tools. I have listed several tools here that I used in the past with great success. Any of these tools can assist you in your application discovery and analysis process:

- Stratusphere by Liquidware Labs
- Network Inventory by Lansweeper
- Baseline Desktop Analyzer by RES Software
- AppDNA by Citrix
- SysTrack by Lakeside Software

For full disclosure as a professional consultant, I maintain active partnerships with Citrix, Liquidware Labs, Lakeside Software, and RES Software. However, I do not resell the products.

Using Stratusphere FIT

Stratusphere by **Liquidware Labs** is one of the market leaders in application performance data collection. This product is used for desktop transformations, enabling IT department's insight into desktop activity with the intent of migrating workloads from physical to virtual. Typically, the agent is deployed and it runs for a minimum of 30 days, although that can be shortened if necessary. The agent runs on the desktop and monitors items such as which applications are run, when they are executed, how long they are used for, the resource consumption, and all versions. This information is collected by a server and can be generated into reports. A sample summary report is show in the following diagram, including which applications are actually used:

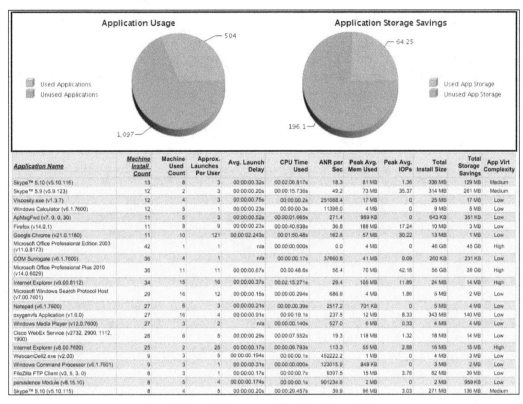

Application Name	Machine Install Count	Machine Used Count	Approx. Launches Per User	Avg. Launch Delay	CPU Time Used	ANR per Sec	Peak Avg. Mem Used	Peak Avg. IOPs	Total Install Size	Total Storage Savings	App Virt Complexity
Skype™ 5.10 (v5.10.116)	13	8	3	00:00:00.32s	00:02:06.817s	18.3	81 MB	1.36	336 MB	129 MB	Medium
Skype™ 5.9 (v5.9.123)	12	2	3	00:00:00.20s	00:00:15.736s	49.2	73 MB	35.37	314 MB	261 MB	Medium
Viscosity.exe (v1.3.7)	12	4	3	00:00:00.75s	00:00:00.2s	251068.4	17 MB	0	25 MB	17 MB	Low
Windows Calculator (v6.1.7600)	12	5	1	00:00:00.23s	00:00:00.3s	11396.0	4 MB	0	9 MB	5 MB	Low
ApMsgFwd (v7, 0, 0, 30)	11	5	3	00:00:00.52s	00:00:01.665s	271.4	959 KB	0	643 KB	351 KB	Low
Firefox (v14.0.1)	11	8	9	00:00:00.23s	00:00:40.638s	36.8	188 MB	17.24	10 MB	3 MB	Low
Google Chrome (v21.0.1180)	11	10	121	00:00:02.243s	00:01:50.48s	162.6	57 MB	30.22	13 MB	1 MB	Low
Microsoft Office Professional Edition 2003 (v11.0.8173)	42	1	1	n/a	00:00:00.000s	0.0	4 MB	0	46 GB	45 GB	High
COM Surrogate (v6.1.7600)	36	4	1	n/a	00:00:00.17s	37660.8	41 MB	0.09	260 KB	231 KB	Low
Microsoft Office Professional Plus 2010 (v14.0.6029)	36	11	11	00:00:00.67s	00:00:48.6s	56.4	70 MB	42.18	56 GB	39 GB	High
Internet Explorer (v9.00.8112)	34	15	16	00:00:00.37s	00:02:15.271s	29.4	105 MB	11.89	24 MB	14 MB	High
Microsoft Windows Search Protocol Host (v7.00.7601)	29	16	12	00:00:00.15s	00:00:00.294s	686.9	4 MB	1.86	5 MB	2 MB	Low
Notepad (v6.1.7600)	27	8	3	00:00:00.21s	00:00:00.39s	2517.2	701 KB	0	5 MB	4 MB	Low
oxygenvfs Application (v1.0.0)	27	16	4	00:00:00.91s	00:00:19.1s	237.5	12 MB	8.33	343 MB	140 MB	Low
Windows Media Player (v12.0.7600)	27	3	2	n/a	00:00:00.140s	527.0	6 MB	0.33	4 MB	4 MB	Low
Cisco WebEx Service (v2732, 2900. 1112, 1900)	26	6	5	00:00:00.29s	00:00:07.552s	19.3	118 MB	1.32	18 MB	14 MB	Low
Internet Explorer (v8.00.7600)	25	2	25	00:00:00.17s	00:00:06.793s	113.3	55 MB	2.88	16 MB	15 MB	High
WebcamDell2.exe (v2.00)	9	3	5	00:00:00.194s	00:00:00.1s	452222.2	1 MB	0	4 MB	3 MB	Low
Windows Command Processor (v6.1.7601)	9	3	1	00:00:00.31s	00:00:00.000s	123015.9	848 KB	0	3 MB	2 MB	Low
FileZilla FTP Client (v3, 5, 3, 0)	8	3	1	00:00:00.17s	00:00:00.7s	9397.5	15 MB	3.76	82 MB	39 MB	Low
persistence Module (v8.15.10)	8	5	4	00:00:00.174s	00:00:00.1s	901234.6	2 MB	0	2 MB	959 KB	Low
Skype™ 5.10 (v5.10.115)	8	4	5	00:00:00.20s	00:00:29.457s	39.9	96 MB	3.03	271 MB	136 MB	Medium

Sample Stratusphere report from Liquidware Labs

According to the Liquidware Labs website, Stratusphere offers the following benefits:

- Assesses and baselines users, applications, and infrastructure resources
- Measures endpoint-to-datacenter network latency
- Rates user and application fitness levels as good/fair/poor
- Supports capacity planning for CPU, memory, and IOPS per application
- Enables design of optimum shared-image strategy
- Allows the creation of remediation plans before migrating desktops to virtual platforms

More information is available at `http://www.liquidwarelabs.com/products/stratuspherefit.asp`.

Utilizing Network Inventory

Lansweeper's Network Inventory product is an agentless utility that runs on a central server on your network. An additional client scanning agent is optional and is recommended for comprehensive data collection. The collected data is written to a database and accessed from a web reporting frontend. Lansweeper can collect the applications that are installed and the ones that are in use across the desktop environment, including generating exclusion or exception reports. The following is a sample of software reports:

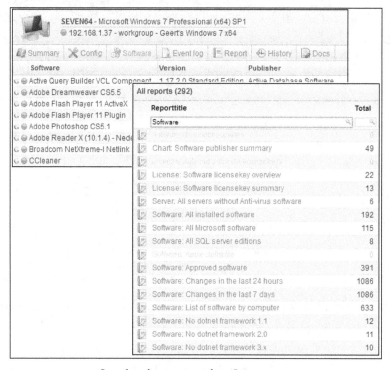

Sample software report from Lansweeper

According to Lansweeper's website, Network Inventory offers the following benefits:

- Software inventory
- Network inventory
- License compliance
- Compliance reporting
- Event log integration

More information is available at `http://www.lansweeper.com/software-inventory-and-software-audit.aspx`.

Using Baseline Desktop Analyzer

RES Software's **Baseline Desktop Analyzer** product provides insight into user context and desktop usage of your existing environment, whether physical or virtual. This is an agentless deploy that is hosted in the Microsoft Azure Cloud, requiring no infrastructure. Baseline Desktop Analyzer collects data on hardware, applications, users, printer topology, and network topology. The following report demonstrates the percentage of different users and the number of devices per domain:

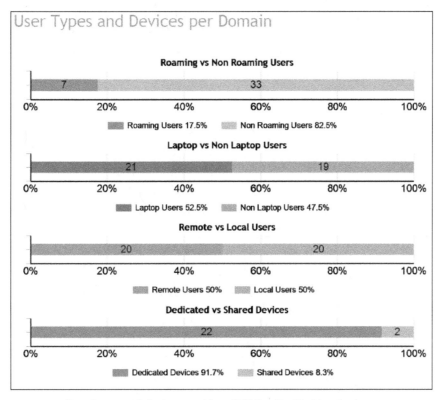

Sample user and device report from RES Baseline Desktop Analyzer

According to RES's website, Baseline Desktop Analyzer provides a quick insight into the user environment using a no-cost software solution and providing quick and easy analysis. This empowers desktop transformation initiatives focused on:

- Application virtualization (App-V)
- Windows 7 migrations
- Citrix XenApp rollouts
- Desktop virtualization projects

More information is available at https://www.resbaselinedesktopanalyzer.com.

Leveraging AppDNA

The **Citrix AppDNA** software enables discovering, automating, validating, and managing applications for faster application migration and virtualization. AppDNA is included as part of the Citrix XenApp 7.5 Platinum License. AppDNA analyzes software installation packages to detect compatibility and interoperability. This includes automated application testing and modeling against target operating environments. The results are presented in a dashboard using a red stoplight format for incompatibility or major issues, yellow to proceed with caution, and green for no issues found, as shown in the following screenshot:

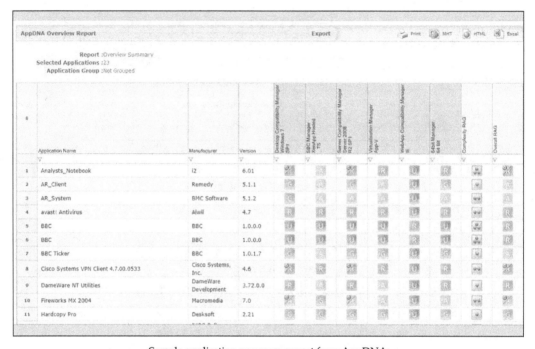

Sample application summary report from AppDNA

According to Citrix's website, AppDNA provides some of the following key features:

- Discover application issues with sophisticated testing
- Model application outcomes to determine the best plan of action
- Automate application remediation and packaging processes
- Manage ongoing application evolution after launch of the migration or virtualization project

More information is available at http://www.citrix.com/products/appdna/overview.html.

Implementing Lakeside Software SysTrack

SysTrack by **Lakeside Software** is another market leader in desktop system and application performance data collection. SysTrack can be used with physical desktops, virtual desktops, and virtual servers, including Citrix XenApp servers. SysTrack can be used to assess current systems prior to virtualization, or it can be used to audit virtual systems to ensure baseline compliance. SysTrack can also be used for chargeback models based on resource utilization.

SysTrack leverages a centralized collection server (based on Windows) and a SQL database. The collection agent is deployed and runs for a typical duration of 30 days, although this can be shortened if necessary. The agent monitors items such as which applications are used, when they are executed, how long they are used for, the resource consumption, and all versions. This information is collected by a server and can be generated into reports. A sample summary report is shown in the following screenshot:

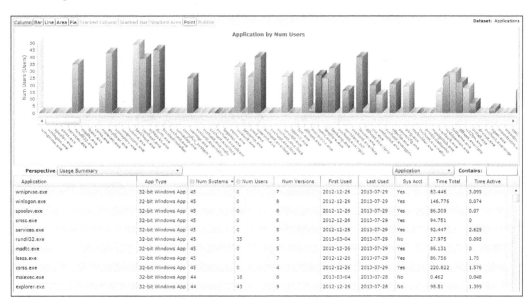

Sample application summary report from Lakeside Software's SysTrack

According to the Lakeside Software website, SysTrack offers the following benefits:

- Ease of use—each client can be deployed remotely in 1 to 3 minutes
- One module for all components (workstations and servers)
- Global system-view capability based on roles and responsibilities
- Out of the box and easy-to-understand interfaces and reports

- Role-based security controls data access
- Detailed performance counter tracking from the ICA stack
- Customizable reporting and alarming
- Application concurrency tracking
- User session tracking

More information is available at `http://www.lakesidesoftware.com/products.aspx`.

The following diagram shows the plan of a SysTrack FastTrack project:

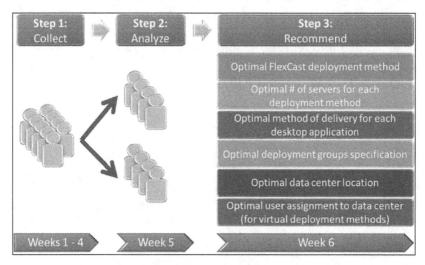

SysTrack FastTrack project plan

SysTrack is also available in conjunction with Citrix as part of Citrix's Project Accelerator. The FastTrack planning tool is based on SysTrack and is part of Citrix's Virtual Desktop Assessment Tool. For more information, please refer to `http://www.lakesidesoftware.com/fasttrack.aspx` or `http://project.citrix.com`.

Completing your software inventory

The tools listed in the preceding section are just a sample of the available tools on the marketplace. Your selection of discovery methods will vary based on scale, costs, and functional requirements. Regardless of which methods or tools you use to generate your software inventory, it should always include the following:

- Application name, vendor, and version number (for example, Microsoft Office 2013)

- Service Pack or Hotfix Level (for example, Autodesk AutoCAD Civil 3D 2014 Hotfix 1)
- Criticality factor (optional, mission critical, and so on)
- Listing of any client/server component
- Known issues, such as bugs or compatibility concerns
- Application owner(s)
- Application-testing methodology

Once all applications and requirements are identified, you should also validate compatibility and supportability. Which versions of Windows does the application support? Will the vendor support this application in a XenApp environment? What is your remediation plan for applications that might not be supported?

Understanding devices

Endpoints are all client devices that the users operate to access the virtual desktop or applications. These include devices such as thin clients, corporate-owned computers, user-owned computers, tablets, and smartphones. This also includes the associated operating system. Defining what is supported, or what needs to be supported, may partially drive the design. Understanding devices will aid in the technical architecture as well as user testing.

Environments with standardized endpoints will only require limited testing. However, organizations with a broad array of devices will need to test against all platforms to ensure the delivered solution is operational.

Endpoints

When defining endpoints, the following factors should be considered:

- Who owns the device (company, contracting agency, or end user)
- Operating system of the device (Wyse ThinOS, Windows, or Apple iOS)
- Security parameters (Active directory membership and time out requirements)
- Connected peripherals
- Number of devices of each type
- Citrix receiver software in use
- Single sign-on agent, if necessary
- VPN client, if necessary

As you define these elements, they should be grouped into categories, as shown in the following diagram:

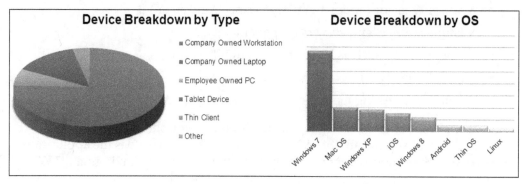

Sample device breakdown graphs by type and operating system

Peripherals

Along with the endpoints device, you must also account for any peripheral. Peripherals are additional components that will need to be operational in your virtual environment. The most common peripheral is client printers. The following list focuses on identifying the most common peripherals; it is not intended to be comprehensive:

- Client-attached printers
- Network printers
- Client hard drives
- Client optical drives
- Client removable drives
- USB and flash memory drives
- Microphones
- Cameras
- Scanners
- Specialty mice and keyboards
- Biometric scanners
- Signature pads
- Credit card readers
- Smart card readers

Each peripheral will need to be identified, cataloged, and tested within the virtualization environment. Some items might work immediately and others might require special drivers or communication channels. The key is to identify the necessary peripherals and components required by your use cases. Once these are identified, they will need to be tested and validated within the solution.

Defining your use cases

Once you have identified and organized your users, applications, and devices into logical groupings, the next step is to clearly define your use cases. This is an iterative process. Some groups might be too broad and should be split into multiple different use cases; other groups might be too tightly focused and can be combined with other use cases. You might also find that two different groups of users have a high rate of commonality and can be merged into a single case, as demonstrated in the following figure:

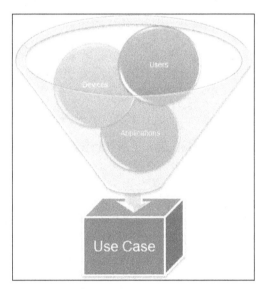

Creation of a use case

The idea is to minimize the number of unique use cases. There should be as many use cases as necessary, but as few as possible. The more unique use cases that are defined, the more iterations of testing will be required. This will carry forward to image design, which we will cover in detail in *Chapter 6, Designing Your Virtual Image Delivery*.

In *Chapter 1, Planning Desktop Virtualization*, we presented several different scenarios to determine the right fit for your organization. Let's take a moment and look at some of these scenarios in the form of use cases.

XenDesktop for Peripheral Support: a medical school was already using thin clients to deliver hosted XenApp applications from within their data center. Through a green initiative, they needed to deploy digital radiology and eliminate X-rays developed on film. This would speed the X-ray viewing process, and it would also reduce the cost and chemicals associated with film development. The new equipment required enhanced USB support and enhanced 32-bit graphics to achieve the proper resolution.

This customer had the following business requirements:

- Eliminating X-ray film development
- Speeding up the X-ray viewing process
- Supporting enhanced USB devices as part of the X-ray process
- Meeting PACS standards for radiology image viewing

The specialty radiology software in use by this customer posed additional constraints on the organization. Although they had an existing XenApp environment for application delivery, the radiology software was not compatible with the Windows Server environment. This forced the design to use XenDesktop to deliver Windows 7 desktops.

This customer initially defined the following four use cases:

- **Radiology image collection**: Enhanced Windows-based computers that require specialty USB sensors to capture X-rays in a digital format and access to the medical records system
- **Radiology image review**: Thin client devices requiring enhanced 32-bit graphics for detailed resolution of digital X-rays and high-resolution monitors for proper clarity and access to the medical records system
- **Back office administration**: Windows computers requiring standard productivity applications and medical records system, supporting USB devices such as scanners and magnetic card readers
- **Student learning labs**: Thin client devices requiring enhanced 32-bit graphics for detailed resolution of digital X-rays for proper clarity and access to a sample medical records system

Through the design process, the customer was able to get the environment consolidated into two use cases:

- A clinical use case with the drivers to support the image collection and image viewing as well as the medical records system client software. This also included the USB drivers for scanners and magnetic card readers, allowing office users and radiology to use a common image.

- A student use case was based on the same base image as the clinical use case, but it was configured for the sample (non-patient) data repository used in training classrooms, thus preventing any data leakage. This also included the radiology software and magnetic card readers.

By consolidating images, you are able to reduce the management footprint of the environment. This includes minimizing update and image maintenance requirements and reducing storage and image streaming requirements.

Planning your strategy

We outlined what it takes to understand your users, applications, and devices. You saw various tools and methods to capture and catalog data. The next step is to plan your analysis and design strategy. Once you collect your data through surveys, automation, or a mix of methods, you will need to analyze the data. You can process the raw data into useful information by creating your defined use cases. Once you define your use cases, you need to define your strategy further.

Which use cases will you tackle first? Do you design for everyone or for a few? Where do you start? How long will it take? What is most important? These are all the important questions to ask and ultimately answer. Consider the following methods:

- **80-20 rule**: According to the Pareto principle, 80 percent of issues are owned by 20 percent of the user population. This 20 percent are your potential problem users or high-demand users. To gain rapid acceptance and early success, focus on the other 80 percent of the users. Then, add the remaining 20 percent later. You may find that the remaining 20 percent requires more effort than the initial 80 percent.

- **Pick the low hanging fruit first**: These are the goals that are easily achievable or do not require a lot of effort. Get the small things out of the way first, and show early success. Some examples of low-hanging fruit may be use cases that are already clearly defined, such as call center departments.

- **Early wins**: Focus on the easy wins up front, especially the highly visible ones. Getting early buy-in from key stakeholders will go a long way for when there are unforeseen delays later. For example, there may be key users or use cases that are highly visible and willing to assist in early adoption.

- **Snowball effect**: This uses the small, early wins to roll up into larger successes. Much like snow rolling downhill, it will pick up momentum. Once the initial users are on board with the project, the feedback will lead to more users getting on board. Positive results will lead to more positive returns.

- **Nothing beats paper**: When in doubt, draw it out on paper (or a whiteboard or Visio). Most people are visual learners. Having a picture to illustrate helps break down language barriers and leads to greater understanding and acceptance. Once you have an idea for a design in mind, draw it out and share it with the stakeholders. This gets everyone on the same page and can lead to further design detail. For an example of a high-level diagram, refer to the end user workflows presented in this chapter or the reference architecture presented in *Chapter 3, Designing Your Infrastructure*.

Summary

In this chapter, we looked at defining our use cases. This included looking at sample use cases, then discussing how to construct our own. To create use cases, we need to understand our user, application, and device environment. Understanding our environment will help us in laying out the business requirements and criteria for success. We also looked at various software tools that can help us in our assessment and definition process. Finally, we discussed formulating a strategy to plan and execute our virtual desktop design.

In the next chapter, we will begin designing our infrastructure. Now that we have a plan in place, we can begin translating it into a reference architecture and high-level design of our infrastructure components, including our virtualization layer, hardware layer, network layer, and storage layer.

3
Designing Your Infrastructure

In the previous chapters, we focused on the analysis that should be performed prior to any design work. Without proper analysis of the organization and use cases, it is impossible to know what problems need to be addressed. Now we can delve into the actual architecture of our virtual solutions based on Citrix XenApp.

In this chapter, you will learn about:

- Creating a reference architecture
- Designing your virtual infrastructure
- Designing your hardware infrastructure
- Designing your network infrastructure
- Designing your storage infrastructure

Creating a reference architecture

Any design of a Citrix environment should include the various tiers of access as illustrated in the following diagram. This is the most basic starting point when developing your reference architecture, but it is nowhere near complete. The basic tiers are:

- **Endpoint tier**: This includes the end user devices
- **Access control tier**: This includes how users get into the environment

- **Delivery tier**: This is where the desktops and applications live

- **Existing infrastructure**: This includes tying into the larger network and resources on the backend

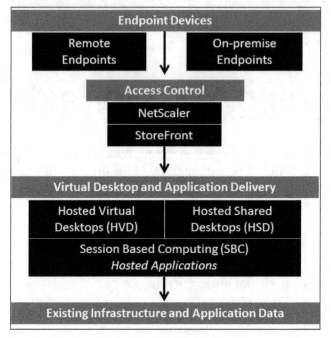

Block diagram of design tiers

A reference architecture diagram

When engaging in a design, the first thing to do is create a **reference architecture**. Think of the reference architecture as the big picture. This should be a logical diagram covering all the major elements of the design. You can draw this out on a whiteboard to get your thoughts straight and ensure you identify all of the components and the flow of the environment. Once you have a basic drawing, you can take the time to create a detailed Visio diagram, similar to the one shown in the following figure:

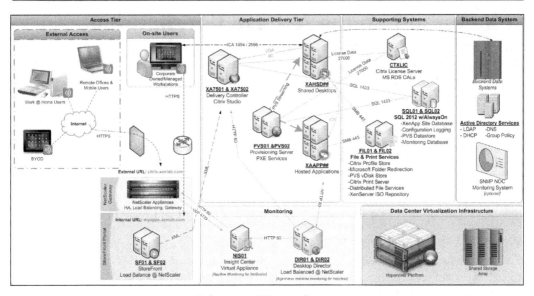

Reference architecture diagram

Once you have the reference architecture diagram compiled the way you want it, both from a logical and aesthetic standpoint, you can then present it to the project stakeholders. Having a visual representation of the desired end-state architecture helps in the ongoing design decisions. This first pass may not be a final diagram, but it makes a great reference point for basing future conversations. This is a work-in-progress and will change as you further define your environment. Sometimes, early assumptions will change as more information is available, but this makes a great starting point.

Visual artifacts such as this diagram also help in breaking down communication barriers, whether they are caused by language differences, style differences, or differences due to proximity. This diagram also facilitates the conversations to move from conceptual to firm design. Let's take a look in further detail.

Understanding the Access tier diagram

The **Access tier** includes both internal and external access. Here we represent our internal on-site users working on our corporate owned and managed workstations. These are our **trusted** resources. They are already authenticated on the network and have direct access to the Citrix solution. These users will typically access a private, internal portal. We also have all of our unsecure resources access the system through the public Internet, coming in through our NetScaler Gateway. This may include remote offices without a direct **Wide Area Network (WAN)** link, mobile users, work-at-home users, and **Bring Your Own Device (BYOD)** users. BYOD may entail contractor-owned, employee-owned, and possibly even corporate-owned devices. These BYOD devices could be laptops or mobile devices such as iPads, which operate on an open wireless network and thus are treated as unsecured devices.

We will cover the Access tier in more detail in *Chapter 4*, *Designing Your Access Layer*. For now, remember that our Access tier consists of the end user devices connecting to Citrix StoreFront, either directly through an internal load-balanced address or remotely through the NetScaler Gateway.

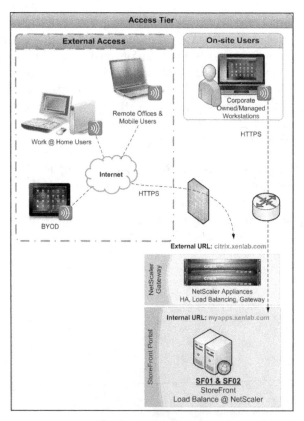

The Access tier diagram

Understanding the Delivery tier diagram

The **Delivery tier** is the core of the Citrix environment, containing the mechanisms for delivering desktops and applications. This is the traditional **XenApp Farm**, though in XenApp 7.5, the term used is **Site**. The Delivery tier will be covered in more detail in *Chapter 5, Designing Your Application Delivery Layer*, and *Chapter 6, Designing Your Virtual Image Delivery*. Using our reference architecture, though, we can see we are planning on having two controllers, two provisioning servers, and two sets of application silos. The use of silos will vary greatly for each environment. For this environment, we will use one silo for shared desktops and the other for hosted applications. Some environments may be able to be delivered using a single image and a single silo, where other environments may need multiple silos. For now, we will use two silos for illustrative purposes, knowing that the actual number of images may vary. For our image delivery, we are assuming the use of Provisioning Services, but will discuss that in much more detail in *Chapter 6, Designing Your Virtual Image Delivery*.

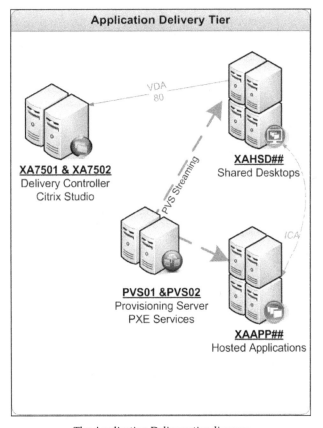

The Application Delivery tier diagram

Understanding the Supporting Systems tier diagram

The **Supporting Systems tier**, shown in the following diagram, contains components required for the Delivery tier to function. This may vary from environment to environment. For this design, we have a dedicated license server, a dedicated SQL server cluster, and dedicated file servers. Other environments may use existing components or even share multiple components on the same server (such as using one cluster for database and file services). These servers will perform auxiliary but critical functions within our virtual desktop solution. The critical takeaway at the moment is the need for these functions; determining where they run becomes a design decision point. These elements are covered in depth in *Chapter 7, Designing Your Supporting Infrastructure Components*.

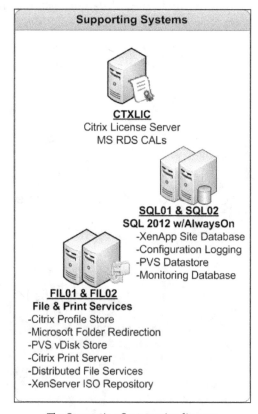

The Supporting Systems tier diagram

Understanding the Backend Data Systems tier diagram

The **Backend Data Systems** is a catch-all for other components, which should still be included in the reference architecture to keep the conversation moving forward and get those creative juices flowing. This can prompt discussions such as "what backend data?" and "what happens if the data repository goes offline?" This is to remind the stakeholders that a Citrix environment is not a standalone environment. It relies on other components outside of the Citrix Site architecture.

In larger environments, the Backend Data Systems can be the source of headaches during implementation, which is why you want to address it up front if possible. Items such as application compatibility, firewall ports, high availability, networking requirements, and performance requirements should all be considered.

The Backend Data System also includes common components in most environments as well, including Active Directory, group policies, and DHCP. We will cover these elements in *Chapter 8, Optimizing Your XenApp® Solution.*

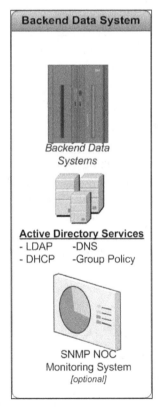

The Backend data system tier diagram

Understanding the Monitoring tier diagram

Breaking out the **Monitoring tier** from backend systems segments Citrix-specific monitoring and serves to highlight some architectural design differences from the existing enterprise systems. Citrix monitoring tools include NetScaler Insight Appliance for monitoring network usage for remote connections and Director for monitoring the end-user experience inside Citrix sessions. Some companies will also use an existing NOC monitoring system in lieu of, or in addition to, dedicated Citrix monitoring. We will delve deeper into monitoring in *Chapter 7, Designing Your Supporting Infrastructure Components*. Have a look at the following figure:

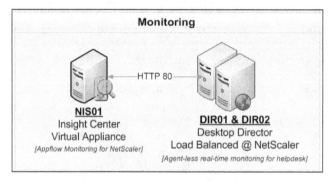

The Monitoring tier diagram

Understanding the Virtualization Infrastructure tier diagram

Finally, we represent the **Virtual Infrastructure tier**. This includes our virtualization platform(s) and storage subsystem(s). These items are covered later in this chapter. For simple, high-level references, we are representing a single cluster of host resources plus a single shared storage array. Obviously, there is more to a virtual infrastructure than just these two elements, but it is enough for a high-level overview.

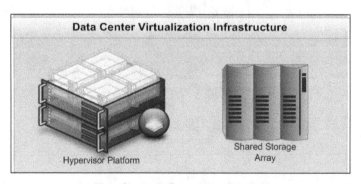

Virtualization infrastructure diagram

Designing highlights

In addition to creating a high-level diagram, it is beneficial to create a list of **design highlights** for executive review. This, along with the picture, helps convey the major decision points without getting lost in the fine details. These components ensure the project stakeholders understand and agree upon the major architectural decisions and allow presentation to the project sponsor. It should also be made clear that this is an early draft design and some decisions may not be finalized and all components are subject to change during the design and build processes.

The design highlights of our environment include:

- **Platform**: XenApp 7.5 Platinum. This version of XenApp will allow us to leverage the most complete feature set and the latest edition.

- **Location**: This environment is designed for a single XenApp site residing in our main corporate data center. Since each site is typically designed for a single datacenter, we can reuse the same design for future regional growth if necessary.

- **Operating system**: Unless specified otherwise, all server components will run on Windows Server 2012 Standard edition. XenApp 7.5 supports both Windows Server 2008 R2 and Windows Server 2012.

- **Image management**: We will be leveraging two unique images; one for hosted shared desktops (including standard applications) and one for specialty hosted applications. With XenApp 7.5, we have the option to use Provisioning Services or Machine Creation Services. Initially, we are planning to use Provisioning Services to stream our disk images, but will review this in more detail later in *Chapter 6, Designing Your Virtual Image Delivery*. Imaging will allow efficient and rapid deployment of updates to XenApp servers and will mitigate the risk of inconsistencies between servers as well as conserve storage space.

- **Scalability**: This design is created to support up to 500 concurrent users. The design is modular and easily scalable. We can support more users simply by adding compute and storage resources for more workload servers (also known as Session Hosts). As we grow the environment, we may need to add additional delivery controllers or provisioning servers based on actual performance and added resiliency; however, the infrastructure should support up to 10,000 and up to 1,000 virtual servers.

- **Application installation strategy**: Applications will be directly installed onto the master server images. Using disk images will ensure consistency among target devices (XenApp servers). Common core applications will be included in the primary shared desktop disk image and secondary and specialty applications will be installed on the disk image for the application silo. **Application streaming** will not be leveraged at this stage.

- **High Availability**: The environment has been designed to eliminate single points of failure for critical components and minimize downtime. All primary Citrix components include high availability and/or fault tolerance.

- **Citrix Receiver**: Citrix Receiver 4.x will be utilized on all devices for access into the environment. Remote users and mobile devices will connect to Citrix StoreFront through the NetScaler Gateway. Internal users will access the StoreFront Receiver for Web site directly.

- **User personalization**: We will leverage Citrix Profile Management to customize user profiles. Citrix Profile Management will store user settings and subsequent connections will maintain the user settings. We will also offload user documents using folder redirection, ensuring users always have access to their data.

- **SQL 2012 databases**: This design requires the use of SQL Server databases. We will be using SQL 2012 with the AlwaysOn feature to ensure high availability.

- **Systems monitoring**: This will be multiphased. Desktop Director will be used for help desk monitoring, end user support, and historical trend reports (including network performance, thanks to the **NetScaler Insight Center™**). The existing network operations center implementation of **Simple Management Network Protocol** (**SMNP**) will be used for automated alerting and notification of the infrastructure servers.

Designing your virtual infrastructure

Once the high-level design or reference architecture is approved, we can start creating the more detailed design elements. All designs are iterative in nature. Like the reference architecture, start with a baseline design and refine as you go. This allows flexibility and provides a frame of reference for all decisions. Just remember, if you change any baselines you must reevaluate your design to ensure everything is still in compliance.

Resource requirements

Once you have a high-level design approved, you can create a spreadsheet detailing the compute, memory, and storage requirements. Do this by listing the necessary resources for each virtual machine that needs to be created to support the design. These numbers are simply starting points in the conversation and should be reviewed and validated for each individual environment. Ideally, the sizing will come from information gathered during the assessment phase of the project. Regardless of how you scale your environment, you must monitor and adjust your scale and baseline based upon production data once it becomes available.

You may want to divide your virtual machine designs into two primary sections: **infrastructure** and **workload**. Infrastructure virtual machines, as shown in the following screenshot, are used to run the environment:

Infrastructure Virtual Machine Requirements							
Role	QTY	OS	vCPU	vRAM	VHD	IOPS	Notes
Citrix XenApp Controller	2	2012	2	4	40	15	All Management Consoles/Tools; XML, STA
Citrix StoreFront	2	2012	2	4	40	10	Citrix StoreFront, LB VIP
Citrix License Server	1	2012	2	4	40	10	All Licensing (CTX, RDS, KMS)
File Server	2	2012	2	4	40	50	File & Print Services, Network Shares
File Server Data	2				500		Folder Redirection, Profiles, vDisks, ISO
Desktop Director	2	2012	2	4	40	20	Director, LB VIP
Provisioning Services	2	2012	4	24	40	20	PVS, Shared HA
Microsoft SQL Server	2	2012	2	8	140	100	SQL 2012 w/Always On
NetScaler VPX 1000	2	NS 10.1	2	4	20	10	NetScaler Appliances
Insight Center	1	XEN	2	3	120	20	NetScaler Insight Appliance

Total VMs:	18	**HOSTS**		Host Specs:	
Est. # vCPUs	36	Min #	1	Model: Cisco UCS B200 M3 Blade	
Est. vRAM	111	Rec #	2	RAM: 128 GB	
Estimated Storage (GB)	1880			PROC: 2 Xeon E5-2680 (16 Cores // 32 Threads)	
Estimated IOPS	480	*Physical Cores:*	32	Storage: Tier 3 - SATA	
		Physical RAM:	256		

Infrastructure resource planning sheet

 Even though one physical host has enough resources to run all of the infrastructure workloads, you always want a minimum of two. This allows high availability, should a host fail. It also allows host-level maintenance without interrupting operations. This follows the *N+1* model of design, always having more resources than required to ensure fault tolerance.

Workload virtual machines, as shown in the following screenshot, are where the users are running their desktops and applications. The workload section is typically the area that is required to grow as you scale up an environment.

Workload Virtual Machine Requirements							
Role	QTY	OS	vCPU	vRAM	VHD	IOPS	Notes
Citrix XenApp 7.5 HSD	25	2012	4	24	40	70	1 GB RAM/Session; 20 Sessions per VM
Citrix XenApp 7.5 APP	12	2012	4	24	40	120	.5 GB RAM/Session; 40 Sessions per VM
							40 GB Write Cache

Total VMs:	37	HOSTS		Host Specs:	
Est. # vCPUs	148	Min #	5	Model: Cisco UCS B200 M3 Blade	
Est. vRAM	888	Rec #	6	RAM: 256 GB	
Estimated Storage (GB)	1480			PROC: 2 Xeon E5-2680 (16 Cores // 32 Threads)	
Estimated IOPS	3190	*Physical Cores:*	96	Storage: Tier 2 - SSD	
		8 Users/Core:	768		
		Physical RAM:	1536		
		Target # HSD Users:	500		

Workload resource planning sheet

By defining the necessary virtual machines early in the design process, we can gauge our resource requirements and the level of effort required to complete the design. By looking at the calculations in the two preceding screenshots, we can estimate that we will need between six and eight physical hosts. If the budget only allows for six hosts, you can determine if you want to operate at risk with no excess capacity for fault tolerance or if there is a need to increase the budget. Alternatively, if the preliminary sizing information is too much, you can have the conversation of which elements to eliminate or delay for now and add in later. This may commonly occur during a proof of concept, where an organization wants to minimize investment and high availability or fault tolerance is not required but may be added in later as part of production readiness.

Determining the right scale and cost can be tricky. If you over-size the environment, you risk needlessly spending more capital up front. If you undersize your environment, you risk project delays and failure by not having enough resources. I tend to err on the side of caution and over-scope my environments during design. This will allow you some flexibility to handle scope creep, environment growth, and ensure you are not resource constrained early in the project.

Virtual machine requirements

Once the general resources are calculated, you can create a secondary spreadsheet listing all of the virtual machines in the environment, as well as any supporting machines. This information is useful for tracking items such as names, IP addresses, resource assignments, host assignment, networking information, and so on. It can also be used as the basis for change control or build requests, depending on your organizational policies and requirements:

Server	IP	CPU	RAM	HD	Role	Host / Pool	
Router	192.168.1.1				Network Router/Default Gateway		
XS-001	192.168.1.2	Infrastructure Pool			XenServer Host	UCS Blade 1	UCS Chassis
XS-002	192.168.1.3				XenServer Host	UCS Blade 2	
XS-003	192.168.1.4				XenServer Host	UCS Blade 3	
XS-004	192.168.1.5				XenServer Host	UCS Blade 4	
XS-005	192.168.1.6	Workload Pool			XenServer Host	UCS Blade 5	
XS-006	192.168.1.7				XenServer Host	UCS Blade 6	
XS-007	192.168.1.8				XenServer Host	UCS Blade 7	
XS-008	192.168.1.9				XenServer Host	UCS Blade 8	
NS01	192.168.1.10	2	4	20	NetScaler VPX 1000	XS-001	NetScaler Appliances
NS02	192.168.1.11	2	4	20	NetScaler VPX 1000	XS-002	
SNIP	192.168.1.12				Subnet IP for NetScaler HA, 1-ARM Mode		
AUTH	192.168.1.14				LB VIP for Authentication		
SFLB	192.168.1.15				LB VIP for StoreFront		
CAG	192.168.1.16				VIP for Access Gateway		
DIRLB	192.168.1.17				LB VIP for Desktop Director		
NIS01	192.168.1.13	2	3	120	NetScaler Insight Server	Infrastructure	
AD01	192.168.1.18	2	2	30	Domain Controller	Infrastructure	Support Services
AD02	192.168.1.192	2	2	30	Domain Controller	Infrastructure	
FIL01	192.168.1.20	2	4	130	File & Print Services	Infrastructure	
FIL02	192.168.1.21				File & Print Services	Infrastructure	
SQL01	192.168.1.22			130	SQL 2012	Infrastructure	
SQL02	192.168.1.23	2	8	130	SQL 2012	Infrastructure	
CTXLIC	192.168.1.30	2	4	40	Citrix License Server	Infrastructure	Citrix Environment Infrastructure
XA7501	192.168.1.31	2	4	40	XenApp 7.5 Controller	Infrastructure	
XA7502	192.168.1.32	2	4	40	XenApp 7.5 Controller	Infrastructure	
DIR01	192.168.1.33	2	4	40	Desktop Director 2.1, Load Balanced	Infrastructure	
DIR02	192.168.1.34	2	4	40	Desktop Director 2.1, Load Balanced	Infrastructure	
PVS01	192.168.1.35	4	24	40	Provisioning Services 7, Shared HA	Infrastructure	
PVS02	192.168.1.36	4	24	40	Provisioning Services 7, Shared HA	Infrastructure	
SF01	192.168.1.37	2	4	40	StoreFront 2.5, Load Balanced	Infrastructure	
SF02	192.168.1.38	2	4	40	StoreFront 2.5, Load Balanced	Infrastructure	
XAHSD01	DHCP	4	24	40	Session Hosts: Desktops (streamed)	Workload	XenApp Hosted Shared Desktops
XAHSD02	DHCP	4	24	40	Session Hosts: Desktops (streamed)	Workload	
XAHSD03	DHCP	4	24	40	Session Hosts: Desktops (streamed)	Workload	
...			25 Total Streamed Servers			Workload	
XAHSD23	DHCP	4	24	40	Session Hosts: Desktops (streamed)	Workload	
XAHSD24	DHCP	4	24	40	Session Hosts: Desktops (streamed)	Workload	
XAHSD25	DHCP	4	24	40	Session Hosts: Desktops (streamed)	Workload	
XAAPP01	DHCP	4	24	40	Session Hosts: Application Servers (streamed)	Workload	XenApp Hosted Applications
XAAPP02	DHCP	4	24	40	Session Hosts: Application Servers (streamed)	Workload	
...			12 Total Streamed Servers			Workload	
XAAPP11	DHCP	4	24	40	Session Hosts: Application Servers (streamed)	Workload	
XAAPP12	DHCP	4	24	40	Session Hosts: Application Servers (streamed)	Workload	

Virtual machine planning and tracking sheet

Determining your virtualization platform

Choosing your platform may impact your design decisions, including scalability, high availability, fault tolerance, and budget. With XenApp 7.5, you also have the option to host on-site or in the cloud. For on-site hosting, there are three primary products for server virtualization: **XenServer**, **VMware vSphere**, and **Microsoft Hyper-V Server**. For cloud hosting, you can use **Microsoft Azure** or **Amazon Web Services (AWS.)** As you can see in the following screenshot, XenApp 7.5 can connect to a variety of platforms for hosting resources:

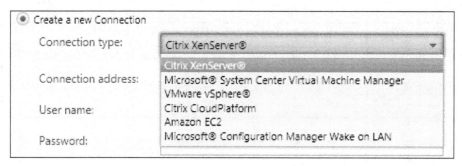

Citrix Studio hosting connection options

Assuming our CIO has mandated on-site hosting, we need to determine our virtualization platform. For XenApp or XenDesktop deployments, the underlying virtualization platform technically does not matter. The Citrix desktop and application virtualization products are hypervisor agnostic. This means they can run equally well on XenServer, vSphere, Hyper-V, or even bare metal. In some environments, the platform is already standardized and is locked in. Other environments might not have standards or may create exceptions based on a given project. Although it does not matter for Citrix per se, you should still identify and design your chosen platform as that will impact other decisions such as storage options, master image creation, and virtual machine templates.

XenServer

XenServer, according to http://www.citrix.com/products/xenserver, is an industry and value leading open source virtualization platform for managing cloud, server, and desktop virtual infrastructures. Organizations of any size can install XenServer in less than ten minutes to virtualize even the most demanding workloads and automate management processes, increasing IT flexibility and agility and lowering costs. With a rich set of management and automation capabilities, a simple and affordable pricing model and optimizations for virtual desktop and cloud computing, XenServer is designed to optimize private data centers and clouds today and in the future.

XenServer is considered a champion in the virtualization vendor landscape, according to Info-Tech, for its combination of vendor and product maturity. XenServer touts the following benefits:

- Cloud-proven virtualization, used by global cloud providers and integrates with the Citrix CloudPlatform and Apache CloudStack.

- Open source, providing community development and integration.

- Cost effective, providing competitive pricing for advanced features as well as free service offerings. Licensing ingrained with other Citrix products as well.

- Highly available architecture using a master/slave model, enabling clustering and live migration of virtual machines.

- Virtual machine snapshots, including automated backup and protection plans.

- Memory optimizations and memory sharing.

- Heterogeneous pools, allowing different hardware within the same cluster.

- Role-based administration, including Active Directory integration.

Have a look at the following diagram:

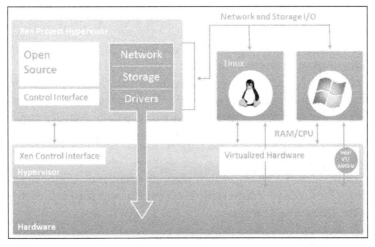

XenServer Server Virtualization Platform (© Citrix Systems, Inc. All Rights Reserved.)

Citrix was founded in 1989 and is publicly traded. Citrix acquired XenSource, makers of the Xen® hypervisor, in 2007. In 2013, Xen was moved to the Linux Foundation and rebranded as XenProject. In June 2013, Citrix moved XenServer 6.2 to a freely available open source platform. Citrix still offers a fully supported commercial option of XenServer that includes updates and product support. The commercial offering is licensed per socket in Advanced, Enterprise, and Platinum editions, or included as part of a XenDesktop deployment.

XenServer is managed with XenCenter®. XenCenter® is a type of client software that communicates directly with the pool master or the individual XenServer. No central server or central database is required.

The XenCenter console for managing XenServer

VMware vSphere

VMware vSphere, also referred to as **VMware ESX** or **VMware ESXi**, is the world's leading virtualization platform for building cloud and virtualization infrastructures. According to `http://www.vmware.com/products/vsphere`, vSphere is designed for organizations that want to virtualize entire data centers and deliver IT as a service; it includes features for transforming data centers into dramatically simplified cloud computing environments that can deliver the next generation of flexible, reliable IT services.

vSphere is also considered a champion in the virtualization vendor landscape, according to Info-Tech, for its combination of vendor and product maturity. vSphere touts the following benefits:

- Shared resources, aggregated into logical pools for the allocation of multiple workloads

- Optimized network services, including advanced virtual switching

- Efficient storage, reducing the complexity of backend storage systems and automation

- Granular and robust object-level security
- High Availability, including live migration of workloads, automated machine and data backup and recovery, replication, and fault tolerance
- Enhanced monitoring and alerting
- Automation, including advanced resource scheduling
- Enhanced storage options, including vSAN
- Enhanced operations management, using vCOps

Have a look at the following diagram:

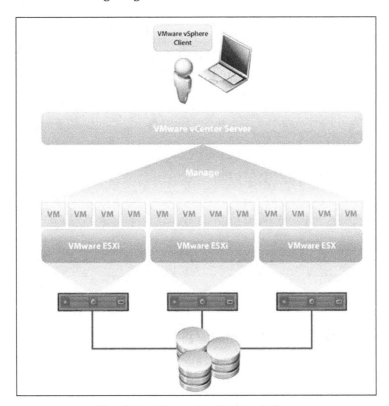

The vSphere Server virtualization platform

VMware was founded in 1998 and later acquired in 2004 by EMC Corporation and now operates as a subsidiary organization. VMware is still a publicly traded company, with their initial public offering in 2007. Although VMware has branched into the desktop virtualization space and the software-defined networking space, their core offering is still server virtualization. vSphere comes in three different editions, each with increasing feature sets and levels of support: Standard, Enterprise, and Enterprise Plus. vSphere is typically licensed per CPU.

vSphere is managed through a dedicated management server called vCenter. vCenter is a centralized management platform that can manage multiple vSphere clusters across datacenters, including real-time statistics, alerts, and historical trends. A client piece of software called the VMware vSphere client is used for the graphical user interface to connect to vCenter. vCenter requires a database to store persistent information, as shown in the following screenshot:

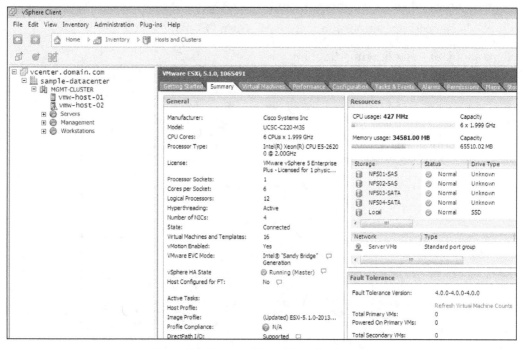

vCenter client for managing vSphere deployments

Microsoft Hyper-V Server

Microsoft Hyper-V Server is a dedicated standalone product that contains the hypervisor, Windows Server driver model, virtualization capabilities, and supporting components such as failover clustering, but does not contain the robust set of features and roles just like the Windows Server operating system. According to http://www.microsoft.com/en-us/server-cloud/hyper-v-server, Hyper-V Server produces a small footprint and requires minimal overhead, which is useful for consolidating servers where no new Windows Server licenses are required. Some of the benefits of Hyper-V Server include:

- Cost-effective virtualization
- Improved scalability and performance over previous versions

- Network virtualization, decouples the server configuration from the network configuration to provide multiple virtual dedicated networks
- Live migration of running workloads between hosts
- Dynamic memory management
- RemoteFX for enhanced graphics
- Multitenancy isolation support

The Hyper-V Server Virtualization Platform is demonstrated in the following diagram:

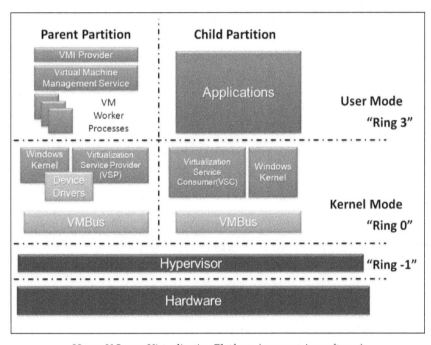

Hyper-V Server Virtualization Platform (source: microsoft.com)

Microsoft was founded in 1975 and is publicly traded. Hyper-V Server was originally introduced with Windows Server 2008 as the successor to the Microsoft Virtual Server platform. Hyper-V Server 2012 is the latest edition, commonly called Hyper-V 3. Hyper-V is not a standalone product, and therefor has no set licensing. Hyper-V is licensed as part of the Windows Server license, which is available in standalone (free), Standard, and Datacenter editions. The Standard edition operates in a 1+2 model, allowing you to run two virtual Windows Server instances at no additional licensing costs on top of the one Hyper-V instance. The Datacenter edition operates in a 1+ unlimited model, allowing you to run unlimited instances of Windows Servers on top of the Hyper-V instance. However, since you are required to license your Windows VMs on other platforms, there are potential savings for running Hyper-V with the Datacenter edition, allowing unlimited virtual instances on the virtual platform.

Hyper-V can be managed through PowerShell commands for automation or remotely using the Hyper-V Remote Management tools from another Windows server or Windows workstation. In a large enterprise, Hyper-V will traditionally be managed through Microsoft System Center. In a virtual desktop environment built on Hyper-V, you may also use the Microsoft System Center Virtual Machine Manager (SCVMM) package.

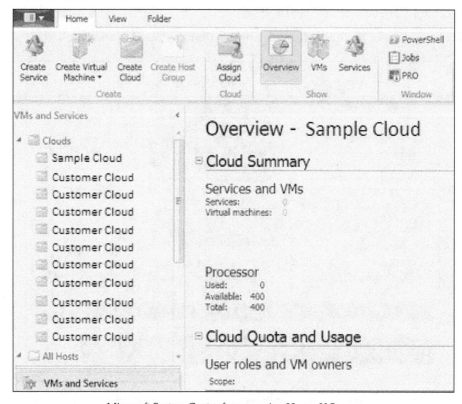

Microsoft System Center for managing Hyper-V Server

Virtualization cluster design decisions

Regardless of the virtualization platform, a common question is whether to use a single cluster or separate clusters. The answer, of course, depends on the environment. This is ultimately a question of costs and scale. Is the environment large enough to have this discussion? Are there enough resources to be able to dedicate a cluster of hosts to the virtual desktop solution environment?

When given the option, it is preferable to have separate clusters. This is preferable for several reasons, including ease of management and consolidation of workloads. Because of the way hypervisors share memory, if all workloads are identical or nearly identical, the overhead on the hypervisor is reduced, thus gaining more resources for the virtual machines. This also provides predictable scalability, so if you are running a cluster of only XenApp Session Hosts as the guest virtual machines, you can easily predict and monitor how many VMs (and essentially how many users) can fit on a given host. If you need to scale up your environment, you can easily predict how many more hosts are needed. If a host or cluster is running many different workloads, resource planning is not as straightforward.

Another reason to separate clusters is high availability and potentially licensing. If an environment is planned properly, you can predict how many users per virtual server and how many virtual servers per host. You can extrapolate that data to estimate how many users will be supported on each physical host. If you plan your environment for redundancy at the host level, you might not need high availability or other advanced features for your user workloads. This could lead to less complexity and possibly lower-tiered licensing, depending on your platform, as shown in the following diagram:

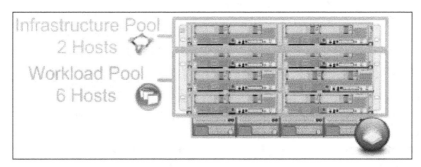

Physical host to resource pool allocation

For the environment in this book, we will be using XenServer as our server virtualization platform. As discussed earlier in this chapter, we are estimating two hosts for an infrastructure pool and six hosts for our workload pool. As our environment grows, our infrastructure pool will remain static or will have minimal growth. Users will primarily hit resources running in the workload pool. As we scale up for more users, we will only need to add resources to the workload pool. We could have all eight hosts in a single pool, which may reduce some of our overall costs by further consolidating servers and needing potentially fewer hosts. However, having separate pools creates scalability and a predictable cost model. If we added XenDesktop workloads at a future stage, we could then create a third pool to host the virtual desktop machines or merge the desktop OS with the server OS in our workload pool.

In the real world, I have seen a mix of VMware vSphere and XenServer, with very limited Microsoft Hyper-V. Most enterprises use VMware for their core infrastructure and their standard virtualization platform; however, Hyper-V is slowly gaining market share and may become more prevalent. These clients may also consider using XenServer for their Citrix workloads (XenApp and XenDesktop) in order to minimize costs and create a single vendor stack. Other enterprises will stick with only a single virtualization provider. A few smaller environments as well as proof of concept engagements tend to favor XenServer. This is not to imply any one platform is better than the other — it is simply a representation of what I have seen. Although I have not worked with Hyper-V 3 in a production environment yet, I have heard of positive reviews and I expect Microsoft to gain a larger foothold in this space. If you would like to see more on Citrix with Hyper-V, check out `http:// blogs.citrix.com/2014/02/18/xendesktop-7-1-on-hyper-v-pilot-guide/`.

According to a survey conducted by ProjectVRC, `http://www.projectvrc.com`, and presented in their *State of the VDI and SBC Union 2014* whitepaper, VMware is the dominant hypervisor of choice, maintaining approximately 79 percent of the market space. That same survey found server-based computing is in use in 78 percent of organizations, with Citrix XenApp being the dominant application / desktop virtualization platform. This supports much of what I have seen in customer engagements.

Designing your hardware infrastructure

Hardware design should come after you have determined how many resources you need and how many virtualization hosts you plan to deploy. In some environments, the hardware may be preselected based on the vendor contracts. Other environments may have pre-existing hardware due to early purchases, surplus, or repurposing other hardware. Even if the hardware is preexisting, design the environment for what is needed first, then compare with the hardware available. If there are not enough resources, you can either trim the design to match, request additional hardware, or possibly phase in the environment to the resources available (design for 1,000 users but only deploy for 500 users until more hardware is acquired).

Selecting between the rack and blade options

When picking your hardware, assuming you have no vendor constraints, you must determine what type of systems you are buying. Server hardware for data centers typically comes in **rack mount** or **blade** configurations. You may also want to consider integrated architectures, such as **FlexPod** or **vBlock** designs, or **converged platforms** such as Nutanix or SimpliVity.

Rack mount servers are typically sized in rack unit measurements notated with a U (1U is a server that takes up one unit of measure in a rack). The size of the rack mount server will depend on several form factors, most notably hard disk drives and cooling fans. Most virtualization systems fall into the 2U and 4U categories. Rack mount servers are popular because you can add as you grow, always getting the latest builds to suit your needs. Rack mount servers tend to be less expensive than their blade counterparts. IBM, Dell, and HP compete heavily in the rack mount server space.

Blade servers require a blade chassis, which shares common components among all blades in the array. This includes network uplinks, power distribution, cooling, and management access. Although slightly more expensive than rack mount servers, blades allow greater density within a data center and overall operating efficiencies. Along with IBM, Dell, and HP; Cisco is a big player in this space with their **Unified Computing System (UCS)** chassis and servers.

Cisco revolutionized the blade server market with their UCS platform. Prior to UCS, hardware vendors were coming across limitations as to how much memory could be assigned to a server based upon memory-modules-to-CPU ratios. Cisco applied their network switching technology to create blades with much higher memory allocation by treating four memory modules as one, ultimately quadrupling the available memory to a server. Because of this increased memory density, UCS is a very popular platform for virtualization. Combined with Cisco's UCS management platform and stateless servers, many environments are deploying UCS for their virtual platform.

Understanding converged platforms

Converged platforms, also called **hyper-converged platforms** or **web-scale architectures**, combine storage, compute, networking, and management into a single appliance. These converted platforms allow all aspects of a virtual platform to be managed from a single console. This also creates a single entity for support and integration, greatly simplifying your infrastructure design and maintenance.

To grow your environment, you simply add another hyper-converged appliance. The resources are then shared, including the local storage, using grid-style orchestration by the platform. This design allows very linear, predictive growth, as shown in the following diagram. The leading vendors in this space are Nutanix (`http://www.nutanix.com/`) and SimpliVity (`http://www.simplivity.com/`).

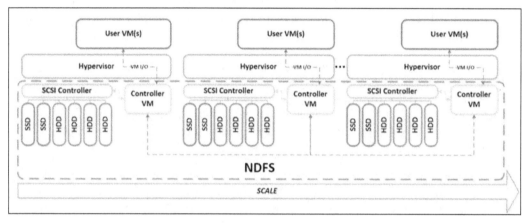

Converged platform architecture (source: Nutanix)

Reconsidering the cloud

When designing your hardware, along with choosing the vendors and models for your compute, storage, and network systems, you will also need to consider implementation and maintenance costs. It doesn't matter if you are using a converged platform, an integration stack, or just standalone components; all of these elements will need to be managed. These elements can become both complex and costly. This is a good opportunity to reconsider using a cloud hosting provider. Leveraging cloud services such as **Amazon Web Services** (**AWS**) or **Microsoft Azure** allow you to increase your hosting infrastructure and delivery capabilities without a large investment in hardware. Your organization's ability to leverage cloud services may be impacted by various elements, such as security, compliance, current hardware availability, application data, and so on.

When looking at cloud platforms, you also need to determine location:

- **Private cloud**: The cloud architecture is hosted on-site and typically owned and managed internally.

- **Public cloud**: The cloud architecture is hosted off-site at a provider location and is connected through the Internet or private WAN circuits. The provider is responsible for purchasing and managing the infrastructure and the user pays a subscription fee for the items utilized.

- **Hybrid cloud**: A mix of public and private cloud. This is typically used for expansion or burst capacity and requires a bridge between the customer-owned data center and the provider data center.

The following diagram shows the hybrid cloud architecture using Amazon web services:

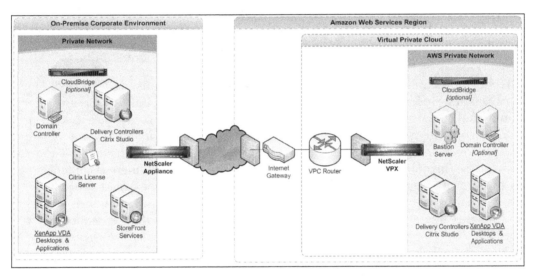

Hybrid cloud architecture using Amazon web services

You also have the option to consider **desktop-as-a-service** (**DaaS**) providers to outsource your entire virtual desktop architecture and management. DaaS providers provide both infrastructure-as-a-service on their cloud platform as well as the VDI platform to deliver desktops and applications. This, as a complete outsourced solution, allows your users to subscribe to desktops for a fixed monthly fee. The biggest risk in using a service provider for cloud or DaaS services is that your desktop or applications may be removed from your backend data and you no longer control the infrastructure.

For our fictional environment, our CIO has requested on-site hosting. However, for your environment, it is worth a second look at cloud offerings.

Designing your network infrastructure

The overall network design usually falls to dedicated network engineers within the client organization since they know the complex network landscape best. In smaller organizations, the virtualization engineer or consultant may be called upon for the network design. Either way, it is important to at least know the networking requirements. This way, the virtualization environment can be planned accordingly, regardless of who will be responsible for the actual network component implementation.

Planning network options

Once the size of the network is determined, network options will need to be discussed and designed. The most basic element is the **default gateway**. In most networks, this is the first address, such as 192.168.1.1, but that is not always the case. Some environments might use the last available address and others use a seemingly random address. The default gateway is used to forward traffic from this network segment to other parts of the network, including outbound traffic.

Other network options include the **DHCP** and **PXE** boot options. DHCP stands for **Dynamic Host Configuration Protocol** and is used to dynamically assign and configure IP addresses in a network environment. DHCP can sometimes become a bone of contention with network and security engineers who may not want dynamic addressing running in the data center. This is another reason why having a dedicated network segment for the Citrix architecture is recommended. If there is contention or concerns by the network engineering team, the DHCP can be isolated to just the scopes that need it. **PXE** stands for **Preboot Execution Environment**, which is used to configure operating systems during the boot process. We will discuss the need for DHCP and/or PXE as part of Provisioning Services in *Chapter 6, Designing Your Virtual Image Delivery*. The key point now is to understand what options are available as part of the network design.

Along with the logical network elements, there is also the physical aspect of networking — the actual switches and routers. These may also be virtually defined as part of the hypervisor setup. XenServer and ESX both support distributed virtual switches to create advanced switching for different workloads, including link aggregation and vLAN tagging. Keeping the entire Citrix architecture on a common network will ease a lot of these design elements.

Designing your storage infrastructure

Storage is another area commonly overlooked in virtual architectures. Like networking, storage is usually managed by a specialized team of engineers. When designing storage for a virtual solution, there are two primary elements to consider: capacity and throughput.

Capacity planning

Capacity is a simple measurement of how much disk space is required. In our sizing spreadsheets we created earlier, we identified that we need 1,880 GB of space for our infrastructure and 1,480 GB of space for our workloads. Simply defining how much space you need, however, is not enough. You also need to consider the speed, or throughput, of that space (how fast the data is written or retrieved). Most enterprise storage systems involve tiered data schemes, allowing you to mix and match storage as appropriate for the workload at hand.

Let's assume we have four tiers of storage: Super high-speed flash storage, high-speed Solid State Disks (SSDs), moderate-speed serial attached SCSI disks (SAS), and relatively low-speed serial ATA disks (SATA). The cost and speed are proportional, so tier 1 is the fastest and most expense tier while tier 4 is the cheapest and lowest performing tier. Infrastructure servers tend to fall into the tier 2 or tier 3 framework. These servers are usually standard Windows Servers with limited data processing expectations. The workload servers are the workhorses of the environment. These virtual machines are the ones processing the user sessions and tasks, thus requiring a tier 1 or tier 2 storage.

In *Chapter 1, Planning Desktop Virtualization*, we looked at the six components of project management success. Storage design decisions impact five of those size elements: scope, costs, quality, risk, and customer satisfaction. Therefore, it is important to get it right. Exactly how you place your storage will depend on up-front analysis and monitoring in steady state operations. Much like virtual infrastructure sizing, if you get it wrong, you are costing yourself either performance or money, and in some cases both.

The disk capacity can be affected by how the size is provisioned. Thin-provisioned space is ideal since it only consumes the actual disk space utilized, not what is allocated. However, this runs the risk of over-allocation as the space is consumed. There may also be a temporary negative performance impact when the thin-provisioned space is required to grow. Thick-provisioned space is fully allocated up front as the space is assigned it is automatically reserved. This can lead to underutilization, but it guarantees the space is readily available. From a virtualization design perspective, there is no significant benefit or drawback to either method as long as it is managed properly.

Measuring throughput

IOPS (inputs outputs per second) is a measure of throughput capacity on the whole of not just an individual disk, but of the entire storage array. IOPS is estimated by the workload type and will vary greatly from environment to environment. IOPS can be measured on existing systems using disk performance counters. IOPS can also be measured from the hypervisor level for each virtual machine. IOPS will also need to be measured for what the storage system can deliver. You may find your bottleneck is in the transport between the virtualization platform and the storage platform, or that your storage platform is taxed and may need more cache space.

Many of the assessment tools mentioned in *Chapter 2, Defining Your Desktop Virtualization Environment,* will provide reports on the IOPS per system. Another useful tool to create artificial throughput and to test IOPS capacity is IOMeter, available at `http://www.iometer.org/`. This runs on a virtual machine; you can identify which disk to test against, how many threads to run, write block size, and distribution of read/write activities. This utility can be used to check whether the virtual machines are getting full access to the IOPS requested, as shown in the following screenshot:

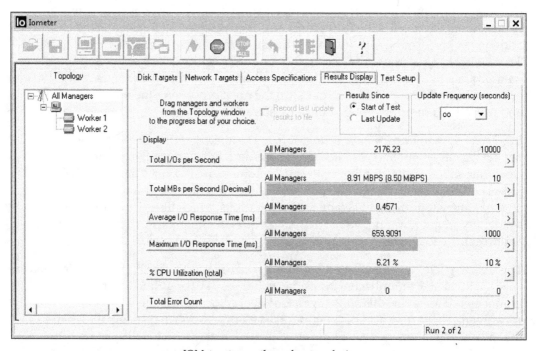

IOMeter storage throughput analysis

A general rule of thumb for Windows Servers is 10–40 IOPS per system. Intense data processing systems, such as SQL and Exchange, will require more IOPS. XenApp and XenDesktop are typically measured with IOPS per user. As with any design, if you are working on general assumptions versus empirical data, it should be noted and discussed.

For our design, we are using several assumptions for IOPS based upon the role of the system in question. Once the design is completed, these values should be measured against production data and all baselines should be updated. We are estimating 480 IOPS for the infrastructure systems. This is an average 15 IOPS for the base systems, plus an increase of IOPS for SQL and file servers. For the workload pool, we are estimating 3,190 IOPS, which works out to approximately 3–4 IOPS per user. The observed IOPS may be different.

If you are in an environment that needs a high amount of IOPS that cannot be delivered with traditional storage arrays, you may want to consider some of the specialty appliances such as Atlantis ILIO, which caches storage commands; dedicated SSD arrays; or flash memory arrays such as Violin for elevated performance. These devices can be used in conjunction with or as a replacement to traditional storage arrays.

Completing the architectural blueprint

At this point, we still have not actually built anything, but we have laid out the plans for all of our components. We should understand our use cases, our master design, and our resources. We have now effectively created a blueprint for our virtualization environment. The purpose of all of this legwork and planning is to have a solid design guide that can then be approved and implemented. When all elements are detailed in advance, the implementation phase can be split into multiple streams. In some organizations, different teams will be responsible for certain points of execution; in other environments, you may want to offload some of the activities to junior resources. Either way, as long as you have a clear and concise master plan, you can feel confident that it will be executed properly.

Summary

In this chapter, we looked at designing our infrastructure. In most environments, the infrastructure will be shared among multiple and different types of workloads. We discussed designing our workload independently of any preexisting constraints to determine where any bottlenecks are likely to occur. We started with defining our reference architecture, creating a picture of what our environment will look like. Based on this reference architecture, we can begin defining our resource requirements and build a design for our environment. We also discussed designing our virtualization platform, determining our underlying hardware components, and defining our networking and storage requirements.

Now we can begin our detailed design and build efforts, starting with our Access layer in the next chapter. In the next chapter, we will explore StoreFront and NetScaler Gateway. We will look at the various user access options to determine what the right fit is for our environment.

4
Designing Your Access Layer

In the previous chapters, we focused on analysis and high-level design. Now that our blueprint is complete, we can begin building our different layers. In this chapter, we will delve into the Access layer, including design considerations, best practices, and recommendations.

In this chapter, you will learn about the following:

- Designing your Access layer with StoreFront
- Designing your Access layer with NetScaler
- Managing end user access

Determining your portal presence

Designing your Access layer will partially depend on how you want users to access the Citrix environment. Will all users connect using the private corporate network only, or do you need to provide remote access to Internet-based connections? Do you support mobile devices or just personal computers? Are all users domestic, or is this a global access? Will users be using Citrix Receiver for direct access, or will they use a web browser? What type of network performance (latency or bandwidth) will the users' network connections have?

To gain the most value out of the flexibility of Citrix, the vast majority of customer deployments provide both local and remote access. This enables work at home as well as BYOD initiatives. This allows users who are remote, traveling, or using unsecured devices to have secure access to your applications and backend data systems.

For our environment, we assume local and secured remote access for a wide variety of devices using both Citrix Receiver and a web page for application access. We will be building our portal using Citrix StoreFront, but first, let's look at a comparison of Web Interface and StoreFront.

Comparing Web Interface and StoreFront

Both Citrix Web Interface and Citrix StoreFront are viable products for creating a web portal. Web Interface is currently at the end of the development phase and is in use in many environments. You can use both StoreFront and Web Interface in the same environment as well, if necessary, such as when using legacy environments or transitioning from one web portal to another.

Feature	Web Interface	StoreFront	Notes
Advanced customization	Yes	Limited	Ability to completely customize the user interface pages
Anonymous logon	Yes	Yes	Only valid for legacy XenApp Farms, not applicable for XenApp 7.5
Application search	Yes	Yes	Users can search for applications by title or description
Auto launch application or desktop	Yes	Yes	Automatic if only a single resource is published; it can be customized
Client deployment	Yes	Yes	Automatic Citrix client deployment
Client proxy settings	Yes	No	Configure user web proxy settings performance
Customize web session timeout	Yes	Yes	Determine web session timeout, the default is 20 minutes
Default IIS page	Yes	Yes	**WI**: Built in; **SF**: Requires HTML redirection page
Drop-down list of domains	Yes	Yes	Configured with authorization settings, including the ability to set a default domain
Error logging in event logs	Yes	Yes	Errors tracked in the Windows Application Event log

Feature	Web Interface	StoreFront	Notes
Explicit authentication	Yes	Yes	Authentication based on domain username and password
Favorite applications	No	Yes	Ability to save application shortcuts to your personal store
Filter or hide applications	Yes	Yes	**WI**: CTX122133; **SF**: Use of keywords and PowerShell
Integration with AppController	No	Yes	Integration with XenMobile
Integration with ShareFile	No	Yes	Requires an AppController appliance
Integration with web and Sass applications	No	Yes	Integration with XenMobile
Java client fallback	Yes	No	StoreFront uses an HTML5 client for fallback
Launch applications	Yes	Yes	Allow users to access hosted applications
Mandatory applications	Yes	Yes	Added feature in StoreFront 2.5 with use of keywords
Messages, notes, and so on	Yes	No	Messages are integrated in the Web Interface console. and they can be added to StoreFront through customizations
Native HTML5, iOS, and Android clients	No	Yes	Purpose-built receiver clients
NetScaler Gateway integration	Yes	Yes	Enable secure access through NetScaler
Parallel resource enumeration	No	Yes	Web Interface enumerates sites/farms serially, which can cause delays
Pass-through authentication	Yes	Yes	Added feature in StoreFront 2.5
Pass-through or mixed authentication	Yes	Yes	A mix of pass-through and explicit authentication
Pre-Launch XenApp applications	Yes	Yes	Session Pre-Launch is a feature of XenApp 6.5
Prepopulated domain	Yes	Yes	Prepopulate and optionally hide the domain field

Feature	Web Interface	StoreFront	Notes
Prevent multilaunch of applications	Yes	No	CTX124612
SmartCard and token authentication	Yes	Yes	Support for use of smart cards
Software Development Kit (SDK)	Yes	Yes	Added feature in StoreFront 2.5
Stateless web sessions	No	Yes	Each request is an independent transaction
Theme support	No	Yes	Design themes and custom style sheets
Tweak ICA parameters	Yes	Yes	Ability to modify the default ICA file settings
User password change	Yes	Yes	Allow users to change their passwords
Web UI change through console	Yes	No	SF requires modifying CSS files

Reviewing the Access tier diagram

As we discussed in *Chapter 3*, *Designing Your Infrastructure*, the Access tier includes both internal and external access. Here we represent our internal on-site users working on our corporate-owned and managed workstations. These are our trusted resources. They are already authenticated on the network and have direct access to the Citrix solution. These users will typically access a private internal portal. We also have all our unsecure resources access the system through the public Internet, coming in through our NetScaler Gateway. This may include remote offices without a direct wide area network link, mobile users, work at home users, and BYOD users.

Our Access tier consists of the end user devices connecting to Citrix StoreFront, either directly or through NetScaler Gateway. Our devices include corporate workstations, work at home computers, and mobile devices running both Android and iOS operating systems. Have a look at the following figure:

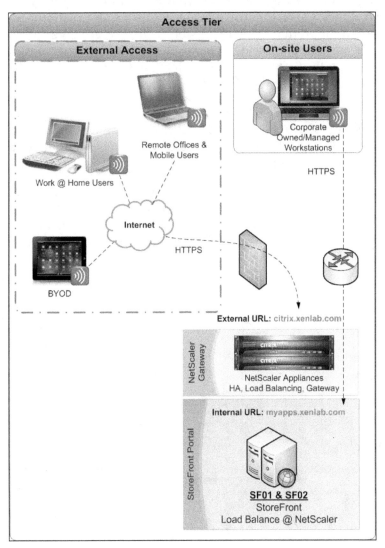

Access tier diagram

Designing with StoreFront

Citrix StoreFront was designed and built from the ground up using HTML5. One of the biggest complaints of Web Interface was the lack of support for the multiple development platforms used as the program was enhanced over the years. By starting fresh with StoreFront, Citrix was able to use a single platform. StoreFront was first released for production with Version 1.2 in July, 2012. Version 2.0 of StoreFront was released to coincide with XenDesktop 7, and it features many improvements over the first-generation production. The latest version, StoreFront 2.5, is part of the XenApp 7.5 release and supports all the latest features.

Although some customers liked the first version of StoreFront, most were not thrilled with some aspects of the architecture. However, the adoption rate quickly rose with StoreFront 2.0, and most new implementations are now using StoreFront. For this chapter, we will focus on StoreFront 2.5.

StoreFront provides the most consistent user experience by retaining users' application selections and presenting a common interface regardless of device or connection method. Using Receiver instead of the web browser maintains the same functionality as the older PNAgent to control how applications appear on the client. StoreFront sites are called **Stores**.

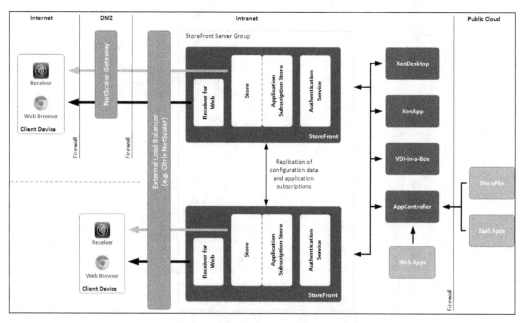

StoreFront architecture; © Citrix Systems, Inc. All Rights Reserved.

Requirements for StoreFront

Citrix StoreFront 2.5 is a lightweight web application. It can be run on standalone systems or combined with other functions on a common server. StoreFront has the following requirements:

- Windows Server 2008 R2 with Service Pack 1 or later
- Internet Information Services roles
- Windows Server 2008 Features: .NET Framework 3.5.1
- Windows Server 2012 Features: .NET Framework 3.5, NET Framework 4.5, and ASP.NET 4.5
- Citrix XenApp 5.0 or later for application enumeration
- Citrix XenDesktop 5.5 or later for desktop enumeration
- Citrix VDI-in-a-Box 5.2 or later for VDI enumeration
- NetScaler 9.3 or later for gateway features

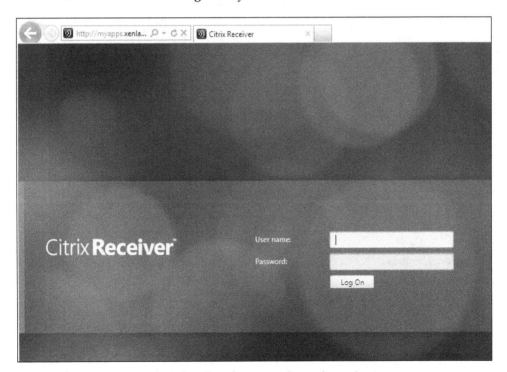

Citrix StoreFront logon page (internal access)

Design decisions for StoreFront

The following design decisions must be made when planning or implementing StoreFront. This decision matrix should be repeated for each store in use, as appropriate for the environment:

Option	Decision	Justification
Version	StoreFront 2.5	2.5 is the latest version of StoreFront
Location	Datacenter	Datacenter or network location StoreFront
Protocol	HTTPS	HTTPS is highly recommended for security purposes, but HTTP can be used
Number of servers	Two	
Hosts	SF01 SF02	List of server(s) hosting StoreFront
Operating system	2012	Base operating system of StoreFront
Server hardware	2 CPU 4 GB RAM 40 GB HDD	CPU, RAM, and disk space for the host machines
Load Balancing / High Availability	NetScaler VIP	How and where StoreFront is load balanced
Base URL	myapps.xenlab.com	Should be the load balancing URL
Authentication	Explicit	Authentication method(s) in use
Store name	Store	Name of StoreFront store
Store URL	/Citrix/Store	
Receiver web URL	/Citrix/StoreWeb	
Delivery controllers	xa7501 xa7502	List of delivery controllers and type (XenApp, XenDesktop, and VDI-in-a-Box)
Remote access	NetScaler Gateway	None for no remote access, no VPN Tunnel for standard gateway access, and full VPN tunnel for full gateway access (requires additional plugin)
NetScaler Gateway appliance	citrix.xenlab.com	Gateway address for remote access in two-arm mode, which is the callback address

Option	Decision	Justification
STA servers	xa7501 xa7502	List of STA servers, which must be the same as listed in Gateway
Trusted domain(s)	`xenlab.com`	
Internal beacons	`myapps.xenlab.com`	Internal URL only

External beacons	`http://www.citrix.com`
	
	`http://www.google.com`
		Any external URL

StoreFront Receiver for web applications, including featured and auto applications

StoreFront recommendations

A common request from many customers is to use the same address for internal and external users, allowing everyone to remember only a single address. According to Citrix, this is *not* supported for mobile devices. Mobile devices should be configured with a separate URL for internal access, if required. Another consideration is that most customers only allow wired connections on the secure network; all wireless mobile devices might be forced to use the NetScaler Gateway to connect. If all mobile devices are considered external, then you may be able to cheat and use the same address for both types of access.

However, if you allow mobile devices on the internal network, they might experience connection issues. Using a single URL also assumes that users will be using Receiver for web functionality, not native receiver functionality on their local computers. Should the customer wish to use a native receiver, separate internal and external URLs should be created. These can point to the same resources, but will require separate addresses.

If you choose to use a single URL for both internal and external access, you might want to leverage NetScaler to provide not only the gateway and load balancing features, but also the SSL offload. This will allow NetScaler to manage the server certificate for the URL and not require any binding on the StoreFront servers. This will also require the same DNS entries to be defined differently, both internally and externally.

For this environment, we are using separate addresses, so `https://citrix.xenlab.com` will resolve to a publically routable address that connects to the Access Gateway, as illustrated in the following figure:

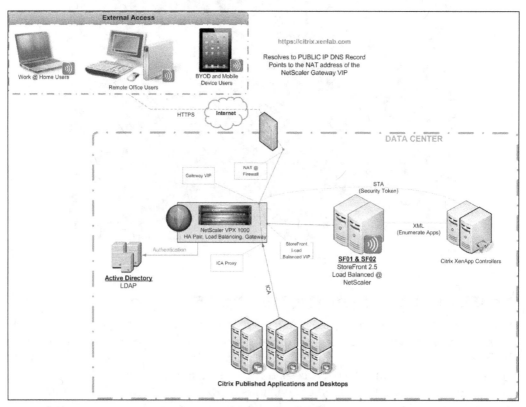

External access communication workflow

Internal and on-network resources will be directed to `http://myapps.xenlab.com`, which will resolve to a nonroutable private address pointing to the load balanced address for StoreFront servers, as illustrated in the following figure:

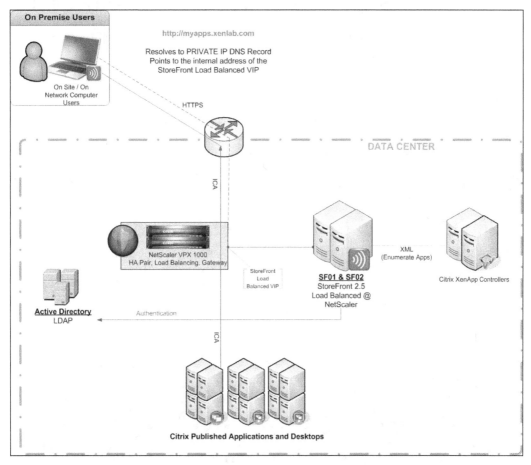

Internal access communication workflow

Customizations

StoreFront is built on HTML5 and can be customized. Much like Web Interface, most customers prefer to keep customizations to a minimum in order to ease troubleshooting and reduce the amount of rework necessary when patching or updating. Sometimes, customizations will be overwritten by updated files during a maintenance window.

The most basic customizations for StoreFront are around how applications are displayed. In a new environment, users will have no default applications. Unlike Web Interface, which shows all applications a user has access to, StoreFront will only show the applications they are subscribed to. Users might have access to hundreds of published applications but might choose to only keep a few on their receiver page. Additional customizations and recommendations can be found in the StoreFront Planning Guide available at `http://support.citrix.com/article/CTX136547`.

Speeding up StoreFront

You might want to apply the changes outlined at `http://support.citrix.com/article/ctx117273`. This involves modifying the `Aspnet.config` file to avoid generating publisher evidence, which is used to verify the .NET framework authenticode signature, and it can slow down the initial load time of the application. This article pertains to Web Interface, but it is applicable to StoreFront as well.

Using the application subscription model

Using the plus sign on the left-hand side of Receiver for the web StoreFront page, users can expand the list of applications. Users can then select the applications they want as part of their subscriptions, which appear on the main page. This limits the cluster on the web page and lets users control what they see. Applications with a green check mark are currently subscribed. This includes all auto and mandatory applications. We will discuss the keywords next.

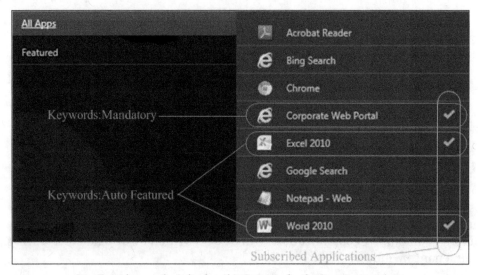

StoreFront keywords as displayed in Receiver for the StoreFront website

Using keywords for StoreFront applications and desktops

To prevent users from seeing a blank screen at first use, or to ensure that all users subscribe to a core application, you can apply keywords to an application description. Some possible keywords are **Auto** to automatically subscribe, **Featured** to include in the features application list, and **TreatAsApp** to have desktops displayed as an application. Multiple keywords, such as **KEYWORDS:Auto Featured**, need to be separated by a space. For more information, check out `http://support.citrix.com/proddocs/topic/dws-storefront-20/dws-plan-optimize-ux.html`.

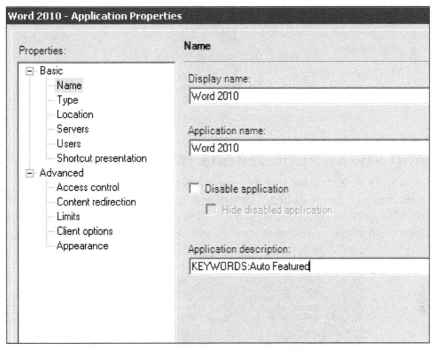

Application properties for StoreFront keywords in XenApp 6.5

For ease of reference, the preceding screenshot shows the application property settings for the Citrix XenApp 6.5 setup, while the following screenshot shows the equivalent settings in the new Citrix XenApp 7.5 interface:

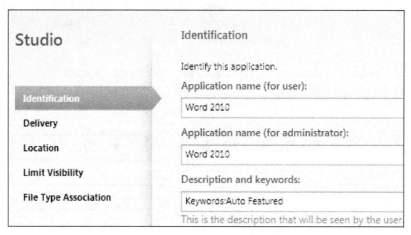

Application properties for StoreFront keywords in XenApp 7.5

Creating sticky applications for StoreFront

Though you have applications published with **Keywords:Auto**, users can unsubscribe from the applications. To ensure an application is forced, you can use **Keywords:Mandatory**. This has the same effect as automatically subscribing the application for all users; it also prevents users from removing the application from their subscriptions, as shown in the following screenshot:

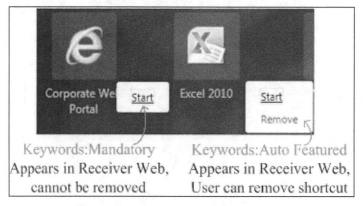

StoreFront mandatory and auto application keywords

Filtering or hiding applications from StoreFront

StoreFront allows you to hide published applications from StoreFront stores. Similar to hiding applications in Web Interface, this is useful when you have a common set of applications in your XenApp site, but due to security reasons, only want to enable an application from select StoreFront stores. This is also a way to hide applications from use without disabling them. The steps are detailed at http://blogs.citrix.com/2014/03/27/hiding-applications-in-citrix-storefront/. Similar to our earlier Web Interface example, we can filter any application with **Keyword:VDIOnly**, using the following PowerShell syntax:

```
Set-DSResourceFilterKeyword -SiteId 1 -VirtualPath "/Citrix/Store1"
`-ExcludeKeywords @("VDIOnly")
```

The Citrix Studio list of applications for each Delivery Group includes the keywords field, making it very easy to quickly see which keywords are assigned to each application. This will help in planning the use of keywords and understanding any impact around filters.

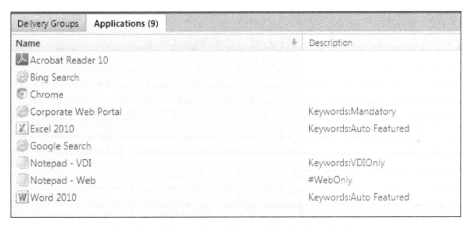

StoreFront keywords as displayed in XenApp Studio

Enabling discovery for mobile clients

StoreFront contains a provisioning file that can be distributed via e-mail to mobile clients. This is the fastest and easiest way for mobile devices to connect. It saves the users' time by not having to manually enter connection information, and it also saves headaches for the IT staff. To easily generate a provisioning file, click on the Activate link, which will create a file called receiverconfig.cr, which is an XML file containing all of the gateway and store information necessary for clients to connect. For more information, check out http://support.citrix.com/article/CTX134667.

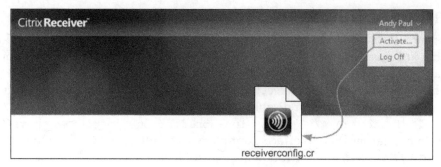

StoreFront discovery for mobile clients

Setting the default IIS page

One of the biggest complaints made about StoreFront is that it does not configure a default IIS site like Web Interface does. This is easily remedied by making a simple default HTML file to redirect users to the full URL of the desired Receiver for Web site. The steps are available at `http://support.citrix.com/article/CTX133903`.

Rebranding the Receiver for Web site

Some customers want to add their own design or branding to the Receiver for Web site. In theory, you can reprogram the entire site by modifying the various source files. Try to keep rebranding simple, just like with Web Interface. There is no need to rewrite the entire site. If you want to make some branding modifications, the best way is to modify the cascading style sheet (CSS) files in StoreFront. Detailed steps are available at `http://blogs.citrix.com/2013/06/26/customizing-receiver-for-web-in-storefront-2-0/`.

Using the HOST file to ease setup

Some administrators find it necessary to modify the local host file of StoreFront servers with two entries—one host file entry for the internal URL and a separate entry for the external (gateway) URL. This ensures the callback and authentication will work without relying on DNS or load balancer routing. To do this, edit the `c:\Windows\System32\drivers\etc\host` file to include entries such as the internal IP for NetScaler Gateway using an external URL and a localhost IP for the internal URL, modified for your environment. Check the following command line:

```
192.168.1.16 remote.xenlab.com #Inside NetScaler Gateway address for Call
Back
```

```
192.168.1.37 myapps.xenlab.com #Localhost IP for StoreFront URL
```

Designing with NetScaler Gateway™

Citrix NetScaler is the Swiss Army knife of network appliances. It can do almost anything and can serve many critical functions. It is a purpose-built appliance that comes in three general models: VPX, MPX, and SDX. The VPX series are virtual appliances; MPX models are physical appliances; SDX models are physical models running multiple virtual appliances, designed for multitenancy. Entire books can (and have) be written on managing NetScaler appliances. For this book, our focus will be on Gateway, Load Balancing, and SSL offload features. Other features, such as global server load balancing, application firewalls, smart access filters, traffic shaping, caching, and acceleration, will not be discussed here.

NetScaler can be deployed in a one-arm or two-arm mode. One-arm means only a single interface is active; this is the simplest and most common deployment. Two-arm means two (or more) interfaces are active, typically an internal link and a DMZ link. If you are using the two-arm mode, you should set the default gateway of the NetScaler appliances to the outbound router in the DMZ. Also, if you are using the two-arm mode, you might need to set route statements so you can manage/direct your internal traffic. Finally, if you are using a two-arm deployment, you might need to configure a second gateway address internally to use as a callback address for StoreFront.

For our environment, we use NetScaler VPX 1000 appliances deployed in a one-arm mode. We will be leveraging high availability, load balancing, NetScaler Gateway, and SSL offload features. Our VPX appliances will run on XenServer using NetScaler Version 10.1.

For more information on one-arm and two-arm deployment scenarios, I highly recommend Rick Rohne's article at http://www.thegenerationv.com/2009/09/netscaler-1-or-2-arm-mode-which-is.html. He details single-arm and multiple-arm configurations in an easy-to-understand manner.

Requirements for NetScaler VPX

NetScaler requirements will vary depending on which model of NetScaler appliance you are deploying, how many interfaces you choose to use, and the deployment platform. In general, you will need:

- VPX deployments:
    - XenServer 5.6 or later (VMware ESX 3.5 or later and Hyper-V 2008 are also supported)
    - 2 virtual CPUs
    - 3 GB RAM

- ° 40 GB drive space
- ° One 1-Gbps network interface (two or more for the two-arm mode)

- MPX or SDX deployments:
  - ° Physical appliance(s) installed in rack with power and network connection(s)

- License files (NetScaler licenses are registered to the primary interface MAC address)

- Requisite IP addresses:
  - ° One **NetScaler IP** (**NSIP**) per appliance, which is the management IP address.
  - ° One **Subnet IP** (**SNIP**) per subnet, including the primary network. The primary network SNIP is used for HA, and additional SNIPs allow for communication to devices on these separate network segments.
  - ° One IP per Virtual server / Virtual interface (VIP).

 To better understand the roles of mapped and subnet IP addresses, check out http://support.citrix.com/article/CTX120318.

In addition to the minimum requirements, design engineers and customers should do the following, including requesting a block of at least 10 IP addresses, however more or less may be needed:

- Reserve one IP address for the NetScaler Gateway to be used for remote/public access. This IP address will be publically accessible.

- Reserve one IP address for the StoreFront load balance interface for internal access.

- Reserve one IP address for the authentication services load balance interface, used to balance LDAP requests among multiple controllers on the internal network.

- Reserve one IP address for the DNS load balance interface to distribute DNS requests to multiple servers on the internal network (optional).

- Reserve one IP address for the desktop director load balance interface on the internal network (optional).

- Reserve one IP address for the load balanced XML broker interface, connecting to the controllers on the internal network (optional).

- Reserve one internal IP address for the NetScaler Gateway callback interface for StoreFront (optional, may be necessary in a two-arm deployment).

- When using gateway features for public access, request and install a public certificate, including an intermediate certificate to ensure the certificate chain is complete.

- Also, if using multiple domains, create separate authentication load balance interfaces along with a separate NetScaler Gateway interface and URLs per domain.

- If you are designing different authentication types (such as two-factor for authentication for Internet-based users, and single-factor authentication for partner-network users), create separate gateway interfaces.

Configuring the base settings for NetScaler

The initial configuration of NetScaler is done through the console. In a VPX appliance running on XenServer, this is available using the XenCenter console. For physical appliances, this is achieved using the direct console connection. Upon startup, you must supply the NetScaler appliance with an IP address, subnet mask, and gateway. This IP address becomes the NetScaler IP, or NSIP, and is used for all future management of the appliance.

To get started, you can download the VPX appliance from Citrix and then import the virtual appliance into XenServer using the XenCenter utility. Once the appliance is imported and powered on, you can begin the base configuration as shown in the following screenshot:

```
inetd cron httpd monit sshd .

!There is no ns.conf in the /nsconfig!

Start Netscaler software
tput: no terminal type specified and no TERM environmental variable.
Enter NetScaler's IPv4 address []: 192.168.1.10
Enter Netmask []: 255.255.255.0
Enter Gateway IPv4 address []: 192.168.1.1
-------------------------------------------------------------------
Netscaler Virtual Appliance Initial Network Address Configuration.
This menu allows you to set and modify the initial IPv4 network addresses.
The current value is displayed in brackets ([]).
Selecting the listed number allows the address to be changed.

After the network changes are saved, you may either login as nsroot and
use the Netscaler command line interface, or use a web browser to
http://192.168.1.10 to complete or change the Netscaler configuration.
-------------------------------------------------------------------
    1. NetScaler's IPv4 address [192.168.1.10]
    2. Netmask [255.255.255.0]
    3. Gateway IPv4 address [192.168.1.1]
    4. Save and quit
Select item (1-4) [4]:
```

NetScaler base configuration

Once the base configuration is complete, and the NetScaler appliance is rebooted, all other configuration activities will be performed through the NetScaler Java-based graphical user interface available at the management (NSIP) address. The default username is nsroot, and the password is nsroot. It is highly recommended that administrators change the nsroot password immediately. The main management console is shown in the following screenshot.

 Firefox or Chrome browsers perform better than Internet Explorer when using the graphical user interface console for NetScaler. There are some known issues with the Java applet. For more information, check out http://support.citrix.com/proddocs/topic/ns-faq-map-10-1/ns-faq-config-utility-ref.html.

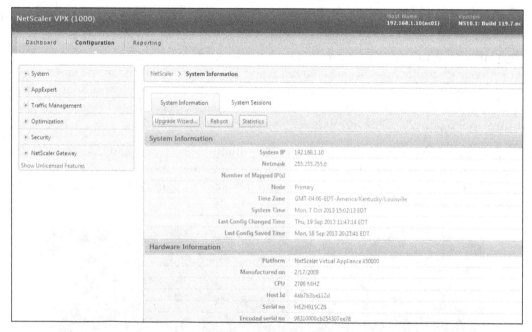

NetScaler configuration console

Configuring load balancing services

The NetScaler load balancing feature distributes requests across multiple servers to optimize resource utilization and ensure a level of fault tolerance. This prevents a single server from becoming overloaded while also providing health checks to ensure a server is available before a request is forwarded. A load balancer configuration consists of four components:

- **Server**: This is defined as the IP address of the backend target server that will host the actual client services. In our case, we will define a server for each of the servers running StoreFront.

- **Monitor**: Monitors are probes attached to each service type and are used to check the health of a target server. If a server does not respond within a specified response timeout, and the specified number of probes fails, the service is marked as down and taken out of load balancing until it becomes available again. In our scenario, we will use the custom monitor for StoreFront.

- **Service**: Services map a monitor to a server to define which service is being used. Alternately, service groups can be defined instead of individual services. We create two defined services, one for each StoreFront server, using the StoreFront monitor.

- **Virtual server**: A virtual server is hosted on NetScaler and is defined by an IP address and port. Services are bound to the virtual server, creating the load balance set. The virtual server IP address is the one used to connect to the load balance cluster of servers. We define a single virtual server to load balance StoreFront services among our two StoreFront servers.

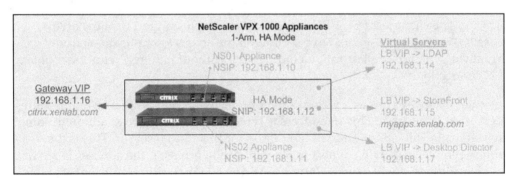

NetScaler connections planning diagram

In our environment, we have load balancing virtual servers defined for our LDAP authentication as well as StoreFront and Desktop Director, as noted in the preceding figure and displayed in the following screenshot:

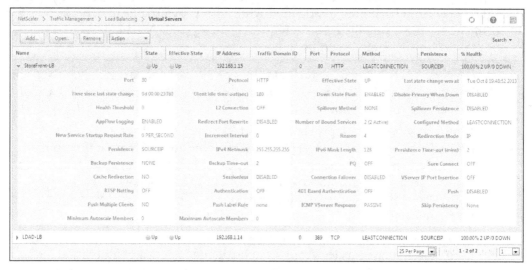

Defined load balanced servers in NetScaler, with load balancing details

Configuring NetScaler Gateway services

Citrix NetScaler Gateway is a secure desktop and application access solution that runs on a NetScaler appliance. It provides SSL VPN capabilities for application and/or network access. Full VPN access requires an additional NetScaler Gateway plugin for Receiver. Application and desktop access only requires the Citrix Receiver software. The client-less SSL VPN is the most common solution to allow access to users. This enables users to have secure remote access to applications from virtually any device or platform, including iOS, without having to run a secondary VPN connection.

NetScaler Gateway runs as a virtual server on the NetScaler appliance and requires a dedicated IP address. This IP address is typically a DMZ address, although some environments will use an internal IP address for this virtual server. This is the address remote users will connect to for application access; if the address is not a routable address, it will need a **Network Address Translation (NAT)** entry at the firewall level. As shown previously in the *External access communication workflow* diagram, remote users will attempt to access the URL (for example, citrix.xenlab. com). This will trigger a DNS lookup that should resolve to a public IP; the public IP will in turn be translated at the firewall to the NetScaler Gateway virtual IP.

Before you deploy NetScaler Gateway, you will need to configure the following, some of which may be done with load balancers:

- **IP Address**: Used for the NetScaler Gateway virtual server.

- **Firewall NAT Entry**: Firewall network address translation to translate the public IP address to the internal NetScaler Gateway virtual IP address.

- **URL**: Planned web address with DNS entries pointing to the public IP address.

- **Configure server certificate**: This is to request a signed SSL certificate and install it on NetScaler. It includes the root and intermediate certificates, to ensure the SSL chain remains intact. Some clients will generate an error when the intermediate certificate is not available, such as when using GoDaddy issued certificates, as shown in the following screenshot. For more information on installing and linking certificates, check out `http://support.citrix.com/article/CTX114146` and `http://support.citrix.com/article/CTX128539`.

Error due to missing an intermediate certificate

- **Configure authentication**: NetScaler can use multiple types of authentication, including LDAP, RADIUS, and RSA, among others. For our environment, we will use LDAP for domain authentication configured through a load balanced virtual server.

- **Access policies**: Policies define what criteria are required to allow access. This includes regular expressions to determine valid connections. Access policies also define where the connections connect once they are validated.

- **Secure ticket authority**: This is used as added security for Citrix XenApp and XenDesktop sessions to ensure the user is authorized to make the application request, since the request is generated after the user has authenticated to establish the session. This helps prevent a "man-in-the-middle" attack by client spoofing. The STA servers are typically the same as XenApp controllers or XML brokers; however, in larger environments, these roles may be split.

For more planning guides, check out `http://support.citrix.com/proddocs/` `topic/netscaler-gateway-101/ng-checklist-10-1-con.html`.

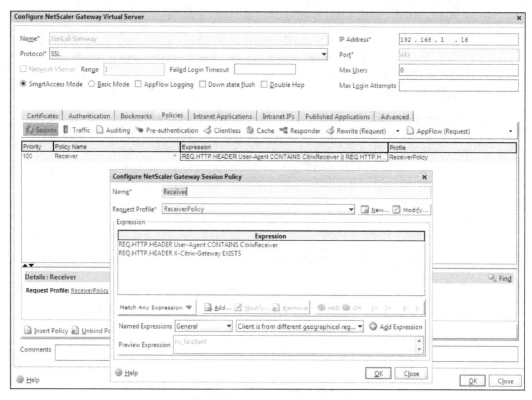

NetScaler Gateway configuration

Tying it all together

Designing and building a new Citrix environment involves a lot of moving pieces. For example, you cannot fully build StoreFront without having XenApp servers to connect for XML services, and you cannot launch applications until you build your XenApp servers and publish the applications. On the other hand, you cannot effectively test XenApp until you have StoreFront built and you can validate your applications. The same goes for NetScaler; do you define your load balanced servers first, or do you build your individual components first and then define your load balanced servers?

This creates a lot of *chicken and egg* problems. That is why planning is so important. At this point, refer to *Chapter 3, Designing Your Infrastructure*, particularly the reference architecture and the virtual machine planning spreadsheet. You can see that we laid out what we will do long before we do it. Since we know what will be defined where, we can build elements and define references to objects that might not be built yet. Once we have all the individual components built, we can tie them together and complete our testing.

You might find the following guides useful:

- Citrix StoreFront Implementation Guide: `http://support.citrix.com/article/CTX133185`
- Citrix XenDesktop 5.6 with Receiver StoreFront and Access Gateway: `http://support.citrix.com/article/CTX132787`

Since there are many parts to integrating StoreFront and NetScaler, it is easy to get lost. To make this process easier, you can follow this handy cheat sheet when building new environments.

Identifying the base requirements

Gather your design principles and basic settings, such as:

- NetScaler Gateway
- Load balancing features
- SSL offload
- High Availability
- Other

Gathering all the prerequisites

Based on your design elements, document the following key decisions:

- Identify target URLs for internal and external access:
  - Request SSL certificates for each address
- Determine deployment mode (one-arm or two-arm)
- Secure IP address for NetScaler appliances:
  - One address per appliance (NSIP)
  - One address per subnet (SNIP)
  - One address per Virtual Server (VIP)

Installing NetScaler appliances

Install physical appliances or import virtual appliances, and then configure your appliances:

- Assign the management IP address, subnet mask, and the default gateway and reboot your system
- Connect via web browser to management IP address and complete configuration:
    ◦ Change NSROOT password
    ◦ Install license files (based on Mac address of appliance)
    ◦ Configure SNIP
    ◦ Install certificate(s)
- Configure second appliance:
    ◦ Enable HA mode

Installing and configuring StoreFront servers

Deploy your virtual servers for StoreFront using your standards and then perform the following tasks:

1. Modify the host file:
    ◦ Create an entry for the base URL using the localhost address
    ◦ Create an entry for the Gateway callback (if necessary)

2. Install StoreFront 2.5 on two (or more) servers:
    ◦ IIS will be installed if it is not already

3. Create a new deployment:
    ◦ Assign a base URL
    ◦ Assign a store name
    ◦ Add delivery controllers

 ° Select **Remote Access** (no VPN tunnel)

 Enter NetScaler Gateway information

 Enter STA server address

 Select/unselect **Enable Session Reliability**

 ° Create deployment

4. Configure StoreFront:

 ° Update **Authentication Method**

 Add domain pass-through for local receivers

 Configure trusted domains

 Modify password options (optional)

 ° Review store settings

 ° Review NetScaler Gateway settings

 ° Review/manage beacons

5. Install StoreFront on the second server:

 ° Modify the hosts file

 ° Install StoreFront

 ° Join existing server group

 Click on **Add Server** on StoreFront #1

 Enter authorization code in StoreFront #2

 ° Verify all settings copied properly

Configuring load balance virtual servers on NetScaler®

Once your StoreFront (or Web Interface) servers are configured, you can create the load balancing configuration on NetScaler:

1. Sign in to the NetScaler web console and select **Load Balancing** under **Traffic Management**:

 ° Enable feature, if necessary

2. Select **Servers** and add a server for each target:
   - ° Enter name and IP address for each server

3. Select **Monitors** and add specialty monitors, as necessary:
   - ° Create StoreFront Monitor using the custom type **STOREFRONT**
     Use **Store name**, but keep **Host name** blank
     This allows one monitor to be reused
   - ° Create an LDAP monitor using custom type LDAP
     Check out `http://support.citrix.com/article/CTX114335`
   - ° If using Web Interface, create a monitor using **CITRIX-WEB-INTERFACE**
     Use the URL of the website logon page
   - ° If using XML load balancers, select **CITRIX-XML-SERVICE**

4. Select **Services** and add services to monitor servers:
   - ° Alternately, you can use service groups instead of individual servers
   - ° Name services by the monitor and server in use, such as LDAP-AD01

5. Select **Virtual Servers** and create the load balance groups:
   - ° Enter name and IP of the LB VIP
   - ° Select the protocol and port
   - ° Select the services (or service groups) to balance
   - ° Select the method and persistence
   - ° Apply the SSL binding, if necessary
   - ° The suggested load balanced servers are:
     LDAP
     StoreFront
     Web Interface
     XML

6. Verify load balancers are operating correctly.

Configuring the NetScaler Gateway™ virtual server

Finally, once all other components are completed, you can configure the Gateway virtual server:

1. Sign in to NetScaler Web Console and select **NetScaler Gateway**:
   - Enable feature, if necessary

2. Select **Policies, Authentication**, and **LDAP**:
   - Create LDAP authentication policy
   - Assign name and add server
     Define Authentication Server, and use IP for the LDAP LB VIP
     Use the service account name with rights to read the directory
     Click on **Retrieve Attributes to verify**
   - Add the TRUE expression

3. Select **Policies** and **Session**:
   - Create a session policy
   - Assign name and create new profile
     Name Policy
     Configure Client Experience, Security, and Published Applications tabs
   - Create expressions:
     REQ.HTTP.HEADER User-Agent CONTAINS CitrixReceiver
     REQ.HTTP.HEADER X-Citrix-Gateway EXISTS
   - Create a second policy for **Web Only** used as fallback/failsafe policy

4. Select **Virtual Servers** and add a new virtual server:
   - Assign a name, an IP address, and a certificate
   - Assign an authentication policy
   - Assign session policies
   - Insert a clientless policy:
     Create a new CVPN policy for URL rewrite
   - Publish apps and add secure ticket authorities

5. Validate remote access through NetScaler Gateway.

6. Add additional preauthorization and session policies, as required.

NetScaler Gateway logon page

Summary

In this chapter, we looked at designing our Access layer. In most new environments, StoreFront will be utilized. However, some legacy environments might still use Web Interface. There is no wrong answer; as we saw in the comparison matrix, there are pros and cons to either platform. Some environments will use both. A web portal is secured and extended using NetScaler Gateway. The biggest takeaway is pre-planning since you will need at least one and possibly multiple SSL certificates, depending on your environment.

We will begin designing our application delivery in the next chapter. We will step through the key design elements for our XenApp 7.5 site, including infrastructure, delivery groups, and application delivery strategies.

5
Designing Your Application Delivery Layer

In the previous chapters, we focused on analysis and high-level design and began filling out our environment starting with the Access layer. In this chapter, we will delve into the Application Delivery layer, including design considerations, best practices, and recommendations.

In this chapter, you will learn about the following:

- Designing your XenApp deployment
- Configuring XenApp controllers
- Configuring XenApp session hosts
- Using Delivery Groups
- The application of delivery models

Welcome to XenApp® 7.5

This book is written about XenApp 7.5 Platinum Edition. This feature set was chosen because it is the most current XenApp release at the time of writing as well as the most feature rich. XenApp 7.5 was released on March 26, 2014. XenApp 7.5 and XenDesktop 7.5 have been fully merged into the same product set, so many of the features we discuss will be common with XenDesktop. This is a radical change from the previous editions of XenApp.

What's new in XenApp 7.5?

In the *Preface*, we briefly discussed what is new in XenApp 7.5, but let's take a deeper dive.

XenApp 7.5 uses **FlexCast Management Architecture (FMA)**, which was first introduced with XenDesktop 5; this replaces **Independent Management Architecture (IMA)** used in the previous XenApp versions. FMA offers more scalability and removes the management layer from the operating system. This makes it easier to manage multiple versions of Windows. With this change of architecture, XenApp 7.5 currently supports Windows Server 2008 R2 and Windows Server 2012 as valid server operating systems. However, by moving away from IMA, there are some features that have been lost. These will be covered later in this chapter.

XenApp 7.5 now supports **hybrid cloud provisioning**. This gives administrators the ability to provision and deliver desktops and applications from **Citrix CloudPlatform** as well as **Amazon Web Services**. This might be done for burst capacity, transitional workloads, and leveraging outsourced **Infrastructure-as-a-Service (IAAS)**.

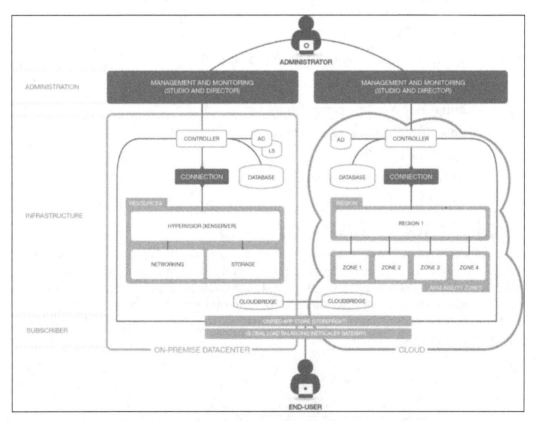

Hybrid cloud design; © Citrix Systems, Inc. All Rights Reserved.

The full feature set of **AppDNA** is available for XenApp and XenDesktop Platinum Edition customers. This was covered in *Chapter 2, Defining Your Desktop Virtualization Environment*.

Receiver and **StoreFront** enhancements include support for anonymous logins, domain pass-through authentication, mandatory apps, and smart card authentication. This also includes extending support for **Web Interface 5.4** officially. These features are covered in *Chapter 4, Designing Your Access Layer*.

Citrix Director is a replacement for **EdgeSight**®. Director is a real-time agentless monitoring utility introduced with Citrix XenDesktop 5, which also supports Citrix XenApp 6.0 and higher. Director communicates directly with the controllers and uses the controller interface to read from the backend database. Director uses **Windows Remote Management (WinRM)** and **Windows Remote Assistance** to communicate directly with the session or desktop on demand. This allows Director to have real-time information without extensive network communication previously required by EdgeSight. Based on licensing levels, this data can be retained for up to a year. When combined with NetScaler and HDX Insight Monitoring Appliance, this can include end-to-end user network data as well. This is covered in more detail in *Chapter 7, Designing Your Supporting Infrastructure Components*.

Integration with **XenMobile**, including cross-promotional licensing with XenMobile Enterprise, is now part of XenApp and XenDesktop 7.5.

Updated concepts in XenApp 7.5

In the *Preface*, we laid out a table comparing XenApp 7.5 terms with the previous versions. Let's take a closer look at some of these updated concepts.

FMA replaces the IMA used in previous versions of XenApp, which we already mentioned. However, FMA introduces several changes in architecture. Previously, **farms** were the top-level objects in the XenApp architecture; each farm could be composed of multiple sites. In XenApp 7.5, the **Delivery Site** is the highest-level item. Sites offer applications and desktops to groups of users. FMA also requires domain membership.

XenApp 6 introduced the concept of **Controllers** and session hosts. Controllers, derived from the earlier **Zone Data Collectors** (**ZDC**), ran the management software and were responsible for the farm operations, including brokering connections with the XML service. Session hosts were responsible for user workloads; this is where users would connect to run their applications and desktops. The controllers are also capable of running user workloads, but are generally reserved for management purposes only. With XenApp 7.5, the **delivery controller** role is similar, but instead of **Election Preference** to define a most preferred controller, all controller functions are distributed among all controllers in a site.

Application servers in XenApp 6.x belonged to **Worker Groups**, which made for efficient management of application assignments. Earlier versions required applications to be published individually on a server-by-server basis. With XenApp 6.x, administrators can manage all session hosts in a worker group as a single entity for application deployment and load balancing. Within the farm, **folders** were used to organize applications and servers, allowing a delegation of administration. With XenApp 7.5, you use **Machine Catalogs** to manage machines and **Delivery Groups** to manage load balancing and hosted applications or desktops.

In previous versions of XenApp, all servers in the farm required the full Citrix XenApp product set to be installed and were typically designed for a single operating system (for example, XenApp 6 for Windows Server 2008, XenApp 6.5 for Windows Server 2008 R2, and so on). With XenApp 7.5, the session hosts only require **Virtual Delivery Agent** (**VDA**) to be installed, which communicates with the delivery controllers to manage connections. By using a VDA as opposed to a full installation, XenApp can now support multiple operating systems, including Windows Server 2008 R2 and Windows Server 2012, in order to deliver desktops and applications. For those using XenDesktop 7.5 as well, this includes Windows 7 and Windows 8 desktop operating systems, all from a single delivery architecture.

In XenApp 6.5, all farm management was performed through a management console called the **Delivery Services Console**. Earlier versions used consoles under various names, such as AppCenter, Advanced Configuration Console, or Access Management Console. XenApp 7.5 now uses Citrix Studio, the same as XenDesktop, for all management functionality. All commands are also available through PowerShell.

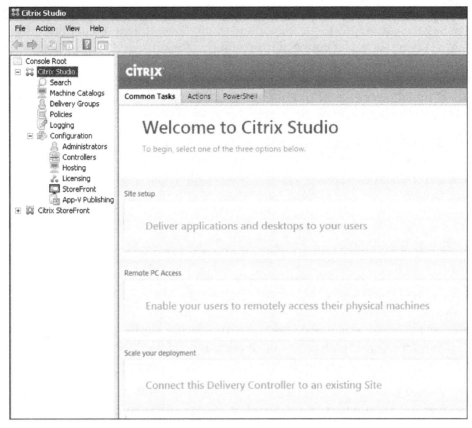

Citrix Studio

Another new feature of XenApp 7.5 that may be new to most XenApp administrators is **Director**, formerly called Desktop Director as part of XenDesktop. Director is a monitoring tool used by Director to monitor environment health, shadow users, and help with troubleshooting issues. It replaces older features such as the shadowing toolbar, health monitoring and recovery (HMR), and EdgeSight.

XenApp 7.5 does not use the IMA datastore, like previous versions, to store persistent configuration information. The IMA datastore could run on multiple platforms, and it only contained configuration settings and no real-time data, which allowed it to go offline with limited effect. Now, configuration and real-time session data are stored in a Microsoft SQL Server database, which is a critical component. We will cover this more in *Chapter 7, Designing Your Supporting Infrastructure Components*.

In the previous versions of XenApp, load evaluators used predefined measurements, such as session count, processor utilization, or memory utilization, to determine the load on a server. New user connections could then be directed to the servers with the least load. XenApp 7.5 uses load management policies to balance load across servers. This is now part of Citrix policies as opposed to separate load evaluators. Although similar in function, one key difference is that load evaluators could be applied at the server or application level; load management policies are applied to the entire Delivery Group.

For XenApp administrators, the administration has changed as well. In the previous versions, you could create custom administrators and assign permissions based on folders and objects. In XenApp 7.5, custom administrators are based on role and scope. A role represents a job function and has defined permissions; a scope represents a collection of objects. We will cover this more in *Chapter 9, Implementing Your XenApp® Solution*.

What's missing in XenApp 7.5?

As with any radical change, some features will be lost. Some of the new features introduced in XenApp 6.x were based on IMA features, and are not available with FMA. Other longtime IMA features have been depreciated. Some of the following features might be added back in future feature packs or version updates:

- **Zones**: Election Preference as well as the Zone Preference and Failover features are not part of XenApp 7.5. XenApp 7.5 is built on the XenDesktop model of sites, with each location being a single site as opposed to a global farm in previous versions. Each site is the logical equivalent of a zone. Since the controllers share all management functions, there is no need for Election Preference. For failover planning, you can use **Global Server Load Balancing (GSLB)** between multiple XenApp sites.

- **Worker Groups**: Introduced in XenApp 6, they are used to create groups of servers for application publishing. This was an improvement on previous versions that required individual resource publishing to each XenApp server. In XenApp 6.x, servers could be a part of multiple Worker Groups. With XenApp 7.5, servers only belong to a single Delivery Group.

- **Direct application publishing**: XenApp 7.5 uses Delivery Groups to publish applications, losing the ability to publish individual applications to select users and groups. For example, if you have 10 servers in a Delivery Group and publish Microsoft Word, all 10 servers should be able to deliver Word. If you only wanted three of the servers to deliver Word, you would need to carve them out into a separate Delivery Group. We will discuss Delivery Groups in more detail later in this chapter.

- **Application streaming**: This is no longer built into the XenApp 7.5 product set. Earlier versions of XenApp allowed the creation of application packages to be streamed on demand to servers or client systems for localized exaction. XenApp 7.5 relies on integration with Microsoft App-V to provide this functionality.

- **Secure Gateway**: This is no longer supported. In previous releases, Secure Gateway was an option to provide secure connections between the server and user devices using a Windows-based server in the DMZ to broker the secure connections. NetScaler Gateway, formerly Citrix Access Gateway, is the replacement for secure external connections and has long been the preferred method.

- **Shadowing**: Shadowing users through the Delivery Services Console and the Shadow Toolbar are no longer available; this has been replaced with the Director component that uses Microsoft Remote Assistance. In previous releases, administrators set policies to control user-to-user shadowing.

- **Legacy printing**: This is no longer supported; it includes legacy client printer names and compatibility for DOS-based and 16-bit printers and Windows 95 or Window NT client systems. This also includes the ability to enable or disable autoretained and autorestored printers.

- **Secure ICA**: In previous releases, Secure ICA could encrypt client connections for basic, 40-bit, 56-bit, and 128-bit encryption. In XenApp 7.5, ICA encryption is available only for 128-bit encryption.

- **Anonymous users**: These are no longer supported in XenApp 7.5. Although not widely used, anonymous rights allowed guest users permission to access applications without user authentication. In XenApp 7.5, no guest permissions are supported. All applications and desktops are allocated through Delivery Groups, which require Active Directory user or group assignment for access permission. This feature is on the road map to be added in future releases.

- **Session pre-launch**: First introduced in XenApp 6.5, it was used to reduce application launch time. This feature is not available in this release, but it is planned to be re-introduced in future releases.

- **Session linger**: Also introduced in XenApp 6.5, it is not currently available in this release. Linger is used to keep a session in standby mode after a user closes; if the user launches another application within the linger window, they will reconnect to the previous session as opposed to launching a new session. This feature is under development and will be added again in future releases.

For more information on session pre-launch and session linger, check `http://blogs.citrix.com/2014/04/15/part-3-new-and-improved-session-pre-launch-and-lingering-coming-to-xenapp-and-xendesktop`.

- **Health Monitoring and Recovery (HMR)**: Available in previous releases, this could run tests on the servers in a server farm to monitor their state and discover any health risks. The monitoring features are now replaced by Director; however, there are currently no built-in recovery features available.

- **Local Text Echo**: Used to accelerate the display of input text on user devices on high latency connections, this is not included in XenApp 7.5 due to improvements to the graphics system and HDX protocol.

- **Local Host Cache**: This is used to create a local cache of the IMA datastore and was designed to allow XenApp servers to continue to operate if the database was inaccessible. In XenApp 7.5, no new sessions can launch if the SQL database is unavailable. An upcoming feature enhancement called Connection Leasing is on the road map, which will allow users to connect to resources even if the database is offline.

- **Smart Auditor**: This is used to record the onscreen activity of a user's session; it is no longer available.

- The **Single Sign-on** feature: This provides password security and is not supported for Windows 8 and Windows Server 2012 environments due to changes in the login process. It is still supported for the Windows 2008 R2 and Windows 7 environments. It is not included in the XenApp 7.5 media, but it is still available for download from the Citrix website.

- **Datastore**: Only SQL databases are supported for this release of XenApp. Previous versions provided support for Oracle databases as well as for Microsoft Access.

- **Virtual IP**: This is used for loopback support. In previous releases, this policy setting could allow each session to have its own virtual loopback address for communication, which may have been a requirement of certain applications for security or licensing. This is not available in XenApp 7.5; however, there is a Microsoft workaround for Windows Server 2012. For more information, check `http://social.technet.microsoft.com/wiki/contents/articles/15230.rds-ip-virtualization-in-windows-server-2012.aspx`.

Designing your XenApp® deployment

When first discussing XenApp, the conversation might lead to questions about *VDI* or *Cloud Computing* and where XenApp fits in. This is an opportune time to remind your fellows that Citrix, with the XenApp line of products, has effectively been providing VDI and Cloud Computing services for 25 years! Even with the XenDesktop 7 line that merged XenApp and XenDesktop into a single product line, there is still emphasis on Hosted Shared Desktops and Hosted Applications for maximum density. We are focusing on XenApp 7.5 Platinum Edition; however, the lessons learned here can apply to older legacy XenApp farms or new XenDesktop 7 implementations. We can even extend our XenApp 7.5 environment into the cloud if necessary, using the concepts discussed in *Chapter 3, Designing Your Infrastructure*.

A XenApp 7.5 site consists of the following primary components:

- Controllers
- Session hosts
- Databases
- Licenses

Within the site, the following multiple configuration elements impact the overall design and function:

- Machine Catalogs
- Delivery Groups
- Applications
- Policies

Requirements for XenApp

Citrix XenApp 7.5 has multiple components. In smaller environments, some of these components may live on the same server, as shown in the following screenshot. In enterprise environments, separate servers will be dedicated to each component. For our environment, we will treat each component separately. We will list the requirements here, but some might be addressed elsewhere in this book.

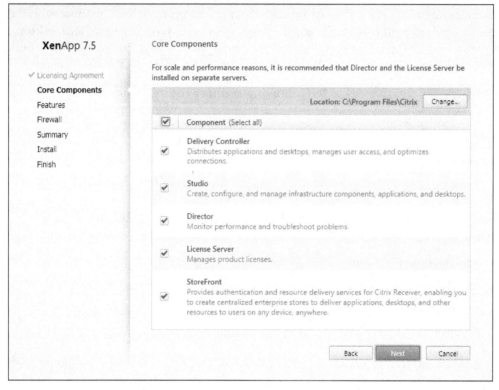

Sample core component installation option

In our environment, we will run Studio on the delivery controllers. We will also use VDA on our deliver controllers, to enable publishing of management resources. This is strictly optional and is not a requirement of XenApp. We run our SQL databases and director services on other systems.

Delivery controller

The delivery controller role, the core component of the XenApp site, requires the following elements:

- Windows Server 2008 R2 SP1 or later

- Windows Server 2008 features: Microsoft .NET Framework 3.5 SP1 and PowerShell 2.0

- Windows Server 2012 features: Microsoft .NET Framework 4.5 and PowerShell 3.0

- Visual C++ 2005, 2008 SP1, and 2010 redistributable packages

Studio

Studio, used to manage the XenApp site, can be installed on controllers, standalone management machines, or both. I typically install my management tools on controllers, but this is not a requirement. To run Studio, you need the following:

- Windows 7 or later or Windows Server 2008 R2 SP1 or later

- Windows 7 or Server 2008 features: Microsoft .NET Framework 3.5 SP1 and PowerShell 2.0

- Windows 8 or Server 2012 features: Microsoft .NET Framework 4.5 and PowerShell 3.0

- The Microsoft management console

Database

The role of the database has changed from the previous versions of XenApp. It is now a core component of site deployment and should be engineered with High Availability and fault tolerance as part of the design. We will cover this in more detail in *Chapter 7, Designing Your Supporting Infrastructure Components*. For now, we need to understand the following database requirements:

- SQL Server 2012 SP1, Express, Standard, and Enterprise Editions

- SQL Server 2008 R2 SP2, Express, Standard, Enterprise, and Datacenter Editions

- SQL Server Clustered Instances

- SQL Server Mirroring

- SQL Server 2012 AlwaysOn Availability Groups

Windows authentication is required for connections between the controller and the SQL Server database.

SQL Server 2012 Express can be installed on the controller as part of a single server deployment or if a SQL server is not available. This is not recommended for a production environment since it supports only a standalone mode with no high availability.

Director

Director can be combined with the controllers in smaller environments. For enterprise-scale deployments, I typically recommend having the Director role separate. For the installation Director, your system must meet the following prerequisites.

- Windows Server 2008 R2 SP1 or later

- Internet Information Services roles

- .NET Framework 4.5 and ASP.NET 2.0

Virtual Delivery Agent (VDA) for the Windows desktop OS

Since we are focusing on XenApp 7.5, we will not be using any desktop OS systems. However, since the XenApp and XenDesktop product sets are merged, you might find the need to include some desktop OS deployments in your environment. VDA for a desktop OS requires the following:

- Windows 8.1, Professional and Enterprise editions

- Windows 8, Professional and Enterprise editions

- Windows 7 SP1, Professional, Enterprise, and Ultimate editions

- Microsoft .NET Framework 3.5 SP1

- Microsoft .NET Framework 4.0

- Microsoft Visual C++ 2010 Runtime (32-bit or 64-bit, depending on the platform)

- Remote PC access uses this VDA, which you install on physical office PCs

- Microsoft Media Foundation recommended for enhanced media redirection (optional)

You cannot install a Version 7.5 VDA on a machine running Windows XP or Windows Vista; however, you can install an earlier Virtual Desktop Agent version on the operating systems if needed.

Virtual Delivery Agent (VDA) for the Windows server OS

VDA does not need to be installed on the controllers. However, it can be installed there if you want to publish the controller desktops or the management tools for convenience. When installing VDA, the following requirements must be met:

- Windows Server 2012 R2, Standard and Data center editions
- Windows Server 2012, Standard and Data center editions
- Windows Server 2008 R2 SP1, Standard, Enterprise, and Data center editions
- The Remote Desktop Services role
- Microsoft .NET Framework 3.5 SP1
- Microsoft .NET Framework 4.5.1
- Microsoft Visual C++ 2005, 2008, and 2010 Runtimes (32-bit and 64-bit)
- Microsoft Media Foundation recommended for enhanced Media Redirection (optional)

Design decisions for the XenApp site

The following design decisions must be made when planning or implementing a new XenApp site. The delivery controllers should be configured with static IP addresses, while the virtual machines used to deliver applications and desktops will use DHCP IP addresses. The following table outlines key decisions related to planning a new XenApp site:

Option	Decision	Justification
XenDesktop version	7.5 Platinum	XenApp 7.5 Platinum is the latest release
VDA version	7.5	7.5 is the most current VDA available
Number of sites	1	Typically, one per data center; might have one additional for testing and development
Number of controllers	2	Typically, two per site for fault tolerance; each controller can support up to 10,000 connections

Option	Decision	Justification
Delivery Controllers	xa7501 xa7502	List of controllers
Controller location	Datacenter	Host cluster or physical location of controllers
Database	LABSQL	Name of SQL database server
Number of users	500	Planned number of users (list both total and concurrent)
Number of applications	30	Planned number of applications to publish
Number of virtual servers	25 desktops 12 apps	Planned number of virtual desktops to host
Number of Directors	2	Typically two per site for fault tolerance
Machine Catalogs	Controllers Legacy Corporate Desktop Development	List of planned Machine Catalogs
Delivery Groups	Line of Business Test Applications Corporate Desktop Controllers	List of planned Delivery Groups
Time zones	EST	Specific time zone of servers, and whether client device time zones will be used
Session encryption	No	Specify whether secure ICA is required
XML encryption	No	Specify whether XML encryption is required
Administrators	CitrixAdmins	List of groups for delegated administration and their roles
Hosting environment	XenServer 6.0.2	Lost hosting environment details, including base platform and connection point; optionally, list planned network and storage as well
Licensing	ctxlic	List license server, license quantity, and license type

Using a decision matrix or table, like the one listed here, helps to make sure that all key decisions are discussed and made in advance. This ensures a smooth implementation process and eliminates the need to wait on other components. Recalling the Application Delivery tier from our reference architecture, as shown in the following figure, we can see a visual of our high-level plan.

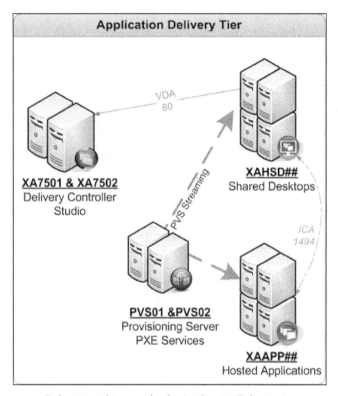

Reference architecture for the Application Delivery tier

Creating your XenApp® site

Once all the planning and design work is complete, we can begin the actual build process. A XenApp site consists of one or more controllers, product licenses, and supporting databases. We have supporting components, which we can use as well. These supporting components include provisioning services, file and print servers, Director, and so on. For now, we will focus on building our XenApp site, starting with our controllers. We will cover some of the other components in future chapters.

Quick start guide to deploy a XenApp site

The following provides a quick start guide or check list to rapidly deploy your XenApp site. The following sections provide more detail, including reference graphics; however, this quick start guide provides a handy reference:

1. Create a standardized server OS template.

2. Deploy a VM from the template for use as a controller.

3. Configure this VM with a static IP address and join to the domain.

4. Make sure the Active Directory machine object is placed in the proper OU.

5. Ensure the proper service accounts and/or Active Directory security groups are placed in the local administrative group. These accounts will be used for all installation activities.

6. Mount the XenApp installation media ISO to the virtual DVD drive of the VM.

7. Sign in with an administrative account, preferably a dedicated service account.

8. Run **Autoselect** from the installation media.

9. On the installation splash screen, click on the **Start** button next to **XenApp**.

10. On the installation screen, select the product to install, in this case **Delivery Controller**.

11. Agree to the software license agreement, and click on **Next**.

12. Select the core components to install, check **Delivery Controller** and **Studio**, and click on **Next**.

13. Select the features to install, uncheck **Install Microsoft SQL Server 2012 Express**, ensure **Install Windows Remote Assistance** is checked, and then click on **Next**.

14. Review **Firewall Ports**, select **Automatically**, and then click on **Next**.

15. Review the **Summary** page, verify all information, and then click on **Install**.

16. Once the installation is complete, leave **Launch Studio** checked, and click on **Finish**.

At this point, the delivery controller is installed, but not configured. When **Studio** launches, click on **Deliver applications and desktops to your users** in the **Welcome to Citrix Studio** screen and perform the following steps:

1. Select the **fully configured site** option and provide a site name, and then click on **Next**.

2. Enter **database server location, database name**, and **test the connection**. Once the database connection is confirmed, click on **Next**.

3. Enter **license server address** and **port**, click on **Connect**, and then select the existing license. Click on **Next** once complete.

4. Enter the hypervisor connection information, selecting the type of hypervisor and the connection information, including the user account. Click on **Next** once complete.

5. Select and name the virtual network resources for use by deployed virtual machines, and click on **Next**.

6. Select the available storage options from the hypervisor for use by deployed virtual machines and click on **Next**.

7. Specify whether you plan to use App-V in this deployment, and click on **Next**.

8. Review the **summary**, and click on **Finish** to finalize **Site Setup**.

Once the site setup is complete, you can configure Machine Catalogs and Delivery Groups, or add additional Controllers. To add a second controller, follow these steps:

1. Deploy a VM from the template for use as a controller.

2. Configure this VM with a static IP address and join to the domain.

3. Make sure the Active Directory machine object is placed in the proper OU.

4. Ensure the proper service accounts and/or Active Directory security groups are placed in the local administrative group. These accounts will be used for all installation activities.

5. Mount the XenApp installation media ISO to the virtual DVD drive of the VM.

6. Sign in with an administrative account, preferably a dedicated service account.

7. Run **Autoselect** from the installation media.

8. On the installation splash screen, click on the **Start** button next to **XenApp**.

9. On the installation screen, select the product to install, in this case **Delivery Controller**.

10. Agree to the software license agreement and click on **Next**.

11. Select the core components to install, check **Delivery Controller** and **Studio**, and click on **Next**.

12. Select the features to install, uncheck **Install Microsoft SQL Server 2012 Express**, ensure **Install Windows Remote Assistance** is checked, and then click on **Next**.

13. Review the firewall ports, select **Automatically**, and then click on **Next**.

14. Review the **Summary** page, verify all information, and then click on **Install**.

15. Once the installation is complete, leave **Launch Studio** checked and click on **Finish**.

16. When Studio launches, click on **Connect this Delivery Controller to an existing Site** in the **Welcome to Citrix Studio** screen.

17. Enter the name or IP address of the first controller, and click on **OK**.

18. When prompted to update the database automatically, select **Yes**.

Configuring your first XenApp delivery controller

Once you have determined how to design and implement your new XenApp environment, you can begin building the components. We will start with our delivery controllers. Our delivery controllers will be statically built and assigned per industry best practices. You need a minimum of two delivery controllers per site. You might need more if you plan on hosting more than 10,000 connections or if you need higher levels of fault tolerance.

The following steps assume you have a standardized Windows Server 2008 R2 or a Windows Server 2012 deployed in your environment, joined to the domain, and ready for use. You should use a service account that has local administrative rights for each machine you are installing these components on. A common practice is to create both a service account and a security group in Active Directory. Place the service account and IT administrators in that security group, and then give that security group local administrator rights on each infrastructure server.

Once you have a machine ready, you can mount the installation media (or access it from a network share) and begin the installation. Citrix has made the installation wizard very straightforward for XenApp 7.5. As soon as you mount the ISO image, or manually execute the **AutoSelect** option from the media repository, you will be prompted to install either XenApp or XenDesktop, as shown in the following screenshot. Since XenApp and XenDesktop now use a common platform, many of the elements are the same.

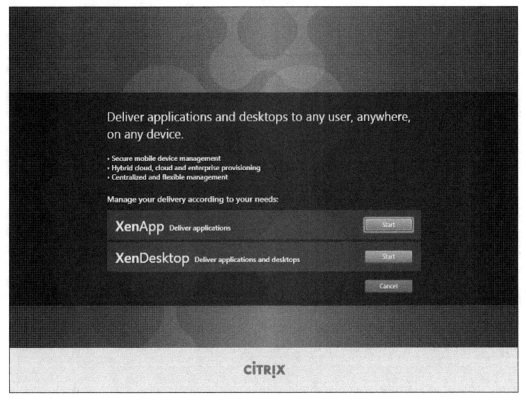

XenApp installation wizard AutoSelect splash screen

Using the installation wizard, you have the option to select the components to install. Since this is our first delivery controller, we will select the **Delivery Controller** option.

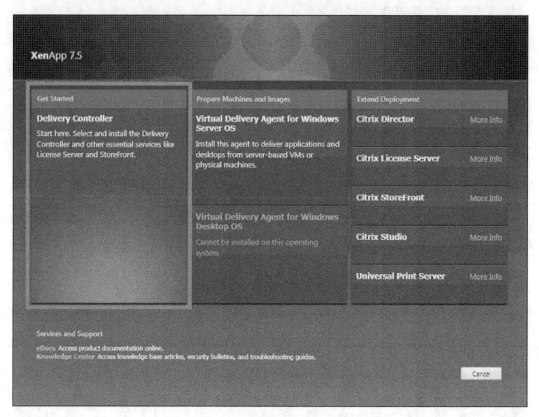

XenApp installation wizard options

When installing the delivery controller, you have the option to select which XenApp infrastructure components you want to install. For a small lab or proof of concept environment, you might want to select all components. For a production-ready environment, you will want to select only the components required. For our environment, we select the **Delivery Controller** and **Studio** features, as shown in the following screenshot:

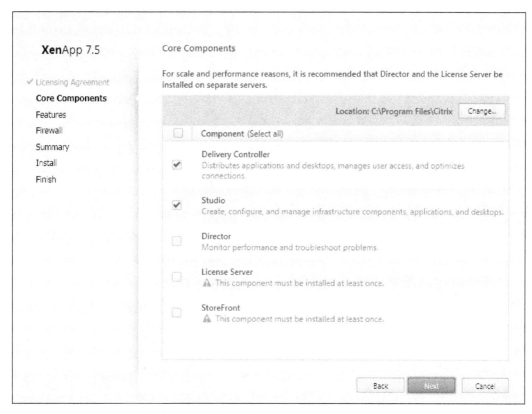

XenApp installation wizard core component selections

After the core components are selected, you can select the supporting features. This includes the option to install SQL Express and the Windows Remote Assistance features. SQL Express should only be used in very small environments, such as testing, development, or proof of concept environments, since it does not have fault-tolerance features. Windows Remote Assistance is used by Director and should be installed to enable monitoring.

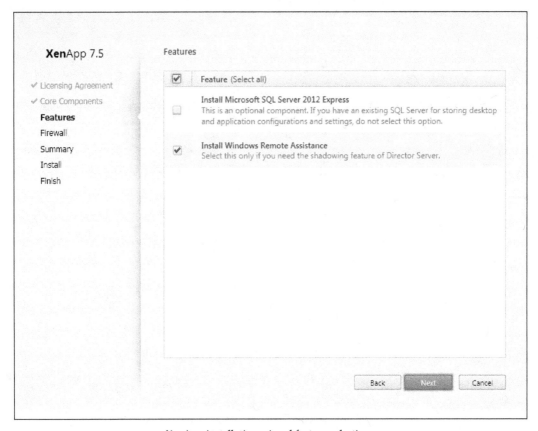

XenApp installation wizard feature selections

Finally, the necessary firewall ports should be opened. For ease of reference, the following screenshot shows the necessary firewall ports for all core components (not just the selected ones.) During installation, only the selected components' firewall ports will opened:

Delivery Controller	Director	License Server	StoreFront
80 TCP	80, 443 TCP	7279 TCP	80, 443 TCP
443 TCP		27000 TCP	
		8083 TCP	
		8082 TCP	

XenApp installation wizard requires firewall ports for all components

The installation wizard will show a summary screen before installation begins, allowing you to change any selected feature or option. This is also a good opportunity to double-check all selections against any planning documentation. The wizard will then show the installation progress and will complete with a summary screen. This summary screen, shown in the following screenshot, verifies all the steps completed, including any supporting component that was installed.

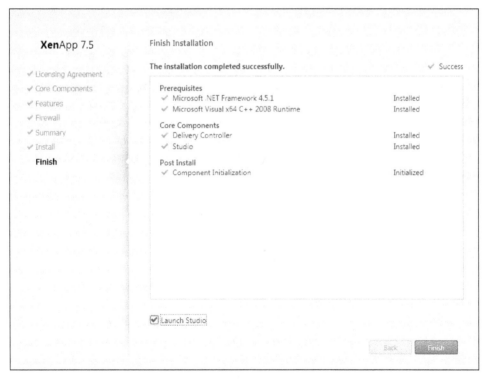

XenApp installation wizard completion summary screen

At no point did we install Remote Desktop Services, formerly known as Terminal Services. Unlike previous versions of XenApp, the controllers for XenApp 7.5 do not require Remote Desktop Services, unless you also install the VDA software.

Configuring your XenApp site

Once the installation of the first delivery controller is complete, you can use Studio to configure your site. Assuming this is a new site, you will click on the **Site setup** option shown in the following screenshot:

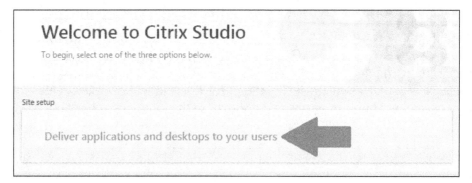

The first step to configuring a site is naming the site. This might seem trivial, but like any naming convention (no matter how arbitrary or logical), it can derail a project through politics. This is a simple item to select in advance. Some organizations use their name, others use their site location, and some others use a mash up of name and location. The name does not matter, so long as you have one. On this screen, shown in the following screenshot, you can select whether to use a full site or an empty one. For this environment, we will use a full site and name it XENLAB to match our organization name.

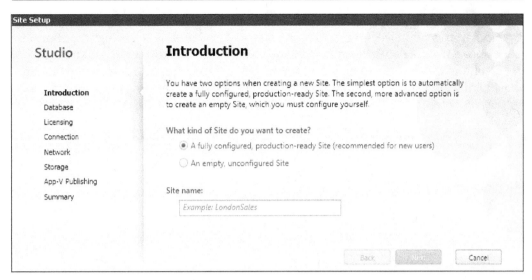

Initial site setup using Citrix Studio

Once you have named your site, you can enter the database information. We will cover more on databases in *Chapter 7, Designing Your Supporting Infrastructure Components*. For now, we know we are placing our databases on our database cluster (cluster name is **LABSQL**; actual servers are SQL01 and SQL02) and instance name. When installing your databases, if your account had DB creator rights in SQL, you can let the wizard create the necessary databases. In a more locked-down environment, you can generate database scripts. Either way, you will need databases created before you can continue. This is demonstrated in the following screenshot:

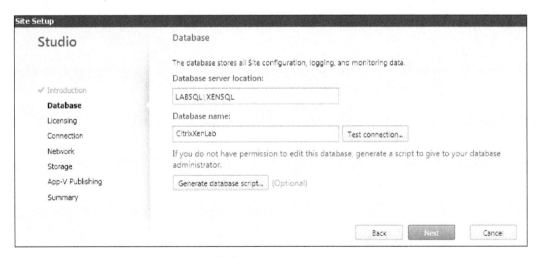

Configuring a database connection for a new site setup

Once the database setup is complete, you are required to define licenses. This step is optional at this point as you can proceed forward and update licensing information later once a license server is built. If you already have a license server or know the name of the future state license server, you can enter it here. You can connect to an existing license server and validate licenses. We will cover more on licensing servers in *Chapter 7, Designing Your Supporting Infrastructure Components*.

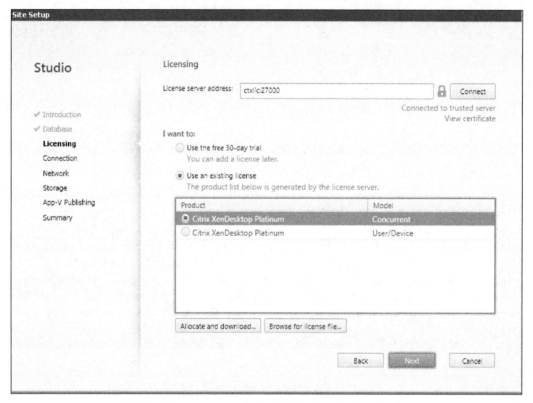

Selecting license server connection information during site setup

The **Connection** settings configure the site to work with your virtualization infrastructure. These settings can easily be modified in Citrix Studio once the initial setup is complete. This includes adding multiple infrastructure connections, if necessary. For this environment, we will use XenServer, as shown in the following screenshot.

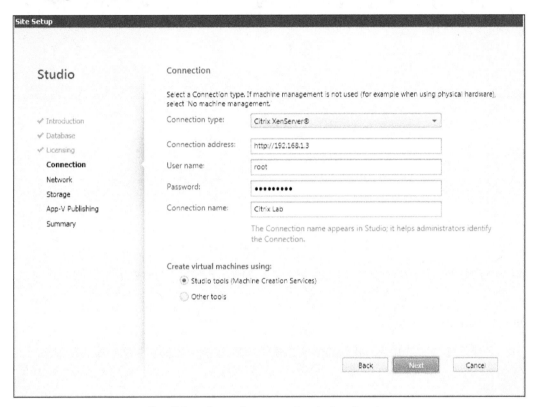

Specifying a hypervisor connection during site setup

The **Network** settings also pertain to the virtual infrastructure and are read from the available networks. This information comes back into play with Machine Creation Services and the PVS XenDesktop Deployment Wizard, which we will cover in *Chapter 6, Designing Your Virtual Image Delivery*.

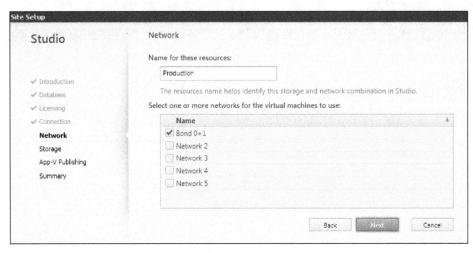

Selecting virtual networks during site setup

Like **Network**, the **Storage** settings are read from the list of available storage repositories identified within the virtual infrastructure. This information can be modified later as storage is added. For now, we will use local storage only, but this might change later.

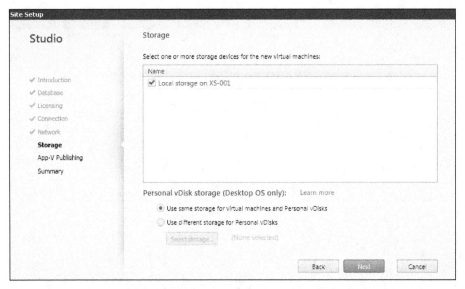

Configuring virtual machine storage during site setup

If you are using App-V for application streaming, you can define that here. Since we are not using App-V at this time, we can set this to No. Once all steps are completed, you can review the site setup information in the **Summary** tab before clicking on **Finish** to finalize.

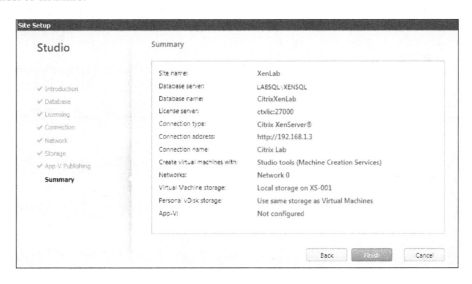

Site setup summary

Once the site setup is complete, you have the option of testing the configuration or setting up Machine Catalogs. We'll come back to Machine Catalogs later in this chapter. Running the site configuration tests includes 178 test points, including database connectivity, hypervisor connectivity, licensing checks, and more. A complete report is available as an HTML file; it is visible as the **Show report** button or by navigating to the current user's AppData\Local\Temp\2\ folder location.

Running site configuration tests

Configuring additional delivery controllers

After your first controller and base site are set up, you can easily add additional controllers. Follow the same basic steps as previously illustrated for the first delivery controller setup. Once installation of the delivery controller and Studio roles are complete, you can connect this new delivery controller to the existing site. In the first launched Studio, you have the option to scale your deployment, as shown in the following screenshot:

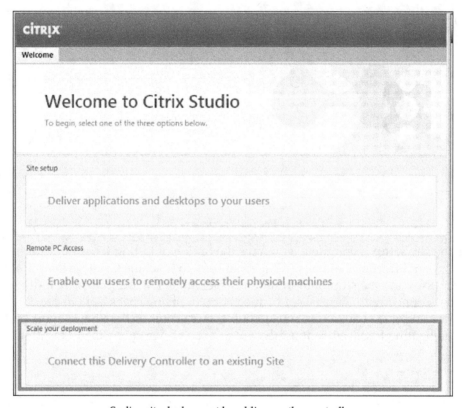

Scaling site deployment by adding another controller

Once you select to add a controller to an existing site, you will be prompted to enter the name of an existing controller. Studio will then query the existing controller to gather site information, including the database connection information. Upon success, you will also be prompted to update the database with this new controller's information.

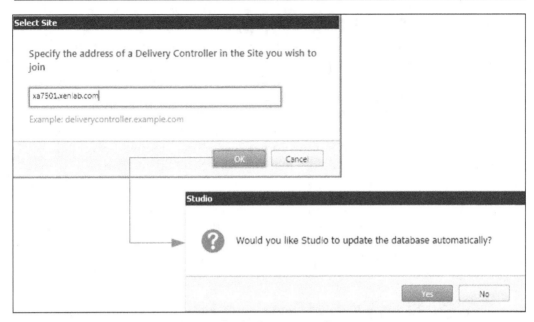

Selecting a site for the new controller to join

Once all steps are complete, you can verify the full list of controllers inside Studio. To do this, open **Studio**, and click on **Controllers** in the navigation pane. All registered controllers will be listed, including the last update time.

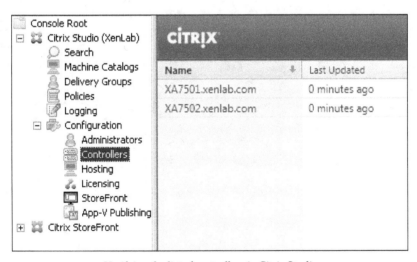

Verifying the list of controllers in Citrix Studio

Configuring your XenApp session hosts

In XenApp 7.5, the official term is VDA. This applies to any system running the Virtual Delivery Agent software. Older versions of XenApp used the terms Presentation Server, Worker Server, or Session Host. For this work, we will maintain the term **Session Host** to highlight the differences between infrastructure servers and desktop workloads. For our sake, a session host is any server we use to deliver desktops or applications. With XenApp 7.5, using the VDA model, we can deliver XenApp workloads from the Windows Server 2008 R2 or Windows Server 2012 machines. This allows more flexibility than previous XenApp versions, which were all tied to a specific operating system.

To install VDA on a server operating system, you can use the same media we used to install the controllers. When you insert this media, you have the option to prepare machines and images, as shown in the following screenshot, which includes the VDA installation process. We will revisit this when we discuss image management in the next chapter.

Starting the VDA installation process

When you install VDA, you either create a master image or enable connections. Creating a master image can be used to prepare a VM for imaging, whereas enabling connections is used to just install VDA on a server. For this, we enable connections on our controllers. Remember, you do not need to have VDA installed on your controllers; this is strictly optional. However, by doing so, we can test connectivity and provide management features through remote access.

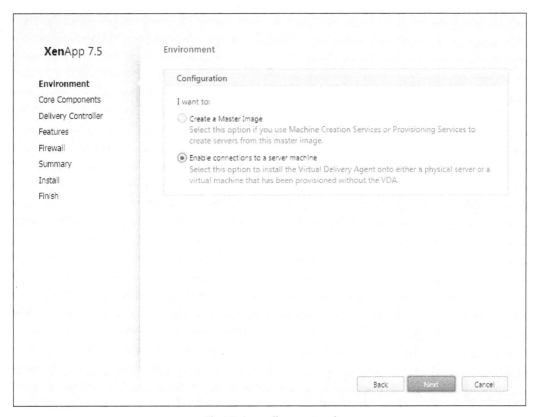

The VDA installation wizard

You may be asking, "Why are you installing VDA on the controllers?". The reason I do this is because I like to have all my management tools available to me remotely. I create a separate Machine Catalog and Delivery Group for controllers, and I limit the access to the Citrix administrative team. This is optional, but I find it very handy. I do not recommend publishing general user applications on controllers.

After selecting the environment options, we need to determine which components we will install. Since we are enabling connections, VDA is automatically selected. We have the option of installing Receiver as well. This is useful if you are publishing full desktops to some or all users, and you want these desktops to pull published applications from other servers. This is sometimes called a Citrix-to-Citrix deployment. This is optional and will depend upon your environment.

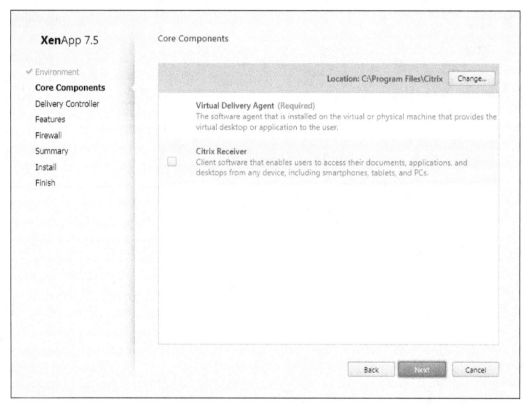

Selecting VDA components for installation

Next, we need to configure our **Delivery Controller** selection. The primary purpose of VDA is to register with the controllers. We have four options, as shown in the following screenshot. For this environment, we will use a manual list of delivery controllers. This can be changed later, either by running the wizard or by leveraging the auto-update feature (this is enabled by default).

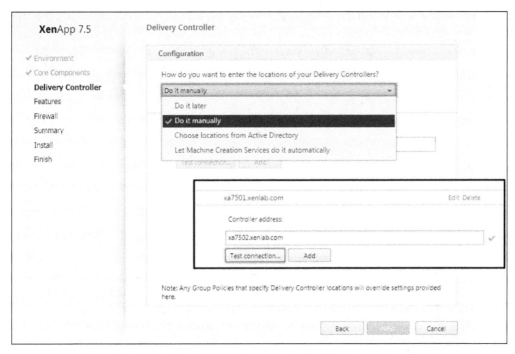

Specifying delivery controllers as part of the VDA installation

There are three configurable features as part of the VDA installation. Typically, each is selected with the default options, but these can be changed:

- **Optimize performance**: Runs the target optimization tool
- **Use Windows Remote Assistance**: Allows shadowing through Director
- **Use Real-Time Audio Transport for audio**: Used for Voice-over-IP optimizations

Selecting features as part of the VDA installation

The firewall ports, listed in the following screenshot, identify the default ports required for the selected features. These firewall ports should be noted not only for the VDA machine but also for any access control list or firewall between network segments.

Controller Communications	Remote Assistance	Real Time Audio
80 TCP	3389 TCP	16500 - 16509 UDP
1494 TCP		
2598 TCP		
8008 TCP		

Required VDA firewall ports

Once all selections have been made, you have the chance to review the summary before completing the actual installation. This is a good opportunity to verify the correctness of your choices and document all settings, if you had not done so already. If the Microsoft **Remote Desktop Session Host** role and **Microsoft Desktop Experience** feature are not already installed, they will be configured as part of the VDA installation process. This will require an additional reboot during the installation process.

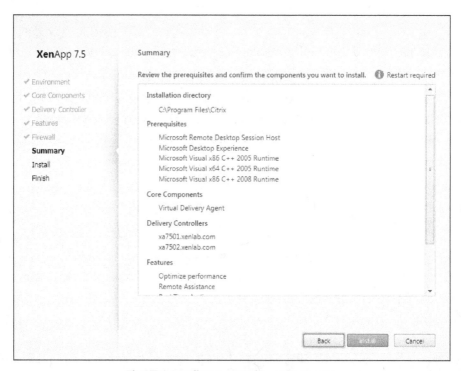

The VDA installation wizard summary screen

Once the configuration changes are complete and all reboots are successful, you should see VDA as successfully registered inside Citrix Studio. Now that we have session hosts configured, our next step is to set up our Machine Catalogs and Delivery Groups.

Managing your XenApp® site

Once the base XenApp site is created, even if we have not added additional controllers, we can begin managing and growing our site. This includes creating the Machine Catalogs and Delivery Groups used to grant access to our users.

Getting started with Machine Catalogs

A Machine Catalog is a collection of physical computers and virtual machines that you assign to users through the Delivery Group. What the user sees depends on the machine type. When creating a Machine Catalog, you must select one of the following types:

- **Server OS and applications**: Users experience a Windows Server environment. This lets multiple user sessions share a single Windows Server environment. This option is appropriate for users who perform well-defined tasks and require only minimal personalization. This is a random desktop environment that lets users connect to any available Windows server environment and is similar to the traditional XenApp Published Desktops. This model is commonly called a **Hosted Shared Desktop (HSD)** model.

- **Desktop OS and applications**: Users experience a Windows client environment. This lets users log in to a Windows client environment in a one-user-per-machine setup. This option provides static or random desktop environments. Static desktops may also be called stateful, persistent, or dedicated. Random desktop environments are sometimes known as stateless, nonpersistent, and pooled. Different documentation standards might use different terms, but virtual desktops will essentially fall into one category or the other. This model is commonly called the **Hosted Virtual Desktop (HVD)** model.

- **Remote PC access machines**: This provides users with remote access to their physical office desktops while maintaining security and the HDX protocol features. This can also be used for blade PCs, where users require enhanced hardware.

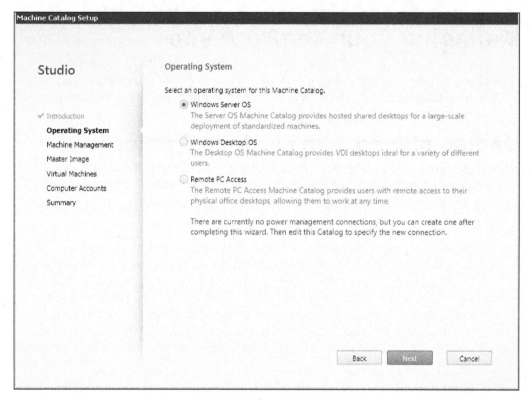

Machine Catalog setup wizard

A Machine Catalog cannot contain a mixture of these types; it must include only server OS, desktop OS, or remote PC access machines. Any given machine, physical or virtual, can only belong to a single catalog. Each machine in a catalog should be configured and managed alike, including ensuring all applications and features are the same.

Each catalog will have only one type of power management and one type of deployment mechanism. The power options are either power managed or not power managed. Power managed machines are typically in the data center, such as virtual machines, which may be powered on and off based upon need. Machine deployment options include **Machine Creation Services (MCS)**, **Provisioning Services (PVS)**, or others (which includes manual deployment as well as template-based deployments). We will cover deployment more in the next chapter, but for now, we will use "another service" since we are importing our static controllers into a Machine Catalog.

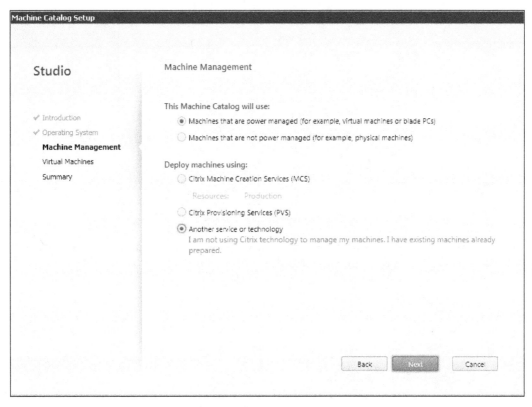

Machine Catalog management options

Since we are using another service, we must manually add or select our machines to be a part of the Catalog. If we were using MCS or PVS, we could select the master image or collection from those technologies. Since we have defined our hypervisor connection during site setup, we can browse all of our defined virtual machines and select the ones we want.

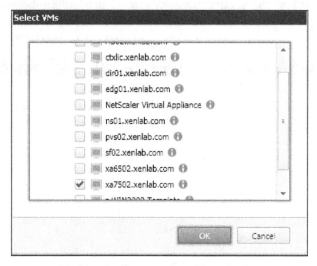

Machine Catalog manual machine selection

When manually importing machines, you might need to associate the computer's Active Directory account with the virtual machine object.

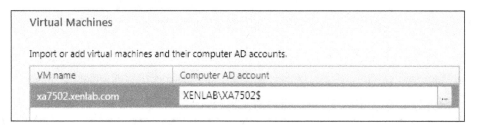

Machine Catalog machine computer account assignment

After we have selected all of our machines, we can provide a catalog name and description. In this case, we create a controllers catalog.

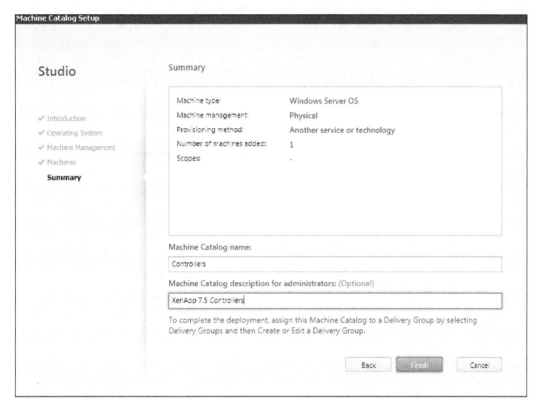

Machine Catalog setup wizard summary

Once the Catalog creation is complete, you have the option of testing the configuration or setting up Delivery Groups. Running the catalog tests includes 25 test points, including hypervisor connectivity, controller connectivity, active directory association, and more. A complete report is available as an HTML file and is visible as the **Show report** button or by navigating to the current user's `AppData\ Local\Temp\2\` folder location.

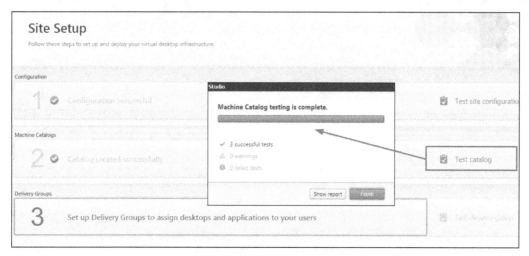

Citrix Studio catalog test process

Once we complete our first Machine Catalog, we can move on to Delivery Groups. However, we will come back to some additional options of Machine Catalogs later.

Getting started with Delivery Groups

Delivery Groups are designed to deliver applications and desktops to users. A Delivery Group can contain machines from multiple catalogs, and a single catalog can contribute machines to multiple Delivery Groups. However, a given machine can belong to only one Delivery Group. For this reason, most organizations keep Machine Catalogs and Delivery Groups in a one-to-one mapping for simplicity, but this is not a requirement. Ideally, you manage the software running on the machines through the catalogs to which they belong. You then manage user access to applications through the Delivery Groups.

When creating a Delivery Group, you can pull machines from one or more catalogs. Since we only have one catalog, with only a single machine defined, our choices are limited at the moment. We can add more catalogs and machines later, if necessary.

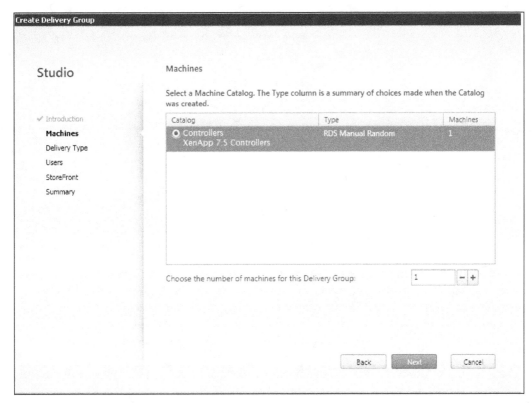

Delivery Group setup wizard

When choosing a delivery type, you have three options:

- **Desktops**: Users will see only a desktop icon for this delivery group
- **Desktops and applications**: Users will see a desktop icon as well as all defined applications for this delivery group
- **Applications**: Users will only see the defined applications in this delivery group

This can be changed later, if necessary.

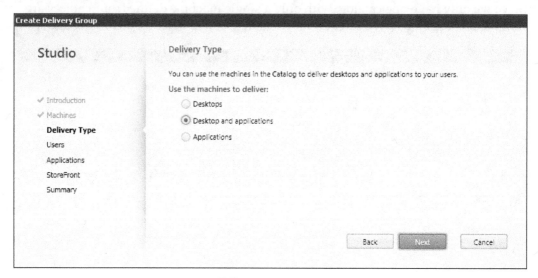

Delivery type options

You will then need to select which Active Directory users or groups will have access to in the Delivery Group. The best practice is to use clearly defined Active Directory security groups for access. These may be existing groups, or new groups created for your XenApp environment, which contain nested user groups. For now, we are simply using **Domain Users**, but we can modify this later, if necessary.

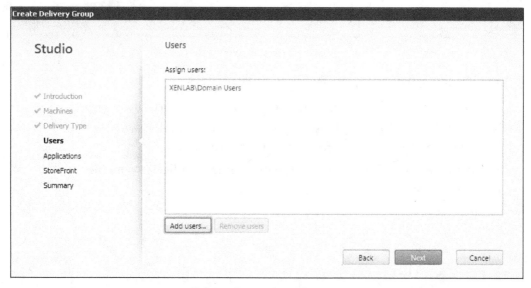

Delivery Group user assignment

When adding applications, the **Delivery Group** wizard will attempt to identify locally installed applications available for publishing. In order for this discovery to succeed, the target server must be powered on; assuming the machine is power-managed, XenApp will start the VM, if necessary. You can select one or more of these applications, or you can manually select an application.

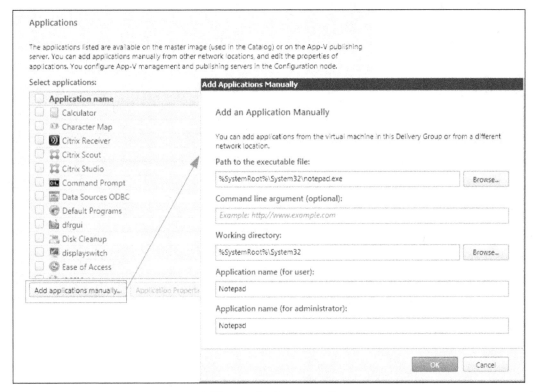

Adding applications manually

Once all applications are selected, you can define the StoreFront connection for Receiver. We will not use this on our controllers since we will not be running Receiver. However, if you define desktops that need to seamlessly access other hosted applications, you can configure the setting. For now, we can review our summary, check for any errors, and then finish our wizard. The **Display name** field is what users will see on the StoreFront site.

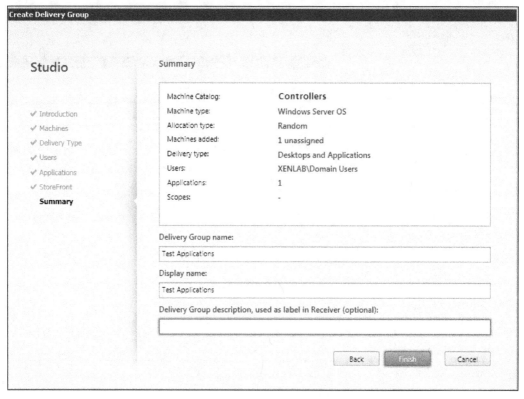

Delivery Group wizard summary

Once the Delivery Group setup is complete, you will return to the Studio with your site fully configured and ready for enhancements. Like before, with Site setup and Machine Catalog setup, you can test to verify the success of your Delivery Group. All these tests can also be repeated in Studio under **Common Tasks**, for future testing.

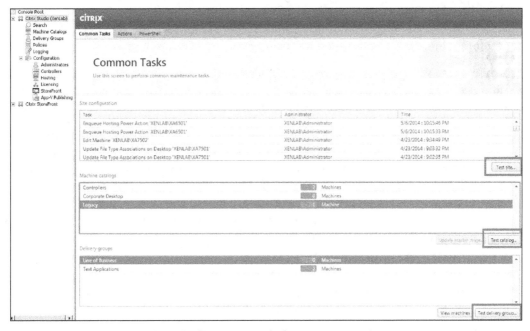

Citrix Studio common tasks for component testing

Application delivery models

XenApp 6 used a utility called the Publish Application Wizard to prepare applications and deliver them to users. In XenApp 7.5, we can use Studio to create and add applications to Delivery Groups, making them available to users who are assigned to that Delivery Group. Using Studio, you first configure a Site, create and specify Machine Catalogs, and then create Delivery Groups. The Delivery Groups determine which users have access to the applications you deliver.

One of the key decisions to make is how to deliver your applications to your users. Within XenApp 7.5, there are several delivery option models we can use. This is similar to previous versions of XenApp, with some minor differences:

- **Locally installed applications**: In this model, all applications are installed in the master images assigned to each catalog. These applications are managed within the image lifecycle management of the master image. The applications might be manually installed or pushed as part of an application management system. Locally installed applications are one of the most common deployment methods, but they might require multiple master images for each type of application set.

- **Virtualized applications**: This leverages virtualized applications packages, created and delivered through Microsoft App-V. In this instance, only the universal applications are installed in a master image. All other applications are streamed on demand using App-V. This allows one master image to service multiple business units, but it also requires the added administrative overhead of App-V.

- **Second-tier hosted applications**: This is the Citrix-to-Citrix scenario we mentioned early and relies on two or more master images. The first image, ideally, is a landing pad where users connect to a virtual desktop. This desktop will contain the core company applications locally installed, with departmental or line-of-business applications hosted on other XenApp application servers. This gives the best of both worlds, but might require additional resources since users might be accessing sessions on multiple servers.

- **Hosted applications**: This is the traditional XenApp application publishing model where users connect to a StoreFront site and launch the individual published applications. These applications might come from different Delivery Groups, and they are typically locally installed on the XenApp servers.

- **Hosted virtualized applications**: This is similar to hosted applications, but these applications might be locally installed on the XenApp servers or they might be streamed to the XenApp servers using App-V. It is transparent to the users, but allows administrators to minimize the number of unique master images.

Getting the most out of Machine Catalogs and Delivery Groups

Since Machine Catalogs and Delivery Groups are new concepts, or at least significantly different concepts from the previous versions of XenApp, prior planning is important. This section contains some helpful tips on planning and managing these new elements as well as ways to emulate older XenApp functionality.

Planning your Machine Catalogs and Delivery Groups

When planning your deployment, you might want to create a matrix of Machine Catalogs. A sample matrix is provided in the following table. This will help ensure your design meets your business needs and aligns with your overall organization.

Catalog name	Machine type	Platform	Image management	# Machines	Master image or collection
Controllers	Server OS	XenServer	Physical	2	
Legacy	Server OS	XenServer	PVS	10	2008 Legacy
Corporate desktop	Server OS	XenServer	PVS	25	Production
Development	Desktop OS	XenServer	MCS	10	DEV001

You can do the same for Delivery Groups. Some organizations will match their Delivery Groups directly to catalogs. Others will use a large catalog, but smaller Delivery Groups, to tightly restrict access or allotment of resources. This is common in organizations using virtual desktops with a charge-back model.

Delivery group name	Catalog	# VMs	Delivery type	Users	Display name
Line of business	Legacy	10	Applications	Domain users	Legacy LOB
Test applications	Development	10	Desktops	Developers CTXADMINS	Development
Corporate desktop	Corporate desktop	25	Desktops and applications	Domain users	My desktop
Controllers	Controllers	2	Desktops and applications	CTXADMINS	Controller

Leveraging PowerShell

All commands used in Studio have corresponding PowerShell commands, which can be used to automate processes or make bulk changes. When using PowerShell, you need to make sure you load the Citrix modules. This can be done with the `Add-PSSnapIn Citrix*` command when running PowerShell on a controller, or by using the start menu shortcut for Import System Modules that will preload all modules. If you are unsure which commands to use, you can perform an action in Studio and then look at the **PowerShell** tab to see the associated commands. Most commands will begin with either `Get-Broker` or `Set-Broker`. In the PowerShell console, type `get-help get-broker` to see the full list of commands.

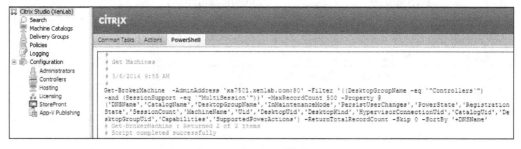

Citrix Studio PowerShell tab

Moving machines between catalogs

What happens if you need to move a machine from one catalog to another? This will typically only happen for physical or nonpower controlled machines. When using PVS or MCS for machine management, the catalogs will rarely change. Although moving a machine is not a necessity, since a Delivery Group can pull from multiple catalogs, you might want to do this as part of organizational changes or housekeeping. There are two options to move machines among catalogs. The first option is to completely remove the machine from the catalog using Studio, and then manually add the machine to the other catalog.

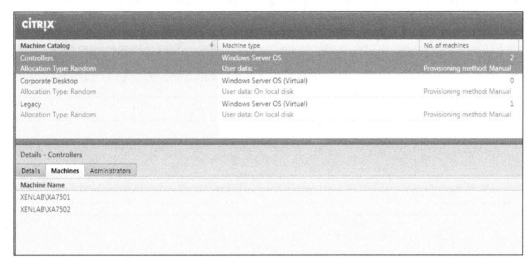

Citrix Studio Machine Catalogs and allocated machines

Secondly, you can use the PowerShell command, `Set-BrokerMachineCatalog`, to change catalog membership, but the old and new Catalog must be of the same type. Changing a Catalog this way does not change any Delivery Group assignment for a machine.

Additional Delivery Group properties

Once a Delivery Group is created, additional properties can be set. This includes modifying user access rights, the delivery type, and application settings. Application settings include the description, limiting the number of desktops, modifying color depth and Secure ICA settings. Access policy settings tie into Smart Access rules as part of NetScaler. Restart schedule allows the control of automated reboots—these are useful when combined with image management to ensure the operating system is always up to date.

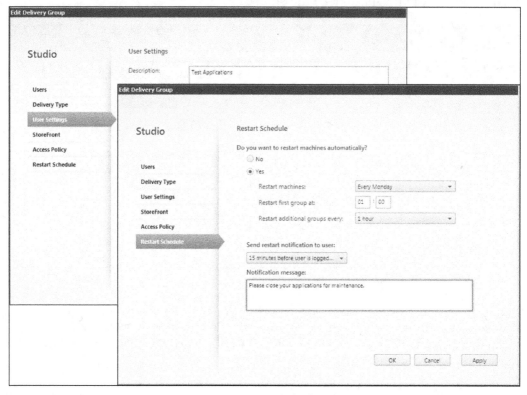

Additional Delivery Group properties

Publishing multiple applications at a time

When adding applications to a Delivery Group, you can add multiple applications at the same time. Once added, each application will be independent of the other applications.

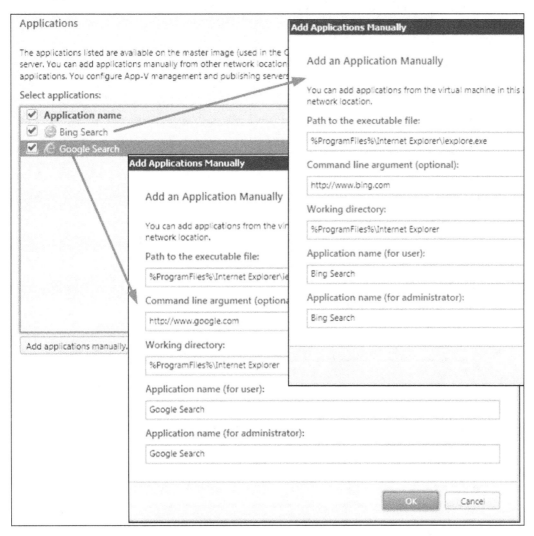

Publishing multiple applications

Additional application properties

Once applications are created, you can modify their properties in Studio. This includes changing the application name and **Keywords** (as mentioned in *Chapter 4, Designing Your Access Layer*.) Here, you can also change the Icon, category, shortcut creation (for Receiver) working directory, and command line options. You can also limit the visibility of applications so that they do not appear (but are still accessible) to certain users.

Additional application properties

Publishing resources to multiple Delivery Groups

So far, we have seen applications assigned to a single Delivery Group, but what if we need the same application(s) published in multiple Delivery Groups? Say, for example, we have separate Delivery Groups for each business unit, but each Business Unit runs some common applications we want to make sure are visible to everyone. One way to do this is with PowerShell. We can use the `Get-BrokerApplication` to view our published applications and properties. We can use the `Add-BrokerApplication` to add a published application to additional Delivery Groups. In the following screenshot, we add our Bing Search application to a second Delivery Group:

```
PS C:\Users\administrator.XENLAB> Add-BrokerApplication "Bing Search" -DesktopGroup 2
PS C:\Users\administrator.XENLAB> $app = Get-BrokerApplication -BrowserName "Bing Search"
PS C:\Users\administrator.XENLAB> $app


ApplicationType                 : HostedOnDesktop
AssociatedDesktopGroupPriorities : {0, 0}
AssociatedDesktopGroupUids       : {2, 1}
AssociatedUserFullNames          : {}
AssociatedUserNames              : {}
AssociatedUserUPNs               : {}
BrowserName                      : Bing Search
ClientFolder                     :
CommandLineArguments             : www.bing.com
CommandLineExecutable            : %ProgramFiles%\Internet Explorer\iexplore.exe
CpuPriorityLevel                 : Normal
Description                      :
Enabled                          : True
IconFromClient                   : False
IconUid                          : 3
MetadataKeys                     : {}
MetadataMap                      : {}
Name                             : Bing Search
PublishedName                    : Bing Search
SecureCmdLineArgumentsEnabled    : True
ShortcutAddedToDesktop           : False
ShortcutAddedToStartMenu         : False
StartMenuFolder                  :
UUID                             : 49dcf749-f998-4e54-843d-982ca9f6e1c8
Uid                              : 7
UserFilterEnabled                : False
Visible                          : True
WaitForPrinterCreation           : False
WorkingDirectory                 : %ProgramFiles%\Internet Explorer
```

PowerShell commands to add an application to multiple Delivery Groups

Making sure machines are available

In order to create a Delivery Group, you must have available (unassigned) machines in at least one Machine Catalog. You can create a Delivery Group and then remove machines. However, if you try to create a Delivery Group with no available machines, you will trigger an error. If you come from a XenApp 6.x environment, you might think of Delivery Groups as Worker Groups, but they are really more like silos that require some additional planning since they are not quite as dynamic.

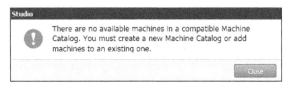

Citrix Studio delivery group creation error

Summary

In this chapter, we looked at designing our application delivery layer, which includes the ability to deliver both applications and desktops in our server environment. We stepped through designing and creating our site, machine catalogs, and delivery groups. Some of these concepts might be new, and some might seem old, depending on which versions of XenApp and XenDesktop you have experience with.

In most environments, a mix of delivery options will be utilized since rarely does one size fit all. Commonly, a mix of hosted applications and published desktops will be leveraged, but this will vary greatly from one organization to another.

Now that we have our application delivery platform built, we can greatly extend it in the next chapter as we look at image management. This will include a dive into Machine Creation Services and Provisioning Services.

6
Designing Your Virtual Image Delivery

In the previous chapter, we discussed how to design our Application Delivery layer. This includes the ability to deliver both desktops and applications through Citrix XenApp 7.5. We delved into designing our delivery site, Machine Catalogs, and Delivery Groups.

With this chapter, we will dig further into our design with the image delivery design. Two of the machine catalog types we touched on in the last chapter are based on **Machine Creation Services (MCS)** and **Provisioning Services (PVS)**, which we will cover here. These are two of the primary delivery engines for image management.

In this chapter, you will learn about the following:

- An overview of image management
- Determining the right fit for your environment
- Understanding Citrix Machine Creation Services
- Designing Citrix Provisioning Services

An overview of image management

Image management, which is sometimes called disk image management, is the idea of creating a reusable copy of a virtual machine's hard drive. This is typically the operating system and any locally installed applications. The key concept behind disk image management is reusability, which allows us to deliver the necessary operating systems to most of the users using as few unique images as possible. By reusing a common image, we can save on the overall management (time to update, configuration changes, and so forth) as well as resources (the storage capacity and disk utilization.) This is a key reason why the use case design, as discussed in *Chapter 2, Defining Your Desktop Virtualization Environment*, is so important.

VIRTUALIZE	STORE	STREAM
Capture server operating system and application into a virtual image	Store the virtual image on the network	Stream the virtual image to multiple target devices

The image management concept

Citrix offers you two products as part of XenApp 7.5: Machine Creation Services and Provisioning Services. We will cover both of these in greater detail later in this chapter, but for now, we will focus on the larger concept of image management. Using image management enforces consistency, since all target devices (virtual machines) use the same disk image. Lack of consistency, especially in a XenApp environment, can cause a lot of headaches, including performance issues and application availability as well as print driver management.

Having image management also enables the rapid deployment of additional systems. What if you acquire another organization and need to expand the environment by adding another 20 session hosts to your XenApp deployment. If you have a master image, you can deploy these additional servers in minutes as opposed to days using a conventional server build process. Because it is the same production image, it is already validated and ready; there is no need to have the new servers tested for functionality.

Of course, using image management might also change how you manage application changes and regular updates. Specifically, if you typically push Windows Update once a month, do you really want to push these updates to all targets or just to the master images? What about antivirus updates? What about emergency patches?

Imagine having to manage 600 servers—all with the same operating systems, service packs, and applications. In a traditional environment, all 600 serves will need to be managed separately. However, in an environment with good image management, a single image can be used and deployed on all 600 servers. This enables a single point of management. Taking this process one step further through the change process, you can prepare and test a new version of the application. Once the new version is approved, you can deploy the new configuration on all 600 servers at the same time by updating the base image, using image management to assign the image, and rebooting the target devices. If an issue is discovered after the release, then you can roll back the changes for all servers at the same time. Once a server reboots, it will use the latest image for which it is assigned.

Determining the right fit for your environment

As previously mentioned, Citrix offers two different technologies for image management: MCS and PVS. We will cover specific details later in the chapter, but as of now, we will discuss them at a high level in order to understand the key differences.

Both MCS and PVS are viable solutions for image management. PVS has been around longer and is the more mature technology, but it also requires more infrastructure than MCS. MCS is built directly into the Studio (allowing a single point of management) where PVS requires separate servers, network considerations, its own console, and the database. Both technologies leverage master images, allowing multiple target servers to run the same configuration.

When deciding between MCS and PVS, the final solution always depends on what you need to do and the impact on the organization. I have a preference for PVS and will typically implement that solution, but MCS has matured quite a bit since its introduction in XenDesktop 5. Barry Schiffer offers a keen insight into the decision-making process, including a decision tree (shown in the following diagram), on his blog at `http://www.barryschiffer.com/provisioning-services-vs-machine-creation-services-2013-revision/`.

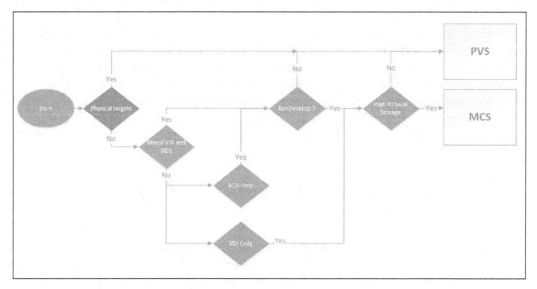

The MCS-PVS decision tree. Source: www.barryschiffer.com

Most Citrix architects, myself included, view PVS as the more scalable solution since it implores a farm configuration for the scalability and workload distribution. Although there is no technical limit to MCS, there are practical limits. PVS uses streamed disk images and can easily scale into the thousands. MCS uses a linked clone technology and relies heavily on the hypervisor management layer and the storage layer. The update process for MCS can be slow as image updates must be copied to all of the storage locations. This requires extensive snapshots and copies behind the scenes. When looking at deployments of more than 500 machines, this can become burdensome. The update process for PVS can be nearly instantaneous since the target machines are reading the updated image from a central repository (upon the reboot), but this places the bulk of utilization on the network layer.

From a storage perspective, MCS typically takes around 20-30 percent more IOPS, but it is generally evenly balanced between read/write. PVS requires less IOPS and significantly less storage, but it is very write-intensive. Nick Rintalan has written a comprehensive article discussing these points at `http://blogs.citrix.com/2013/08/12/pvs-vs-mcs-revisited/`.

Finally, when discussing MCS and PVS, you might want to look at the reusability of the disk images. MCS is only valid for virtual machine workloads where PVS can be used across different platforms. Also, when looking at multiple site deployments or even multiple Citrix deployments within a single location, the PVS architecture can be reused and the disk images can be copied between sites. However, MCS is much simpler to deploy since it does not require a dedicated infrastructure, network booting, or disk streaming.

PVS is one of my absolute favorite Citrix technologies. Along with the benefits of single image management, it forces environments to have strong change management processes. It also ensures consistency, which I find lacking in many legacy environments. When auditing environments, I always look for consistency or the lack thereof, as inconsistency can lead to numerous problems. With PVS, a reboot takes a server or desktop back to the golden image so that any inadvertent changes are removed.

At one previous company, I was the manager of our delivery services team as well as the lead Citrix architect and part of the change management/deployment team. We developed and hosted a set of custom applications across 200+ servers at the time. It was a challenge deploying and auditing all of the custom .exe and .dll files required during each update process and each new server build. Leveraging PVS will allow such builds to be reduced from 2 days for building and testing to as little as 5 minutes for the image deployment. Software update cycles can be reduced to a small downtime window; simply assign a new image and reboot!

In short, MCS is typically used in smaller deployments, whereas PVS is commonly used in larger enterprise deployments. Our reference architecture leverages PVS, but for the sake of demonstration, we will utilize both methods.

Now, you might ask what if you cannot use MCS or PVS? Although this situation is exceedingly rare, it might arise due to technical limits, policy restrictions, or the political landscape of your organization. What can you do? Luckily, there are some alternatives. These are not nearly as dynamic or as useful as MCS and PVS, but they can still make your life easier.

- **Virtual machine templates** can be used to create a master template of your application server image(s) and can be used to deploy new servers quickly. Using templates for the machine deployment in this manner allows for rapid growth but does not take into account future changes, nor does it provide some of the storage benefits of MCS or PVS. Once a machine is deployed, it must be managed and updated individually. For a small environment (less than 10 machines), this might be sufficient, but for larger environments, this is unwieldy.

- **Software management solutions**, such as Microsoft's System Center Configuration Manager, can be used to manage application deployment and configuration as well as operating system configuration changes across multiple servers. A well-managed and maintained change control and software management system can ease a lot of the concerns around consistency. However, since each system is still independent, there is the risk of inconsistency.

- **Regular auditing** is a must in any environment, especially in a XenApp environment that does not use image management. This should include checked items such as application file versions, DLL file versions, operating system patch levels, and application configurations. You can use custom scripts to check these items or some of the tools we discussed in *Chapter 2, Defining Your Desktop Virtualization Environment*.

Understanding Citrix® Machine Creation Services

Machine Creation Services is based on **linked clone** technology. Linked clones were first implemented by VMware. A linked clone is made from a snapshot of the parent virtual machine. All files and settings available on the parent at the moment of taking the snapshot are available on the linked clone. Any changes to the parent do not affect the linked clone, and changes to the linked clone do not affect the parent. This is due to the linked clones using a private snapshot as opposed to the actual base disk.

MCS uses the hypervisor **application programming interface (API)**, which is the underlying operating command of the various hypervisor platforms. MCS is compatible with any hypervisor for which XenApp 7.5 Studio has defined hosting connections, as detailed in *Chapter 3, Designing Your Infrastructure*. MCS uses these API commands to create, start, stop, or destroy the virtual machines from the machine catalog. When creating a machine catalog using MCS, a **master image** is selected. All of the virtual machines in the catalog are based on this one image. If you want to use different master images for different use cases, you can create multiple different catalogs.

To gain a better understanding of the overall process and API integration points, see `http://blogs.citrix.com/2011/06/28/machine-creation-services-primer-part-1/`.

The storage impact of MCS

When deploying machines using MCS, the first step is to define the master image. This master image can be a base virtual machine or the snapshot of a virtual machine. Once this master image is selected, MCS will create a private use snapshot of the virtual machine. This private use snapshot will then be copied to all available storage repositories defined in Citrix Studio under the hosting configuration.

This snapshot will be the same size as the defined base disk of the master image. So, if the base disk is 60 GB in size, each snapshot will be allocated 60 GB of space. Assuming that you have five storage locations defined, the master image snapshot will be created on the first storage location and copied to the other four. This snapshot copy is only placed once per storage location and not per virtual machine. Each virtual machine then creates a linked clone to this master image snapshot. Each linked clone is a temporary snapshot, called a difference disk that also consumes the drive space. Although the disks show you the amount of space allocated, they will only consume what is actually written, which will be much less. This is done through a process called **thin provisioning**.

When using MCS, machine catalogs can be set to random (pooled) assignments or dedicated assignments. For our XenApp environment, we are using the server OS with a random assignment. In a random or pooled assignment, the virtual machines are reverted to the assigned master image snapshot upon each reboot. This keeps the temporary snapshot size low, but it might grow up to the size of the original snapshot depending upon the number of changes made and the frequency of reboots. When using dedicated deployments, the snapshots do not revert automatically.

Each machine has an identity file as well as the snapshot file for that clone. The exact files might vary based on the hypervisor level. For example, in a VMware environment, each virtual machine will also have a machine definition file (vmx) as well as a memory swap file (vswp). Please note that while a difference disk might be allocated the full size of the base disk, the consumed space will typically be much less.

Disks			
Name	Size	Virtual Machine	
Application Servers-baseDisk	60 GB		Master Image Snapshot
XAAPP01_IdentityDisk	16 MB	XAAPP01	Linked Clone Identity Disk
XAAPP01-diff	60 GB	XAAPP01	Linked Clone Difference Disk
XAAPP02_IdentityDisk	16 MB	XAAPP02	
XAAPP02-diff	60 GB	XAAPP02	

The MCS disk created on the XenServer storage repository

For more information on the storage impact of MCS, please see
`http://www.thegenerationv.com/2011/03/xendesktop-5-deep-dive-machine-creation.html`. This article is written for MCS on XenDesktop 5 using VMware vSphere, but the process is still valid.

Along with the storage impact, we must also look at the performance impact. The cloning process can put a strain on the hypervisor processor and the storage array controllers, depending upon the master image size and the number of defined storage repositories. The true impact in your environment should be monitored and managed accordingly. From an operational perspective, plan for the **IOPS** (a measure of throughput) to be approximately 25 percent higher than PVS with an even distribution between read and write. So, if you are assuming 3–4 IOPS per user and 20 users per hosted desktop, we can assume 70 IOPS per virtual desktop server. If we are using MCS, we should plan our storage to handle 60 GB of space and 87 IOPS per virtual server.

Preparing a master image for MCS

If you decide to use MCS, the first step is to create or identify the target machine that will be the master image. The master image is the template from which all other servers will be deployed. This master image should have the base operating system, the VDA software, and any application software that is required fully installed and configured.

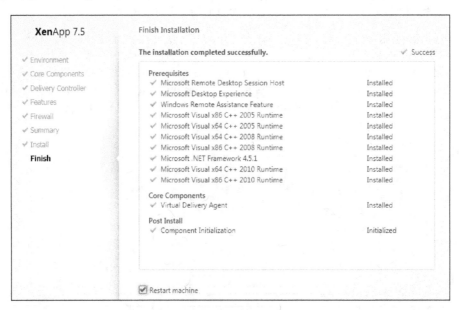

Preparing a master image

Once a master image is identified and ready, you can create your machine catalogs in Studio.

Creating an MCS catalog using Studio

Using Citrix Studio, you can create a new Machine Catalog. Our Machine Catalog will be based on the server OS since we are using XenApp. When defining the catalog, we can choose MCS as a deployment mechanism.

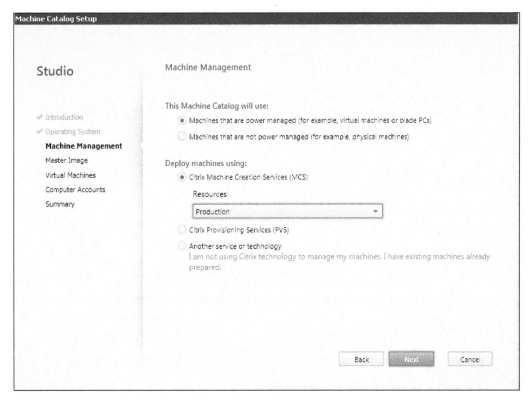

Creating a MCS machine catalog

Next, you can select the virtual machine for use as your master image. You can choose a base machine or an existing snapshot, if required. For our environment, we are using a virtual machine that we have prepared called **XenAppMaster**.

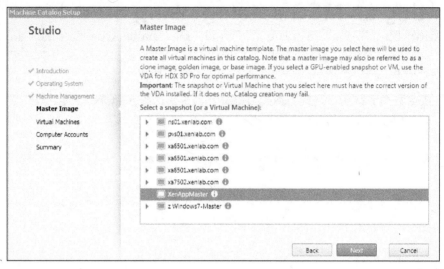

Selecting a master image for MCS catalog

After selecting the source machine for the master image, you can use the **Machine Catalog Setup** wizard to specify how many virtual machines are to be deployed as well as their compute resources. You can change the number of virtual processors and the assigned memory, but you cannot change the disk size.

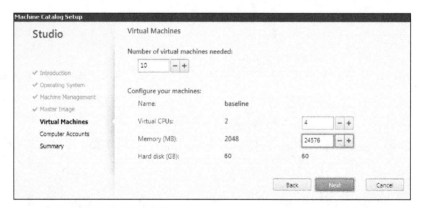

Specifying virtual machine properties when creating an MCS catalog

Once the number of machines are entered, you can then specify the naming standard and Active Directory location of your target virtual machines. The machine accounts will be created using the credentials of the person running Studio so that user or service account must have machine account creation rights in the target OU.

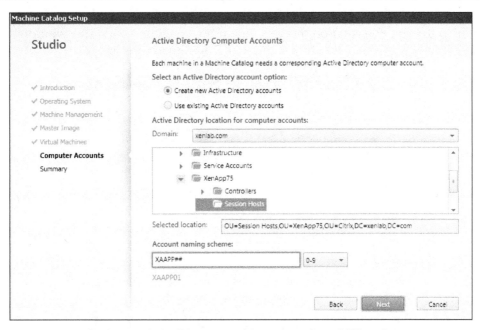

Configuring Active Directory machine accounts for an MCS catalog

On the summary screen, you will specify the Machine Catalog name; in our case, we simply named these *Application Servers*. Please note that this is *not* the delivery group. The step for the creation of the delivery group is separate; this is just the catalog.

The MCS catalog creation summary

After reviewing the summary to ensure that all settings are correct, you can click on **Finish** to begin the creation services. In Studio, you will see a status window. As mentioned previously, the first step is **Copying the master image**.

MCS creation progress

Once the process of creating the MCS catalog is complete, you can see the new Machine Catalog, as shown in the following screenshot:

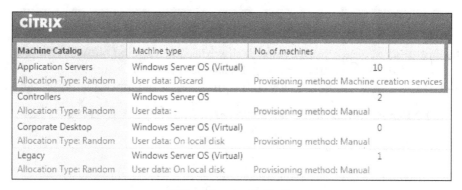

Machine Catalog	Machine type	No. of machines	
Application Servers	Windows Server OS (Virtual)	10	
Allocation Type: Random	User data: Discard	Provisioning method: Machine creation services	
Controllers	Windows Server OS	2	
Allocation Type: Random	User data: -	Provisioning method: Manual	
Corporate Desktop	Windows Server OS (Virtual)	0	
Allocation Type: Random	User data: On local disk	Provisioning method: Manual	
Legacy	Windows Server OS (Virtual)	1	
Allocation Type: Random	User data: On local disk	Provisioning method: Manual	

MCS catalog view in Studio

Now that the Machine Catalog has been created and the virtual machines deployed, you can create a Delivery Group or allocate the new machines to an existing Delivery Group.

Updating an MCS catalog that reflects changes to the master image

Now that we have the machine deployment complete with MCS, you might be thinking "that's easy enough, but what about updates?". Updating MCS catalogs is very similar. Update the master image to the point where it is ready for production deployment, and then right-click on the MCS catalog and select **Update Machines**.

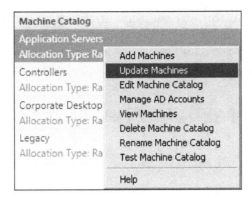

MCS Update Machines

Just like the initial deployment, select the virtual machine or the virtual machine snapshot that is to be used for the update process.

The MCS update process—the machine selection

Once you have selected the proper snapshot or virtual machine, the last step is to decide when to deploy the updates. Do you want to update immediately or upon the next reboot? The most graceful method is **next reboot** and it uses the **scheduled reboot** feature of the delivery group. Either way, the new image will not be in use until after a reboot.

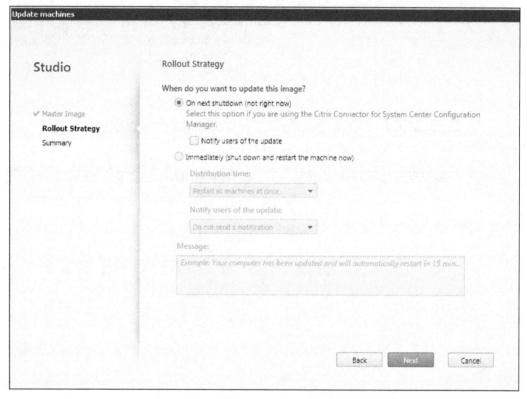

The MCS update rollout strategy

What happens if you update the catalog but realize that you want to revert to a previous image? Simply run the process to update machines again, selecting the previous snapshot or image for use.

Designing Citrix® Provisioning Services

Citrix Provisioning Server provides workstation and server disk images on demand using streaming technology. The proper use of Provisioning Services allows better image management, faster desktop and server deployments, greater resource flexibility, and total cost reduction (through both operational cost savings and storage savings). Provisioning Services is not without a cost since it requires multiple PVS servers (to ensure fault tolerance), its own database, and potential modifications to the change-management processes that might already be in place.

Provisioning Server is independent of any other Citrix technologies. It can be used to deliver server OS or desktop OS workloads, but it is not limited to delivering only XenApp or XenDesktop images. It can stream images to physical devices or virtual machines hosted on any hypervisor platform (Hyper-V, vSphere, or XenServer).

PVS manages virtual disk images, which are called **vDisks**, and streams the content to one or more target devices. These vDisks are based on Microsoft's **Virtual Hard Disk (VHD)** format. By using the streaming technology, only the required disk information is pulled across the network. Once this information is pulled to the local device, all execution is performed locally on the virtual machine. In a typical deployment scenario, a single image is streamed to multiple devices. This ensures that all the target devices are identical since they are using the same source image. Any changes are written to a write cache location (more on that later.) Once a target device is rebooted, it is reset back to the base image, which is also known as a **golden image**.

The storage impact of PVS

The disk image files, which are called vDisks, are organized into centralized containers called stores. PVS can use local stores on each server, creating a distributed high-availability model or a shared repository, creating a centralized model. Whether you use a centralized model or a distributed model, you need to ensure that your vDisk files can be accessed from all PVS servers in order to ensure high availability. For our environment, a shared vDisk store will be created using a CIFS share on our distributed filesystem namespace (\\xenfs\dfs\vdisks). Each virtual disk image should be designed to support the greatest number of user groups and applications in order to minimize the storage and PVS server resource utilization.

Because the PVS servers are responsible for streaming the vDisk to each target, there are a couple of elements to scalability.

- **The number of unique images**: This applies to the base storage (local or centralized) in order to ensure that there is enough drive space to store the image files. Even if a vDisk is set to dynamic, there should be enough space as if it were a fixed size file. This also impacts the PVS server memory since each vDisk is loaded into the system cache as part of the streamlining process. A good rule of thumb is 2 GB of RAM for each unique desktop OS vDisk and 4 GB of RAM for each unique server OS vDisk.

- **The number of target devices**: Out of the box, PVS is configured for 20 streaming ports and 8 threads per port. This allows for 160 devices per server. You can increase the number of ports and/or the number of threads per port in order to meet your anticipated demand. This can be modified under **Advanced Server Properties** for each PVS server.

For more information on PVS scalability, please see `http://blogs.citrix.com/2011/07/30/virtual-provisioning-server-a-successful-real-world-example`.

Each vDisk is comprised of multiple file types:

- **VHD**: The base disk image that uses Microsoft's virtual hard disk format
- **AVHD**: The difference disk, used for versioning, based on Microsoft's virtual hard disk format and leveraging the disk-chaining technology
- **PVP**: Properties file
- **XML**: The manifest file used to synchronize and track the version information
- **LOK**: The utilization lock file

When replicating disks between servers, stores, or sites, all of the PVP, VHD, AVHD, and XML files must match. If the files do not match, a replication error might occur, and the out of sync servers will not be able to stream the vDisk until all files match. For more on vDisk files and image versions, please refer to the *vDisk version and files* screenshot.

By using a central store for vDisks, PVS allows for a reduction in the overall storage requirements. Along with the vDisk files, each target device requires a location for the write cache. Since the base drive is streamed in a read-only format, any changes must be written into a temporary location, which is called the write cache. Typically, this is a small virtual hard disk that is attached to each virtual machine. This drive will host the write cache file, the system page file, and any persistent data that you wish to retain. My rule of thumb is to size this drive to two times the assigned RAM, but you should test and verify this within your own environment. The size of the write cache file is impacted by the amount of changes and the frequency of reboots. During the boot process, the write cache file is deleted.

A new feature of PVS 7.1 is to use the **Cache in Device RAM with Overflow on Hard Disk** option. This greatly optimizes the IOPS and the overall performance of the write cache activities using the virtual machine's memory as a buffer and only writing to the disk in 2 MB blocks as opposed to the more frequent 2 KB blocks. This results in less writes and greater performance. For more information, please see `http://blogs.citrix.com/2014/04/28/the-new-xenapp-reducing-iops-to-1/`. We will discuss write cache options later in this chapter.

The network impact of PVS

Since PVS leverages disk streaming over the network, you are trading the traditional disk read IOPS for the network bandwidth. PVS streaming uses **User Datagram Protocol (UDP)** to transmit the disk image from the PVS server to the target device. The PVS target device software includes flow control and retransmission settings. The data is streamed on demand, as requested by each target device. The initial boot requires 100 MB of bandwidth; ongoing streaming services will vary based on number of target devices and the frequency of data requests. In most environments with a 10 gigabit network fabric, there are no bandwidth constraints; however, you should monitor and plan according to your environment.

Target devices connect to the PVS farm during the boot process. You must use one of the following boot options to leverage Provisioning Services:

- **Network Boot (DHCP Options)**: Using **Dynamic Host Configuration Protocol (DCHP)** options requires the configuration of DHCP scope options 66 and 67. This leverages the DHCP architecture to provide the boot server (option 66) and boot file (option 67). When using DHCP options, the target device will request the IP address and boot information from DCHP. A load-balanced server name or a round-robin DNS alias should be used for option 66. Option 67 will typically be `ARDBP32.bin`.

- **Network Boot (PXE)**: PXE stands for **preboot execution environment**. In this scenario, target devices request an IP address from the DHCP infrastructure. During the boot process, a PXE request is also transmitted and answered by the PXE servers (potentially, the PVS servers). The PXE servers will then transmit the ARDBP32.bin file using **Trivial File Transfer Protocol (TFTP)**, which typically runs on the PVS servers.

- **Boot Device Manager (BDM)**: The boot device manager is a utility that is available on the PVS servers that can create a bootable CD-ROM image (ISO), a boot partition, or a USB device. BDM can leverage DHCP, or it can be used to manually assign IP addresses. BDM is generally used when network boot options are not viable, possibly due to the network security or a conflicting network service.

 I prefer to use the second option mentioned in the preceding list: the PXE boot. I like to let each PVS server act as a TFTP server and manage PXE requests. This creates an easily scalable and fault-tolerance architecture. For more on the bootstrap options, please see: http://support.citrix.com/proddocs/topic/ provisioning-7/pvs-bootstrap-wrapper.html.

Designing your PVS farm

Provisioning Services is a product that is separate from XenApp and XenDesktop. Platinum level licensing, like what we are using, includes the rights to use PVS. Since it is separate, it has its own design considerations. We are using a single site for our PVS farm with two PVS servers and shared infrastructure. The following figure illustrates some of the PVS farm concepts:

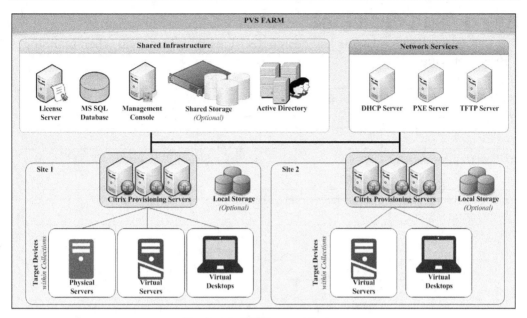

The Sample PVS Farm architecture

Requirements for Provisioning Services

PVS 7.1 has the following requirements:

- Windows Server 2008 R2 SP1 or higher
- Windows Server 2008 features: Microsoft .NET Framework 3.5 SP1, PowerShell 2.0
- Windows Server 2012 features: Microsoft .NET Framework 4.5, PowerShell 3.0
- SQL Server database, preferably with High Availability

Additional elements will be installed as part of the PVS installation wizard.

Key design decisions

The following table represents key design decisions that were used when planning a PVS deployment:

Option	Decision	Justification
PVS version	7.1	7.1 is the latest version
Hotfix		
Provisioning servers	PVS01 PVS02	List of PVS servers
The PVS server's operating system	Windows Server 2012	
CPU	4	Four vCPUs to maximize streaming threads
Memory	24 GB	Maximizes the system cache
Networking	1 network	The production vLAN
DHCP	Runs on another computer	Leverages existing DHCP
PXE	Runs on this server	PXE will be used for the network boot
TFTP	Enabled	Required to deliver the network boot file
UDP ports	6910-6930	Default
Threads per port	8	Default
Console SOAP service	54321	Default
Farm name	XENLAB	The PVS farm name
Administrators	xenlab\CTXAdmins	The list of administrators
Provisioning Services database location	LABSQL\XENSQL	Database servers for the PVS database
Provisioning Services data store name	Provisioning Services	The database for PVS
Database authentication	xenlab\svc-pvs	Requires Windows authentication. A dedicated service account should be used for all Citrix communication.
Site name	LAB	The list of sites. Typically, one site per geographical location.

Option	Decision	Justification
Collection names	Hosted shared desktops Master images desktops	The list of collections. Typically, a collection matches a Machine Catalog.
High Availability	Centralized HA	Centralized or distributed
Active directory machine account password management	Yes, 7 days	Required for proper machine account password changes
Location of vDisk stores	`\\xenfs\dfs\vdisks`	Lists of stores and paths
Location of write-cache	Cache in device RAM with overflow on hard disk	This will vary by vDisk but will typically be the client's local hard drive where a persistent drive is attached to each target VM. The write cache will be directed to this persistent drive.
Offline database support	Enabled	In the event that the PVS database is unavailable, the administrative functionality is lost, but target devices will continue to function normally.
vDisk volume licensing mode	KMS	Required to leverage Microsoft's volume licensing
vDisk boot option	PXE	The boot device manager, PXE, and DHCP are all valid boot options

Preparing a master image for PVS

When using Provisioning Services, just like with MCS, the first step is to create or identify the master target machine that will be used to create the first golden image. The nice thing with PVS is that once you perform an image capture, you can reuse that same image simply by copying the vDisk file. I recommend that you perform the image capture against an image with only the following items:

- The base operating system and service pack
- Virtualization tools (such as XenTools or VMTools)
- Virtual Desktop Agent and related software (refer to the *Preparing a master image* figure)
- The PVS target device software

Once you install the target device software from the PVS media, you can run the Imaging Wizard that will walk you through the image capture process. This is the process that will convert the local c: drive into a VHD file on the PVS store. All future updates, such as application installations and configuration, can be applied to future versions or additional copies of the base image, making the capture a one-time event. However, if you want to update any drivers that might interrupt the PVS stream process (such as newer hypervisor tools or network drivers), you might need to *reverse image* converting the vDisk back to a standard virtual machine in order to perform these updates.

Once the target device software is installed, **Provisioning Services Imaging Wizard** is available. Using the imaging wizard, you can select the drive to be captured and the target vDisk.

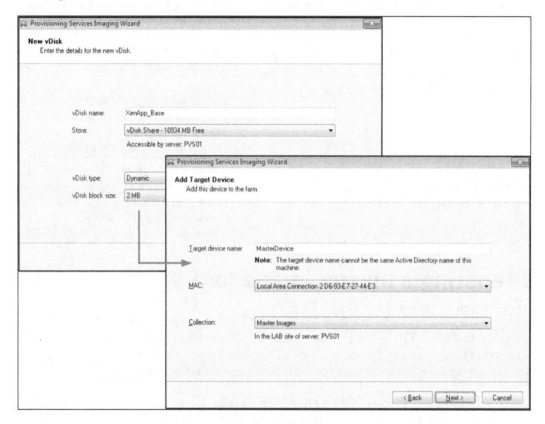

PVS Imaging Wizard

Once the initial image capture is complete, you will need to place the vDisk in standard mode. This enables the vDisk to be streamed to multiple targets in a read-only mode. This also enables the vDisk to use version controls and be leveraged by the deployment wizards.

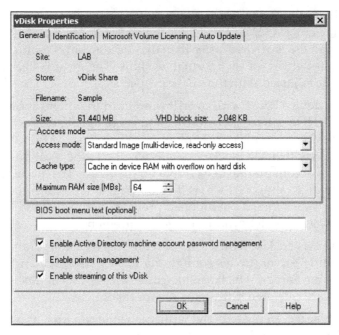

PVS vDisk Properties

vDisks can have one of the following access modes defined:

- **Private**: This allows full read/write access and is only accessible by a single target device at a time. This emulates how a traditional hard disk works and is typically only used for initial image captures. In previous versions of PVS, this was also required for vDisk updates; however, this functionality can now be achieved through version control.

- **Standard**: This allows read-only access by multiple target devices. Any changes are written to the write cache. vDisks in the standard mode can be streamed to multiple targets. Additional versions of standard vDisks can be created, allowing for test, maintenance, and production updates.

vDisks can have one of the following write cache types defined:

- **Cache on device hard drive**: The write cache exists as a file in the NTFS format, located on the target device's hard drive. This write cache file is deleted during each reboot until the vDisk access mode is set to private.

- **Cache on device hard drive persisted**: The write cache exists as a file in the NTFS format, located on the target device's hard drive. This write cache file persists. This method is an experimental feature and is only supported for Windows 7 and Windows 2008 R2 or higher. It also requires a different bootstrap file (CTXBP.BIN).

- **Cache in device RAM**: The write cache can exist as a temporary file in the target device's RAM. This provides the fastest method of disk access, since memory access is always faster than disk access, but it requires additional memory resources for each virtual machine. The default size is 4 GB, but this can be adjusted with the vDisk properties.

- **Cache in device RAM with overflow on hard disk**: This write cache method uses the VHDX differencing format and is only available for Windows 7 and Windows Server 2008 R2 or higher. When the RAM is fully consumed, the least recently used block of data is written to the local differencing disk in order to accommodate newer data on the RAM. The amount of specified RAM (default value of 64 KB) is the non-paged kernel memory that the target device will consume. As mentioned previously, this method has the greatest positive impact on IOPS and storage requirements.

- **Cache on server:** The write cache file can exist as a temporary file on a Provisioning Server. In this configuration, all writes are handled by the Provisioning Server, which can increase the disk I/O and network traffic. These files are deleted during the device reboot.

- **Cache on server persisted**: The write cache file can exist as a file on a Provisioning Server. In this configuration, all writes are handled by the Provisioning Server, which can increase the disk I/O and network traffic. These files are not deleted during a device reboot and can be used to simulate multiple devices operating in the private mode.

For our environment, we will leverage standard mode vDisks with **cache in device RAM with overflow on hard disk**, as it provides the greatest overall performance.

Creating a Machine Catalog using the PVS deployment wizard

Using the Provisioning Services console, you can run **XenDesktop Setup Wizard** or **Streamed VM Setup Wizard** at the site level. Both wizards will create the virtual machines as targets for streaming. Using **XenDesktop Setup Wizard** is applicable for XenApp 7.5 as well as for legacy XenDesktop deployments. The **Streamed VM Setup Wizard** option can be used for legacy XenApp as well as non-Citrix workloads. Since we are using XenApp 7.5, we can use **XenDesktop Setup Wizard**, which will save us a few steps by automatically creating the Machine Catalog in Studio for us. If we used the older **Streamed VM Setup Wizard**, we would need to create the PVS-based Machine Catalog manually and link it to our PVS farm.

PVS XenDesktop Setup Wizard

You will need to specify your hypervisor platform and select your virtual machine template. The hypervisor connections are read from the controller hosting connections defined in Studio. If you are running **Streamed VM Setup Wizard**, you will be prompted to select the hypervisor type and connection information. You must choose the virtual machine template to be used by the wizard; this *cannot* be a standard virtual machine.

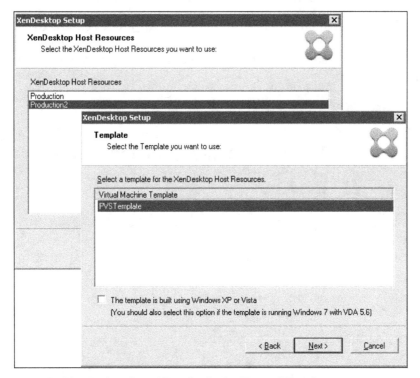

PVS XenDesktop Setup Wizard, selecting Host and Template resources

After selecting a template, you can choose your vDisk. It must be a standard mode vDisk. This is easy to change post the deployment, if required.

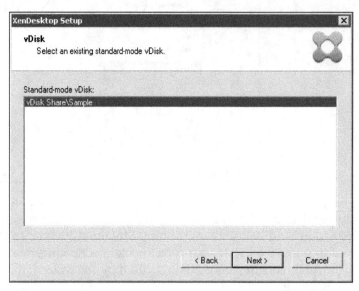

PVS XenDesktop setup wizard, selecting the target vDisk

After specifying the standard mode vDisk to be used, you can choose to create a new catalog or use an existing one. If you use a new catalog, you must select **Windows Desktop Operating System** or **Windows Server Operating System**, as shown in the following screenshot:

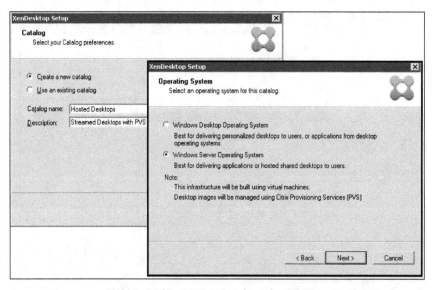

PVS XenDesktop setup wizard, catalog selection

Next, you can use the **XenDesktop Setup Wizard** option to specify how many virtual machines are to be deployed as well as their compute resources. You can change the number of virtual processors and the assigned memory as well as the disk size. Since we are using the *cache in device RAM with overflow on hard disk* option for the write cache, we must have a client hard disk defined.

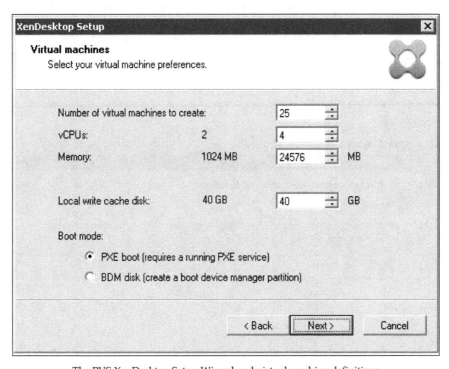

The PVS XenDesktop Setup Wizard and virtual machine definitions

The write cache file will vary in size based on the number of changes made during operations and the frequency of reboots. When using a client device hard disk on a virtual target, I generally size the VM hard disk to be double the amount of RAM since the page file will also go to this same drive automatically. Logfiles as well as any persistent data can reside on this client drive. For larger deployments, I can reduce this size to a logical round number; in this case, we used 40 GB. This will allow for a 24 GB page file, event logs, anti-virus update files, as well as the write cache file itself. Regardless of initial size, the write cache file should be monitored for growth to ensure proper sizing.

After specifying the machine properties, you can choose to let the wizard create the necessary machine accounts, including the proper OU. The user account running the wizard will need machine object creation permissions in the OU for this to work. The wizard will check to see whether a machine account exists. If it does, it will move to the next name based on the naming scheme. If the name does not exist, it will create the machine account and virtual machine with the target name.

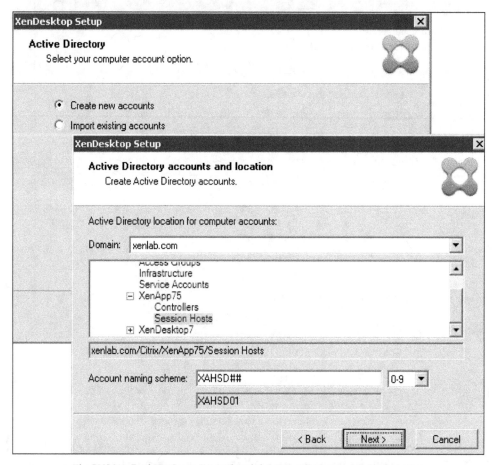

The PVS XenDesktop Setup Wizard and the Active Directory account creation

A progress bar will show you the status of the wizard, including the active directory account creation and machine creation. Once the wizard is complete, you can see the machines in Citrix Studio as a Machine Catalog based on Citrix Provisioning Services.

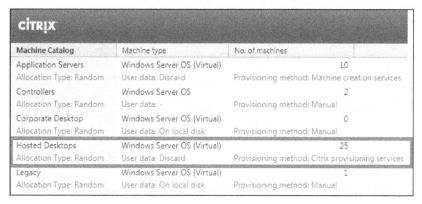

The Citrix Studio list of Machine Catalogs

You can also see the created machine on the hypervisor layer as well as a new **Device Collections** inside **Provisioning Services Console**.

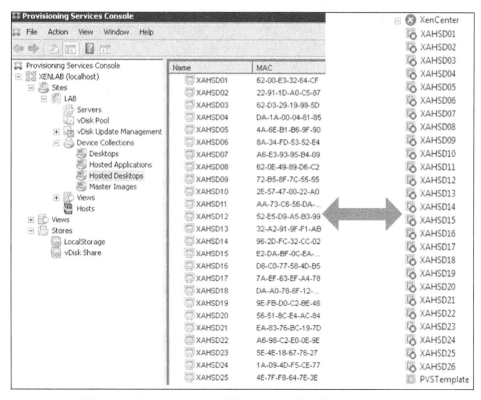

PVS created devices as seen in PVS Console (left) and XenCenter (right)

Now that **Machine Catalog** is created and the virtual machines are deployed, you can create a Delivery Group or assign the new machines to an existing Delivery Group.

Managing images using PVS

Provisioning Services includes a built-in mechanism for managing multiple vDisk versions. In earlier versions of PVS, you had to copy a vDisk to make changes. Version management was introduced in PVS 6 and made the process very streamlined.

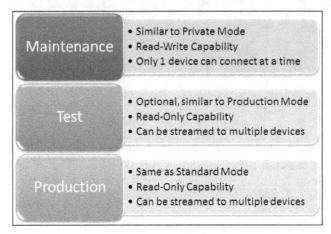

vDisk access levels

Within PVS, each device is defined as one of three types: **Maintenance**, **Test**, or **Production**. These assignments are part of **Target Device Properties** and can be modified. Typically, only a single device is assigned for maintenance.

Assigning the target device type

The levels of maintenance, test, or production map to the version control of the assigned vDisk. Versioning is only available for vDisks set to standard mode. Right-click on the target vDisk and select **Versions...** from the menu to access the **vDisk Versions** control panel, as shown in the following screenshot:

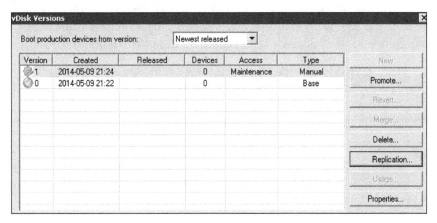

The vDisk versions console

From the vDisk versions menu, you have the following options:

- **New**: This allows you to create a new version. New versions are automatically tagged at the Maintenance level and the version number is incremented by one.

- **Promote**: This allows you to promote a version from the **Maintenance** level to **Test** or **Production**. If you have a test version, you can promote it to **Production**. When promoting to **Production**, you can chose **Immediate** or **Scheduled**. Devices will only use the new vDisk version upon the reboot, so even if you choose **Immediate**, it just means that the vDisk version is immediately available. It will not necessarily be in use right away, just on the next reboot of the target devices.

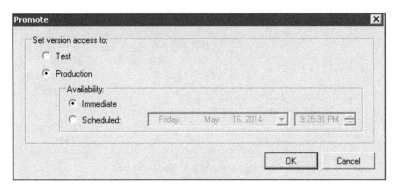

The vDisk version's promotion options

- **Revert**: This allows you to roll back a version promotion. You can revert from **Production** to **Maintenance** or from **Test** to **Maintenance** mode. Reverting will shut down any devices that are currently using that vDisk.

- **Merge**: Combine the chained files, either merging the difference disks (AVHD files) or creating a new consolidated base disk (the VHD file). You can also choose the access level of the new version. Citrix recommends that you keep the chains to 5 versions or fewer in order to optimize operations.

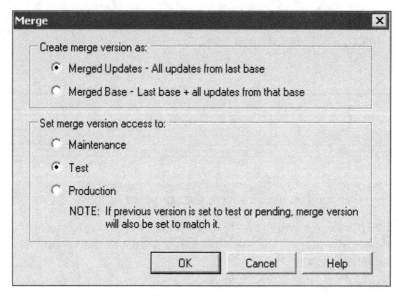

vDisk's merge options

- **Delete**: Remove a vDisk file that is no longer in use. This could be due to a bad version that we reverted, or it could be due to obsolete files from a merger.

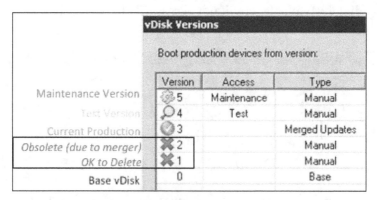

Meanings of the vDisk version's icons

- **Replication**: The replication monitor is used to validate that all the necessary files have been replicated and are fully accessible by all servers. This checks the file signatures against all stores and servers, so it does not matter what your replication method is (manual, scripting, DFS-R, and so on). An error in replication will prevent a server from servicing the streaming request for that vDisk.

- **Usage**: This shows you which devices are currently using the selected version of a vDisk. Devices will only access a new version upon the reboot.

- **Properties**: Provide a description for the various vDisk versions.

Each version of the vDisk will create a new AVHD and PVP file. This contains the difference disk and the properties file for each version. So, if your vDisk is called `Sample`, the base vDisk (Version **0**) will be `sample.vhd`. Future versions will carry the name `sample.#.avhd`, where # is the version number, such as `sample.1.avhd`. All of these files will need to be replicated for proper functionality. Some of these might eventually be deleted through mergers or obsolescence.

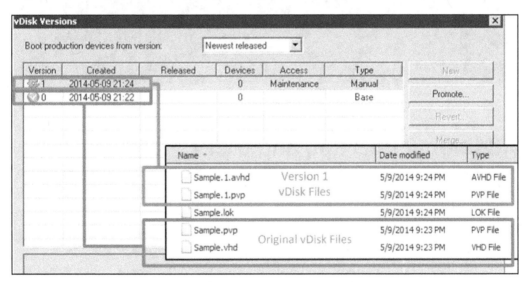

The vDisk version and files

Although this looks like a lot, the process really is very simple. Devices are automatically set for production, so there is no need to modify them. Keep one virtual machine designated as your maintenance machine or master image. When you need to update your vDisk, create a new version, and then use the maintenance machine to apply updates. When you are ready, shut down your maintenance machine and promote the vDisk to production.

The main caveat is that when you boot a maintenance or test machine, you must select the vDisk version from the BIOS screen. So, this requires console access, as shown in the following screenshot:

```
net0: 192.168.1.147/255.255.255.0 gw 192.168.1.1
Booting from filename "ardbp32.bin"
tftp://192.168.1.35/ardbp32.bin. ok

Provisioning Services bootstrap v7.1.0.4022

Copyright (c) 2001-2013 Citrix Systems, Inc. All rights reserved.

Local MAC           : 6200E33264CF
Local IP            : 192.168.1.147
Subnet mask         : 255.255.255.0
Default gateway     : 192.168.1.1
Login server        : 192.168.1.35:6910
Bootstrap loaded at 96CF:0000 Size 4040

Connecting to the Provisioning Services. Please wait...


Boot Menu:
------------------------------------------------------
 1) Sample vDisk.5 [maint]
 2) Sample vDisk.4 [test]
 3) Sample vDisk.3
------------------------------------------------------
Selection [1-3]:
```

The Maintenance target device console screen on start up

Additional PVS tips and tricks

When it comes to Provisioning Services, there is much more material than this single chapter can cover. Our focus is on XenApp, and PVS is a great tool to deliver XenApp workloads. However, before we move on, here are a few additional tips and tricks from the field:

- **The bootstrap file**: The bootstrap file is very important as it tells the devices what servers to connect to in order to boot. This file is also used for fault tolerance and high availability. You can list up to four servers in the bootstrap. This allows the target device software on the client to connect to a second PVS server, should the one it is connected to fail. The bootstrap configuration is available by right-clicking on the individual servers. Make sure that all the servers are configured with their own IP first. To make the process easy, you can click on the **Read Servers from Database** option to pull in all PVS server addresses, and then move the local server to the top.

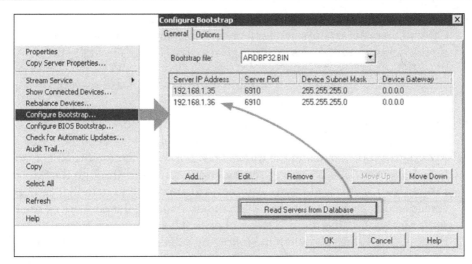

PVS configure bootstrap file

- **Verbose mode**: I'd also like to configure **Verbose mode**, which is part of the bootstrap configuration. Officially, Citrix will say that this is used only for troubleshooting. I like to enable it so that I can see what is happening during the boot process. Did my device check in? What server is it connecting to?

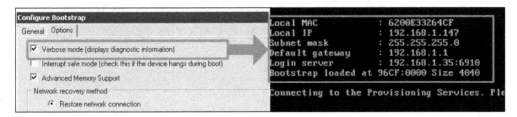

Configure bootstrap for Verbose Mode

- **Separate device collections**: Keeping master images or maintenance devices in separate collections makes the overall management easier. Having production collections separate allows you to quickly assign vDisks or change properties all at once. If you need to assign a new vDisk to an entire collection, you can simply drag-and-drop the vDisk to the collection.

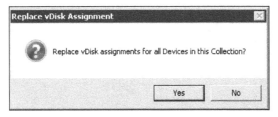

Change the vDisk for an entire collection

- **Registry changes**: Citrix recommends that you disable the Large Send Offload, in order to improve network performance. This can be done on the network properties or through registry changes to `HKEY_LOCAL_MACHINE\SYSTEM\CurrentControlSet\Services\TCPIP\Parameters\DisableTaskOffload = 1`. For more information, please see `http://support.citrix.com/article/CTX117374`.

- **Threads per port**: As mentioned earlier, threads per port can be used to increase the scalability. The default value is eight, but it can be increased as to as high as 60. Increasing the threads per port can increase the CPU load of the PVS server. This is a server setting and is accessible through the **Server Properties | Advanced** menu. Another **Advanced** menu item that can be considered is pacing if you find that you are flooding the network or the PVS server by booting too many devices at once. This allows you to control the boot process. The values shown in the following screenshot are default values:

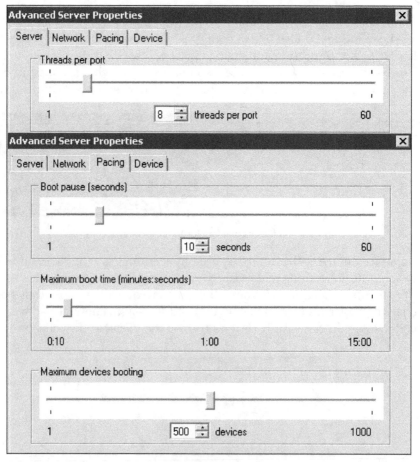

Advanced PVS server properties

Summary

In this chapter, we dove into disk image management, focusing on two Citrix technologies: Machine Creation Services and Provisioning Services. We looked at the pros and cons of each technology. Luckily, with XenApp 7.5, we have the option to use either or both, depending on our situation. Although PVS is the more mature and enterprise-ready option, MCS is a viable candidate as well. Either solution allows us to reuse a master disk image multiple times. This ensures consistency as well as rapid deployment, enabling us to quickly scale out our environments from tens of servers to hundreds or even thousands of servers.

Now that we have our core XenApp infrastructure and our image delivery platforms defined, we can delve further into our supporting infrastructure components, including our database, file, print, and licensing systems.

7
Designing Your Supporting Infrastructure Components

In the earlier chapters, we focused on analysis and high-level design. In the previous two chapters, we dug deep into our XenApp site design and our image management options. In this chapter, we will focus on many of the supporting components of our environment. We will discuss design considerations, best practices, High Availability, and the criticality of these components.

In this chapter, you will:

- Plan your license server
- Design your database platform
- Configure your file services
- Implement monitoring for your XenApp environment

Planning your license server

All Citrix products utilize a common licensing service. This service can run on a dedicated system or it can be hosted on a system that performs other roles. In small environments, licensing might be installed on the first controller using the default installation options. In mid-sized to large enterprise environments, it is recommended that you have a dedicated license server.

The role of the license server in the environment

All Citrix products will check with the license server on startup and user login to ensure the product is properly licensed and there are enough user licenses available. A single license server can support up to 10,000 continuous connections.

The Citrix products for use in our environment, such as **XenApp** and **Provisioning Server**, store a replica of the licensing information, including the number and type of licenses. If a server loses its connection to the license server, the product enters a **grace period** and uses its local record of the licenses to continue licensing the product during this grace period. This record is updated every hour.

Once a license is successfully checked out, the user can connect and run the requested product.

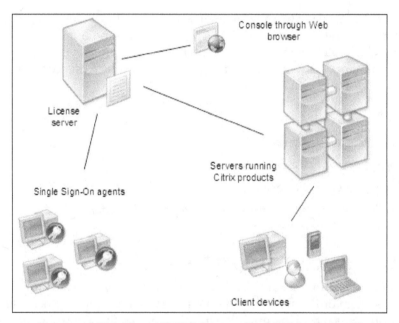

Overview of Citrix License (© Citrix Systems, Inc. All Rights Reserved.)

The requirements for installing the license server

The license server role, a core component of a XenApp site, can be installed on a shared server or dedicated server. The following requirements must be met:

- Windows Server 2008, 2008 R2, 2012, or 2012 R2
- Windows 7, Windows 8, or Windows 8.1
- Microsoft .NET Framework 3.5

The licensing server role is very lightweight. The actual license console is a single-threaded process and only requires a single processor. Memory utilization is negligible. The drive space consumed is less than 2 GB.

Even though this is such a lightweight system, I generally recommend the following for a dedicated license server system:

- Windows Server 2008 R2 SP1 or higher
- 2 vCPU
- 4 GB RAM
- A 40 GB hard drive (or larger, based on your standards)

This enables the Citrix License Server to also function as a licensing server for other production purposes, including the **Microsoft Remote Desktop Services (RDS)** license server and **Microsoft Key Management Service (KMS)** server as well as any other software product licenses.

> Citrix also offers a License Server VPX virtual appliance, which you can use to manage your licenses without requiring a Windows-based server. This VPX appliance is only available for the XenServer hypervisor at this time. If you would like to learn more about the license server VPX appliance, visit http://support.citrix.com/proddocs/topic/licensing-vpx-1112/lic-licensing-vpx-1112.html.

The license service administration console is available locally on the license server, or you can access it remotely through http://licenseservername:8082/ using your browser. You can install an SSL Certificate to enable secure browsing, if required, for your environment.

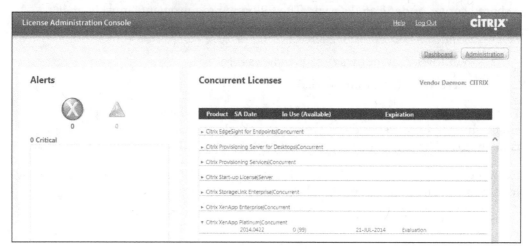

Citrix License Administration Console

High Availability considerations for the licensing server

Citrix licensing is a critical core component to any XenApp design. However, the licensing server does not necessarily require High Availability. All Citrix products include a grace period. This grace period is typically 30 days but can vary depending upon the product. The Windows Event Log indicates whether the product has entered the grace period and calculates the number of hours remaining in the grace period (the starting count is 720). If the grace period runs out, the product stops accepting connections. After communication is reestablished between the product and the license server, the grace period is reset.

Since the system is built with a grace period, fault tolerance is not a critical factor for Citrix licensing. You can create an environment with multiple license servers or even a license server cluster to reduce the impact of failure. However, in most production environments, the license server can be rebuilt, if necessary, within the grace period.

My preferred method of High Availability is to have a single virtual machine dedicated for my license server. Protect this machine using the standard virtualization High Availability and automatic restart policies. This will make sure the virtual license server is migrated and/or restarted in the event of a virtualization host failure. I also recommend keeping a copy of the fully configured virtual machine available for use as a cold spare, should the original VM go offline due to virtual machine or operating system corruption. For more options, visit `http://support.citrix.com/proddocs/topic/licensing-1111/lic-backup.html`.

> The grace period takes place only if the product has successfully communicated with the license server at least once. If you are using Provisioning Services, the last check is based on the master image, not the target device. This can cause issues if a license server is offline, and a target device reboots if the last check in is older than 30 days. For more information and a workaround on this issue, visit `http://support.citrix.com/article/CTX131202`.

Design decisions for the license server

The following design decisions need to be made when planning or implementing licensing for your XenApp site:

Option	Decision	Justification
Number of license servers	1	Typically a single, dedicated license server is used
Name(s) of license servers	CTXLIC	Citrix licenses are assigned by the hostname, which is case sensitive
License server version	11.11	11.11 is the required version for XenApp 7.5 and is backward compatible with other XenApp and XenDesktop versions
License type	Platinum	XenDesktop 7.5 Platinum user/device licenses
License count	99	Number of licenses managed
Hardware platform	Virtual	Physical or virtual
System specifications	2 CPUs 4 GB RAM 40 GB HDD	CPU, RAM, hard drive, and so on
HA/DR plan	VM backup/restore	High Availability / disaster recovery plan

Designing your database platform

XenApp 7.5 uses Microsoft SQL databases for site configuration, change logs, and monitoring.

The role of the database in the XenApp environment

In previous versions of XenApp, the database was important, but it only held persistent information and not session data, so the loss of database connectivity was not a catastrophic failure. With the new FMA architecture, the database is now critical for all operations. The site database contains persistent configuration information, real-time session data, and configuration change logs. It is important to note that if connectivity to the database is lost, no changes can be made to the site (Studio will be unavailable) and new connections cannot be made.

Planning your SQL server requirements

Previous versions of XenApp allowed for SQL, Microsoft Access, or Oracle databases. XenApp 7.5 can only be configured for Microsoft SQL 2008 R2 SP2 or Microsoft SQL 2012 SP1. Server resources vary from one environment to another. Since the database requirements for Citrix tend to be lightweight, the databases can be hosted on a shared SQL environment if one is available. Alternatively, a dedicated virtual SQL environment can be created. This environment should have a minimum of two virtual processors and 4 GB of memory at least; 8 GB of memory is better.

In a small environment, SQL Express can be used. This can be installed during the initial setup. However, it is not recommended for use in a production environment since the management and High Availability options are very limited.

For a complete list of supported databases for all Citrix products, visit
`http://support.citrix.com/article/CTX114501`.

High Availability considerations for databases

Microsoft SQL supports multiple different configurations for High Availability of databases, including:

- **Active-Passive SQL clusters**: This is the traditional Microsoft clustering technology that leverages two servers with shared storage.

- **SQL mirroring**: This requires multiple SQL servers (each licensed separately) as well as a witness server. It ensures the secondary database server, which maintains a copy of the databases, will take over functionality if the primary database server goes offline. This is the preferred method for most enterprise environments; however, this feature is being depreciated by Microsoft. It is available for SQL 2008 and SQL 2012, but it will not be available in future releases of SQL.

- **SQL AlwaysOn availability groups**: This is a new, enterprise-level alternative to mirroring, which was first introduced in SQL 2012. For more information, visit `http://msdn.microsoft.com/en-us/library/hh510230.aspx`.

- **Hypervisor High Availability**: This assumes a greater degree of risk by having a single SQL Server protected with High Availability and automatic restart features of the hypervisor. It is the least expensive option as well as has the highest risk.

Along with High Availability, you should also plan for disaster recovery. This is generally provided through regular database backups, which are then copied offsite and can be used in the event of a catastrophic failure. I generally recommend the following backup routines for SQL databases:

- Weekly full
- Nightly differential
- Hourly transaction log

This will keep database recovery manageable and provide up-to-the-hour recovery windows, if necessary.

 More information on High Availability support is available at `http://support.citrix.com/proddocs/topic/xenapp-xendesktop-75/cds-plan-high-avail-rho.html`.

Planning and sizing your Citrix® databases

The size of the databases greatly depends on environmental variables, such as the size of the site, the number of users, the number of applications, the frequency of changes, and usage patterns. The base site contains a single database that can be split into separate databases for site, configuration logging, and monitoring. I recommend splitting the databases to manage growth and make future searches easier, especially when it comes to the monitoring database.

For detailed planning on sizing, visit `http://support.citrix.com/article/` `CTX139508`. I usually make the following base recommendations, but please adjust it as it fits your environment:

- The XenApp site database
    - 100 MB (can grow as large as 400 MB)
    - Transaction log: 5 GB

- The XenApp monitoring database
    - 5 GB (can grow as large as 12 GB)
    - Transaction log: 1 GB

- XenApp configuration logging
    - 50 MB (can grow as large as 200 MB)

- The Provisioning Services database
    - 20 MB (can grow to 100 MB)

SQL Server design decisions

For our environment, we will be using two SQL 2012 servers with SQL AlwaysOn Availability Groups. These servers will be hosted on our virtual platform with two CPUs and 8 GB RAM each. They will be dedicated to performing SQL functions in our environment and will be used to host only the four previously mentioned databases. SQL01 will be our primary SQL server and SQL02 will be our secondary SQL server, which uses the **Windows Server Failover Cluster (WSFC)** and leverages the group name of LABSQL.

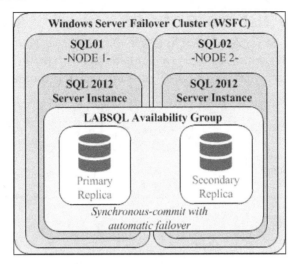

The SQL AlwaysOn design for High Availability

According to `http://www.sql-server-performance.com/2013/alwayson-clustering-failover/`, AlwaysOn Availability Groups is recommended over database mirroring since AlwaysOn overcomes several limitations imposed in database mirroring. These limitations include the following:

- You can have multiple mirrored instances/nodes/replicas (one primary node and up to four secondary nodes) with a combination of synchronous and asynchronous commit modes, both at the same time. The replica setup in synchronous commit mode can be used for higher availability (or for automatic failover), and the replica setup in asynchronous commit mode can be used for disaster recovery.

- You can combine multiple databases together and fail over them as a unit; you don't need to do it for each database separately as you did in the case of database mirroring.

- The secondary replica can be configured as readable, allowing you to offload read-only operations. With a traditional mirror, the replica is always in recovery mode.

- You can also offload backup operations to the secondary replica; this will allow you to have less workload on the primary replica.

Of course, using AlwaysOn requires SQL 2012. If that is not an option, then SQL Mirroring would be the preferred choice for High Availability. For a detailed, step-by-step guide to configure mirroring for an existing XenApp 7.5 site, visit `http://carlwebster.com/changing-production-xendesktop-7x-site-use-sql-mirroring/`.

Managing your databases

During the base site set up, as shown in *Chapter 5, Designing Your Application Delivery Layer*, we only had the option to set up a single database. This initial database contains all the site information, the configuration log, and the monitoring data:

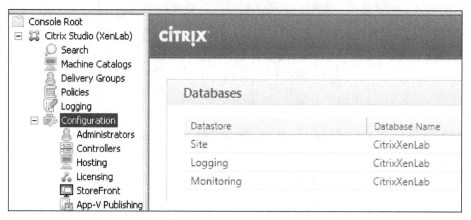

Base database configuration for a XenApp site

The site database, which contains all the configuration and session data, cannot be changed. However, the **Logging** and **Monitoring** databases can be separated. To move the secondary databases, select the database in the center pane of **Studio**, and then click on **Change Database** in the **Actions** pane:

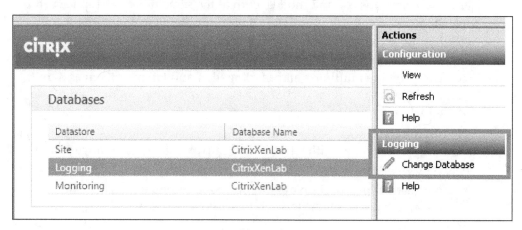

Changing the database location

Using the change database wizard, you can specify the database server and database name. Credentials are based on the current user. If the current user does not have permission to create the database, you can generate a database script that can be run on the database server by a database administrator with elevated privileges:

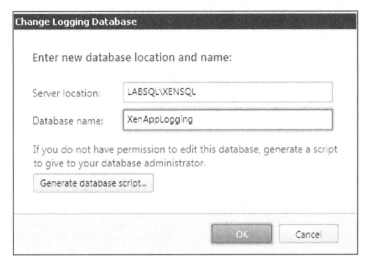

Changing the database location

Configuring your file services

File services are a commonly overlooked component of a XenApp environment design. In this section, we will take a look at some considerations for file services.

The role of file services in the environment

Depending on your specific environment, you may be able to use existing shared file services. Other environments may leverage dedicated file services. The following elements generally require a Windows-type file share:

- The Citrix Profile Store
- Microsoft folder redirection
- The Provisioning Services shared vDisk store
- ISO / Installation Media Repository

These file shares may be hosted on a standalone Windows server, a Windows file cluster, a distributed filesystem that uses **Microsoft DFS-R**, or even on a **Network-attached Storage** (**NAS**) unit that hosts **CIFS** shares.

We discussed the vDisk store previously in *Chapter 6, Designing Your Virtual Image Delivery*. We will cover profile management and folder redirection next, in *Chapter 8, Optimizing Your XenApp® Solution*.

The requirements for file servers

Depending on their role, file servers do not require a lot of compute resources (CPU and RAM), but they may require storage. If you are presenting the shares through a NAS unit or a single host, you can plan your storage requirements using a basic storage calculation and a single network share mapping. Most shared volumes are deployed in 2 TB or 4 TB configurations, but your organizational standards may vary. If you are using a distributed system, you will want to ensure each node maintains enough file space for data replication (so if you determine you need 2 TB of storage space and plan to have two servers replicating the data, you will need a total of 4 TB of storage).

High Availability considerations for file services

File services should be highly available, but their criticality will depend on your environment. If you are not using shared data or shared profiles and using a distributed model for PVS High Availability, you might not need a centralized file repository. However, most XenApp environments will leverage at least profile management if not the other components.

There are several options for High Availability when it comes to file services. Some of these will depend on your hardware and storage platforms. The common options are:

- **Server clusters**: This is the traditional Microsoft clustering technology that leverages two file servers with shared storage.

- **DFS-R**: This is the preferred method; it leverages standalone Microsoft file servers with Distributed File System using replication, creating a multinode data mirror. For more information on creating a DFS-R namespace, visit `http://msdn.microsoft.com/en-us/library/bb540025(v=vs.85).aspx`.

- **Hypervisor High Availability**: This assumes a greater degree of risk by having a single file server protected with High Availability and automatic restart features of the hypervisor. This is the least expensive option as well as has the highest risk.

- **Network-attached Storage**: Using a NAS appliance is common for shared file services. If you are using NAS, it is recommended that you ensure the appliance has fault-tolerant features, such as parity drives and multiple controller units.

All the file data should be backed up and secured offsite for use in disaster recovery as well as for the recovery of accidental deletion of data. These backups can be performed using traditional backup and data protection software or via scripts to remote storage media.

Design decisions

For our environment, we are using two dedicated virtual file servers called FIL01 and FIL02. Each file server has two CPUs and 4 GB of RAM as well as a dedicated 100 GB data drive. We are using Microsoft DFS-R to create a shared namespace with replication. DFS namespaces are domain-specific; they use the following convention: \\<DOMAIN.NAME>\<dfsroot>\<path>. For our environment, the namespace is \\ XENLAB\XENFS. This is a full replication partnership, so anything that is written to FIL01 will be replicated for FIL02, and vice versa.

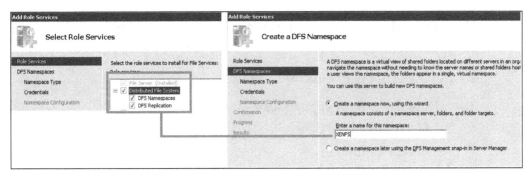

Creating a DFS namespace

We are using DFS-R because it is an easy-to-manage, robust solution with ample fault tolerance and growth capabilities. Should we require more resources, we can easily add more data space or additional file servers. If we ever expand to multiple data centers, we can extend DFS across multiple Active Directory sites.

We will cover this further in *Chapter 8, Optimizing Your XenApp® Solution*, but it is worth noting that Microsoft does not officially support DFS-R for use with user profiles or folder redirection. However, for a single site, I have used this repeatedly without issue. For disaster recovery planning or multiple site distribution, you can use an Active/Passive DFS setup, which is fully supported. For more information, visit http://support.microsoft.com/kb/2533009.

Configuring file share permissions

Any shares used for vDisks or ISO/media files should have full access granted for the XenApp site administrator groups as well as the service accounts. The user data and user profile shares should be configured similar to Microsoft home folders, as described in http://support.microsoft.com/kb/274443:

- **CREATOR OWNER** (Apply to **Subfolders and files only**)
  - **Full control**

- **System** (Apply to **This folder, subfolders and files**)
  - **Full control**

- **Domain admins** (Apply to **This folder, subfolders and files**)
  - **Full control**

- **EVERYONE** (Apply to **This folder only**)
  - **Create folders / append data**
  - **List folder / read data**
  - **Read attributes**
  - **Traverse folder / execute file**

This will allow users to create child folders under the share. Once a user creates a folder, they then inherit the **CREATOR OWNER** rights to that folder, as shown in the following screenshot:

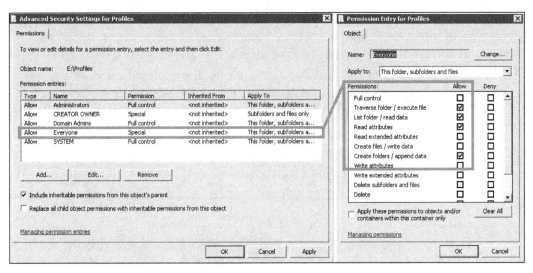

Setting NTFS permissions on shares

Implementing monitoring for your XenApp® environment

Monitoring has significantly changed with the newest version of XenApp. Previous versions of XenApp leveraged **EdgeSight** for all monitoring services. XenApp 6.5 could be monitored with Director 2.1. Now, with XenApp 7.5, all monitoring is built into Director as part of the site deployment.

The role of monitoring in the environment

Director is used to monitor real-time end-user performance as well as historical trends. Users with site administrator and help desk roles have access to log in to and view Director data. Director collects session information, including logon metrics, bandwidth utilization, and user performance. Adding the Insight appliance to monitor NetScaler Gateway will also allow administrators to monitor the network performance of connections. The data retention in Director is based on your licensing level of both XenApp and NetScaler:

- XenApp Advanced/Enterprise edition: Real-time data, 7 days' worth of history and session monitoring.

- XenApp Platinum edition: Real-time data, performance metrics, session monitoring, basic network analysis, and up to 1 year of historical data.

- XenApp Platinum edition plus NetScaler Enterprise: Real-time data, session monitoring, performance metrics, basic network analysis, up to 1 year of historical data, and 1 hour of detailed network data (with HDX Insight).

- XenApp Platinum Edition plus NetScaler Platinum: Real-time data, session monitoring, performance metrics, basic network analysis, up to 1 year of historical data, and unlimited detailed network data (with HDX Insight).

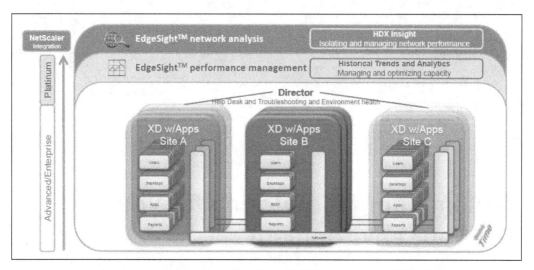

Monitoring integration with Director and NetScaler (© Citrix Systems, Inc. All Rights Reserved.)

For more information, check out `http://blogs.citrix.com/2013/06/04/xendesktop-7-director-and-edgesight-explained/`.

The requirements for installing Director

Director does not require a lot of resources. It can be installed on the controllers in a smaller environment or on dedicated systems in a larger enterprise. Director can be installed on the following operating systems:

- The Windows Server 2012 R2, Standard and Datacenter editions

- The Windows Server 2012, Standard and Datacenter editions

- The Windows Server 2008 R2 SP1, Standard, Enterprise, and Datacenter editions

Director requires the following system components:

- Disk space: 50 MB
- Microsoft .NET framework 4.5
- Microsoft Internet Information Services (IIS) 7.0 and ASP.NET 2.0

The following Internet browsers are supported to view Director:

- Internet Explorer 9 or higher
- Mozilla Firefox
- Google Chrome

The requirements for installing the Insight appliance

HDX Insight is part of the NetScaler Insight Center virtual appliance. This appliance is available for use on XenServer or VMware ESXi. It is not currently available for Hyper-V. The HDX Insight features are compatible with XenApp 6.5 or higher and XenDesktop 5.6 or higher. When integrated with Director, you need to configure the Insight features through the Director dashboard. For more information, visit `http://support.citrix.com/proddocs/topic/xendesktop-7/cds-monitor-config-hdx.html`.

Since Insight Center is a virtual appliance, it has limited configuration requirements. The virtual appliance requires the following components:

- 3 GB of RAM (or more)
- 2 vCPU (or more)
- 120 GB disk space (240 GB is recommended)
- 1 network interface; 100 Mbps is minimum and 1 Gbps is preferred

The appliance can be downloaded from `www.citrix.com` and imported into your virtual infrastructure.

High Availability considerations for Director

Since Director is not a critical component to a XenApp site, High Availability is not necessarily a requirement. If Director is installed on a set of controllers or a set of shared servers, you will inherit the High Availability plan of those elements. Enterprise environments may leverage two (or more) dedicated Directors. These will ideally be accessed using a load-balanced address, such as those created in *Chapter 4, Designing Your Access Layer*.

Alternatively, if using a single Director server, you could rely solely on the High Availability and autorestart features of your hypervisor platform. In the case of Director being offline, you may lose some monitoring data, but the user experience will not be impacted.

Monitoring design decisions

Although Director can be installed on controllers or other shared platforms, I prefer to have dedicated servers. In our case, we have two Director servers: DIR01 and DIR02. These servers are load balanced with a standard load balancing VIP on our NetScaler appliances. We can create a DNS alias called *director* to access the Director dashboard using the load balanced address.

Since Director is lightweight, we do not need to dedicate a lot of resources. Each virtual server has been assigned two virtual processors and 4 GB of memory. This should be plenty of resources for our environment. Each Director should support up to 500 helpdesk connections. If you see your Director servers struggling for resources, you can increase the CPU and RAM allocations for the Director servers or add additional Director servers to the load balancing group.

Using Director to monitor user experience

If Director is installed on the Controller, it is automatically configured. If you install Director on a separate server, you will need to enter a Controller address as part of the installation. Once Director is configured, you can log in with the domain credentials.

Once logged in, the first thing you see is the dashboard, which provides an overview of the currently connected sessions, the overall average logon duration, and the health of the infrastructure, as shown in the following screenshot:

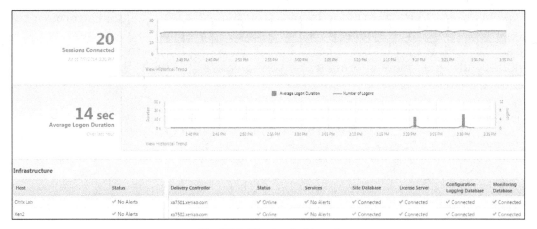

The Citrix Director dashboard

Accessing the **Trends** button at the top of the Director window will allow the administrator to view ongoing trends. These trends can be filtered by delivery group and time period. The default view for **Delivery Group** is **All**, and for **Time period**, it is **Last 24 hours**.

The following screenshot shows concurrent sessions for the past week. Concurrent sessions are the number of users logged in at the same time. This graph shows both the connected and disconnected sessions. Understanding concurrency is important as it can impact capacity and utilization. I find it important to know when users are being connected and the heaviest utilization periods. Watching disconnected sessions is important as well; if this number climbs too high, you may need to reevaluate your session timer policies.

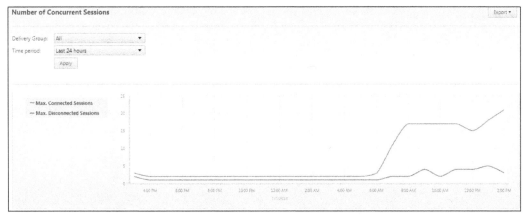

Concurrent usage report from Director

Another useful trend report for administrators to review is the **Logon Performance** report (shown in the following screenshot). This report shows logon performance trends as well as the number of active logons. Hovering the mouse over the data points will expose more information so you can understand how the logon time is calculated.

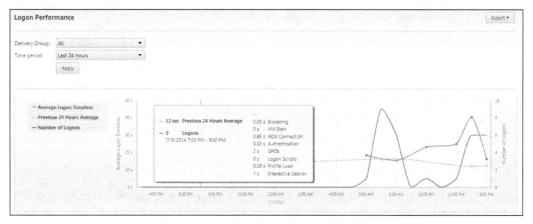

The Logon Performance report from Director

If you are getting poor logon performance, which is a common complaint by users, you can closely examine the various logon steps to determine where slowdowns may be occurring. If it is a single user, the slowdown may be profile-related. However, if it is consistently slow, it may be systemic. For example, the following screenshot shows slow logon processing, primarily due to the speed of the group policy processing. 49 seconds to process GPOs was causing the bulk of the logon performance issues. Once the GPO issues were resolved, the logon speed was reduced to 7 seconds.

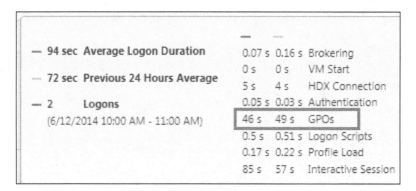

Logon performance metrics

If you find yourself fighting slow logon times, even after reducing GPOs and logon scripts, you can use the Windows Performance Toolkit for more in-depth troubleshooting. This includes XPERF, which is used to trace logon performance. For more details, visit `http://social.technet.microsoft.com/wiki/contents/articles/10128.tools-for-troubleshooting-slow-boots-and-slow-logons-sbsl.aspx`.

To view an individual session, you can look at running sessions or use the search box to find a user by name. You can search by domain name or common name. If more than one name is returned, you can select the target user from the provided drop-down list. If a user has multiple sessions open, you can select the target session from User Activity Manager, shown in the following screenshot. The **Activity Manager** screen allows the helpdesk administrators to view which applications are in use by a user and manage that user's session or profile. Here, the helpdesk operator can shadow a user's session for remote support.

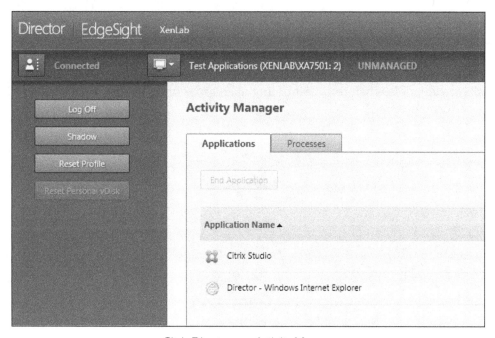

Citrix Director user Activity Manager

Clicking on the **Details** button will switch Director to the user detail view, shown in the following screenshot. Here, administrators can view more details regarding the user and the active session. This includes items such as machine details (which server or workstation they are connected to), session details (including the session state, connection time, endpoint name, and client version), and applied Citrix policies.

Citrix Director session details

The session details screen will also show the logon performance chart for that specific session, personalization information (such as the profile size, location, and folder redirection), as well as HDX channel usage and performance. These details are valuable when troubleshooting user issues or analyzing individual user performance.

Citrix Director additional session details

Summary

In this chapter, we looked at designing our supporting infrastructure components. These are elements that are necessary to support our XenApp deployment, including License Server, SQL databases, file services, and monitoring. We looked at the role and requirements, as well as recommended configurations, for each of these elements.

We took a deeper look at Director as well. Licensing, databases, and file services, although critical, tend to be a "one-time set it and forget routine" for most environments. Director, however, is designed to be used daily, as part of your operations.

Now that we have our primary site built and all the components configured, we can begin looking at optimizing our XenApp solution in the next chapter. This will include managing user profiles, configuring Citrix and Active Directory policies, and configuring printing. These will be the last steps we take to fine-tune our application before we are ready to begin production!

8
Optimizing Your XenApp® Solution

In the earlier chapters, we focused on analysis and high-level design. In the last three chapters, we dug deep into building out our XenApp environment. Now that the environment has been built, we will focus on optimizing our solution in preparation for production workloads.

In this chapter, you will learn about:

- Managing user profiles
- Configuring Citrix policies
- Planning Active Directory policies
- Controlling printing

Managing user profiles

User profiles contain personalization settings for each user. On a Windows system, every user has their own profile. The user profile contains settings such as application settings, registry values, wallpaper settings, and so on.

Types of profiles

In a Windows computing environment, there are three primary types of profiles:

- **Local**: A local profile is created the first time a user logs on to a computer. The profile is stored on the computer's local hard disk and is specific to that one system. This profile is stored locally and is not shared among other computers.

- **Roaming**: A roaming profile is a copy of a locally generated profile that is copied to, and stored on, a network share. This profile is downloaded to any computer as part of the logon process. Changes made to a roaming user profile are synchronized with the server copy of the profile during the logoff process.

- **Mandatory**: A mandatory profile is a type of profile that administrators can use to specify settings for users. Users cannot make changes to a mandatory profile. Any changes made during a session are lost on logoff.

- **Temporary**: A temporary profile is issued each time there is a problem loading a user's profile, regardless of profile type. Temporary profiles are deleted during logoff, so any changes made are lost.

Along with the types of profiles, there are currently two different versions of profiles. Windows XP and Windows Server 2003 leverage V1 profiles; Windows 7, Windows 8, Windows Server 2008, and Windows Server 2012 leverage V2 profiles. Profiles cannot be natively shared between V1 and V2 versions.

There are also multiple third-party add-ons that can be used to further manage profiles. These tools generally get layered on top of Windows and interject during the logon process in order to manage the profile for that session. These tools can typically manage both V1 and V2 profiles and offer enhancements over the native Windows roaming profile. These include, but are not limited to, the following:

- Citrix Profile Management
- AppSense User Environment Manager
- RES Workspace Manager

Why we need to manage profiles

Improper profile management can cause issues in a XenApp environment, including slow logon times and inconsistent settings. If you have an environment that does not need to retain user settings and does not require personalization (such as an application provider that does not leverage customizations), it is possible to use mandatory profiles or even local profiles (although local profiles are never recommended, they might be easy to implement but will have their own management and scalability issues).

Most enterprise environments, especially those offering a VDI solution, require personalization. As administrators, we tend to focus more on the application functionality and performance. However, users care about these items as well as personalization settings, whether it is application preferences, wallpaper settings, or storing Internet favorites. In this case, we need to adequately manage the user profiles for performance and consistency. This rules out local or mandatory profiles since user settings will either not be saved or will not available across multiple servers.

We could leverage roaming profiles, but since Citrix Profile Management is included as part of your XenApp licenses, we will use it. Citrix Profile Management offers many benefits beyond traditional roaming profiles, including:

- Smaller profile size (due to exclusions)
- Faster logon times (due to smaller size and profile streaming)
- Faster logoff times (due to smaller size and active write back)
- More granular controls (only the differences are written instead of the entire profile)
- More reliable roaming experience, including file synchronization

Planning Citrix Profile Management policies

Citrix Profile Management requires three elements to function properly:

- Network share to store profiles
- The Citrix User Profile Manager software agent
- Profile policy settings

We discussed network shares in *Chapter 7, Designing Your Supporting Infrastructure Components*; we will be using this location to centrally store our Citrix user profiles: `\\xenlab\xendfs\citrixprofiles`. Citrix does not *officially* support using Active-Active DFS shares for profile storage. However, for a single site, I have used this repeatedly without issue. For disaster recovery planning or multiple site distribution, you can use an Active-Passive DFS setup that is fully supported. For more information, please refer to `http://support.citrix.com/proddocs/topic/user-profile-manager-5-x/upm-plan-high-availability-disaster-recovery-intro.html`.

With XenApp 7.5, the **User Profile Manager** (**UPM**) 5.1 software agent is installed as part of the VDA installation. In earlier versions, a separate installation was required. If necessary, you can access the UPM installation utility from the XenApp 7.5 media under `\x64\ProfileManagement` or `\x86\ProfileManagement`, as appropriate.

The profile policy can be defined in the following ways, which are listed in order of precedence:

1. Active Directory Group Policy
2. Citrix policy (defined in Studio)
3. Local machine policies
4. Local configuration file (`C:\Program Files\Citrix\User Profile Manager\UPMPolicyDefaults_all.ini`)

We will discuss Citrix policies later in this chapter, including why the preference is to use the Citrix policy engine. To create a profile policy, you can use **Studio**, select **Policies**, and then select **Create Policy**. For now, we will create a Citrix policy called **Profile Management** and use the policy filters to select the appropriate policy elements, as shown in the following screenshot:

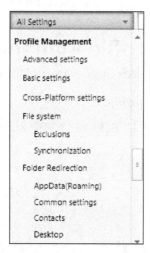

Defining profile management in Citrix Studio

Using the Citrix policy definitions, you can select the various profile management components and choose to configure those items. Anything not configured will revert to default values unless defined elsewhere, such as in the local INI file. As you can see in the following screenshot, we are defining **Active write back**, **Enable Profile management**, **Path to user store**, and **Process logons of local administrators**. We are not defining **Excluded groups**, **Offline profile support**, or **Processed groups**; all of those elements will apply default values (generally disabled or not defined).

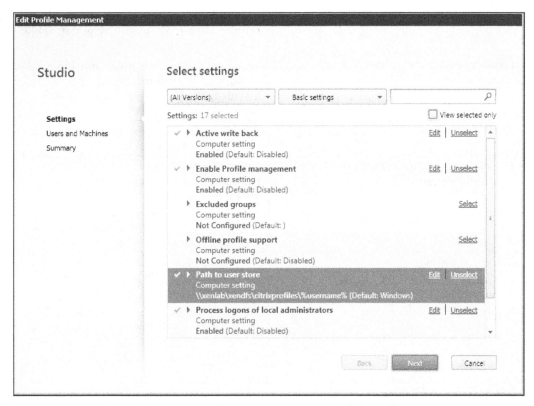

Configuring profile management settings in Citrix Studio

Let's take a look at our recommended sample Citrix Policy. For a full reference of all policy settings and definitions, please refer to `http://support.citrix.com/proddocs/topic/user-profile-manager-5-x/upm-reference-adm-settings-defaults.html`.

Policy settings	Recommendations	Justifications
Basic settings		
Active write back	**Enabled**	Files and folders that are modified are synchronized to the user store in the middle of a session, speeding up the logoff process.
Enable Profile management	**Enabled**	Profile management is not enabled by default. Even if the profile manager is installed, it will not process profiles until it is enabled.
Path to user store	**Enabled**	The absolute path or the path that is relative to the home directory.
Process logons of local administrators	**Enabled**	Specifies whether logons of members of the BUILTIN\Administrators group are processed. This ensures that all users are processed. If you have separate administrative accounts from normal user accounts, you can revisit this.
Advanced settings		
Process Internet cookie files on logoff	**Enabled**	Some deployments leave extra Internet cookies that are not referenced by the Index.dat file. The extra cookies left in the filesystem after sustained browsing can lead to profile bloat. Enable this policy to force the processing of Index.dat, and remove the extra cookies.
File System / Exclusions		
Exclusion list - directories	**Enabled**	The list of folders that are ignored during synchronization. Refer to the following recommended list of exclusions.

Policy settings	Recommendations	Justifications
File System / Synchronization		
Directories to synchronize	Enabled	This is used to ensure that subfolders are synchronized even if the parent folder is excluded. A recommended list of the directories that are to be synchronized is given after the table.
Files to synchronize	Enabled	This is used to ensure that specified files are synchronized even if the parent folder is excluded. A recommended list of files that are to be synchronized is given after the table.
Folders to mirror	Enabled	Mirroring folders allows profile management to process a transactional folder and its contents as a single entity, thereby avoiding profile bloat. A recommended list of folders that are to be mirrored is given after the table.
Log settings		
Enable logging	Enabled	This enables logging. It's only necessary during the initial setup and troubleshooting. Files are written to `%SystemRoot%\System32\Logfiles\UserProfileManager` unless **Path to log file** is configured.
File system notifications	Enabled	Writes filesystem actions to the logfile.
Logoff	Enabled	Writes logoff event processing to the logfile.
Logon	Enabled	Writes logon event processing to the logfile.
Personalized user information	Enabled	Writes user personalization information, including profile path and folder redirection information, to the logfile.
Profile Handling		
Delete locally cached profiles on logoff	Enabled	Users' local profile cache is deleted after the logoff. If this policy is disabled, cached profiles are not deleted, causing a consumption of drive space.
Local profile conflict handling	Enabled / Use local Profile	This defines how profile management behaves if both a profile in the user store and a local Windows user profile (not a Citrix user profile) exist.

Policy settings	Recommendations	Justifications
Streamed User Profiles		
Profile streaming	**Enabled**	Files and folders contained in a profile are fetched from the user store to the local computer only when they are accessed by users after they have logged on. Registry entries and any files in the pending area are exceptions. They are fetched immediately. This will improve the logon speeds for large user profiles.

The following directories are recommended for exclusion and should be entered into the **Exclusion list - directories** entry of the Citrix policy. The paths are relative to the user profile space. For example, to exclude C:\Users\%username%\AppData\Local, you only need to list \AppData\Local:

- AppData\Local

- AppData\LocalLow

- AppData\Roaming\Citrix\PNAgent\AppCache

- AppData\Roaming\Citrix\PNAgent\Icon Cache

- AppData\Roaming\Citrix\PNAgent\ResourceCache

- AppData\Roaming\ICAClient\Cache

- AppData\Roaming\Macromedia\Flash Player\#SharedObject

- AppData\Roaming\Macromedia\Flash Player\macromedia.com\support\ flashplayer\sys

- AppData\Roaming\Microsoft\Windows\Start Menu

- AppData\Roaming\Sun\Java\Deployment\cache

- AppData\Roaming\Sun\Java\Deployment\log

- AppData\Roaming\Sun\Java\Deployment\tmp

- Citrix

The following list of directories should be considered for addition to **Exclusion list - directories** if you are *not* using folder redirection:

- Contacts
- Desktop
- Documents
- Downloads
- Favorites
- Java
- Links
- Local Settings
- Music
- My Documents
- My Pictures
- My Videos
- Pictures
- Saved Games
- Searches
- UserData
- Videos

This is the recommended list of directories that are to be synchronized:

- AppData\Local\Microsoft\Credentials

This is the recommended list of files that are to be synchronized:

- AppData\Local\Microsoft\Office*.qat
- AppData\Local\Microsoft\Office*.officeUI

This is the recommended list of folders that are to be mirrored:

- `AppData\Roaming\Microsoft\Windows\Cookies`

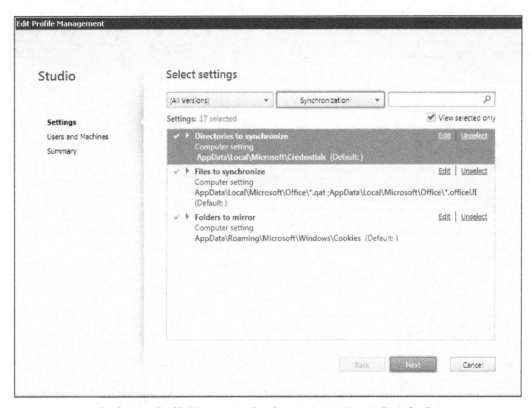

Configuring Profile Management Synchronization settings in Citrix Studio

You should review all of the preceding recommendations in order to ensure that there are no conflicts in your environment. You will most likely need to add additional files and directories to the lists based on your needs. For more information on profile management, please refer to `http://blogs.citrix.com/2012/02/11/citrix-profile-management-and-vdi-doing-it-right/` and `http://blogs.citrix.com/2012/08/05/citrix-profile-management-and-vdi-doing-it-right-part-2/`.

If you are running multiple systems and want to segment profiles, you can create policies with a different path to user store settings. This is common in a mixed environment where you have Windows 7 desktop images and XenApp images. Even though both might be V2 type profiles, which can be shared, they are commonly separated. Or you can leverage different network shares for different organizational units or different deployment locations. For whatever reason, you can easily create and filter policies to fit your needs.

Planning Microsoft folder redirection

Redirecting the user data folders is highly recommended as it separates the user data from user settings. This is important for several reasons, including the reusability of data by multiple systems and protection from profile bloat and corruption. Redirecting user data will also improve the logon performance since these files are not loaded as part of the profile.

Folder redirection has traditionally been implemented through Group Policies by navigating to **User Configuration | Windows Settings | Folder Redirection**, as shown in the following screenshot:

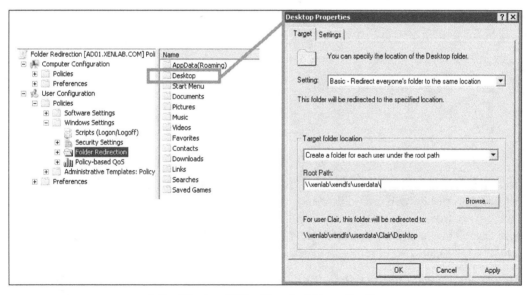

Active Directory GPO settings for folder redirection

However, Citrix has added this capability to the Citrix Profile Management policies natively; it is configurable through Citrix Studio as part of the overall profile management strategy. These settings are available by navigating to **Profile Management | Folder Redirection**.

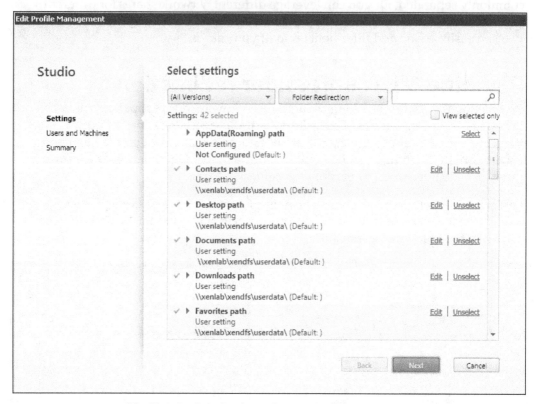

The Citrix Studio policy for configuring the folder redirection

In either scenario, the path is the root path of the network share. The folder redirection policy will create the target folder for each user and then create the necessary subfolders based on policy settings. So, if we define a path of \\xenlab\xendfs\userdata\, and our user Jane Doe (user ID: jdoe) signs in, a folder will be created for \\xenlab\xendfs\userdata\jdoe.

Personally, I prefer to use Citrix Studio to manage the folder redirection as part of profile management. This way, I am not managing profiles in two separate locations. I've also seen GPO-based folder redirection fail due to issues in environments with asynchronous processing. When that happens, the folder redirection was not properly applied, causing issues for users. Using the Citrix policy engine resolves both those issues.

Folder redirection and exclusions

One point of debate is whether or not to add redirected folders to the folder exclusion list that we previously defined. There are a couple of considerations for this. Some engineers will add redirected folders to the exclusions list as a fail-safe, so even if the folder redirection does not work, the user data is *not* placed in the profile permanently. Granted, one drawback of this is that any temporary user data is lost when the user logoff.

Citrix officially recommends that you do *not* exclude redirected folders so that if you change the redirection later, the data can become part of the user profile. There is no technically right answer; just make an informed decision and document that decision and the policy settings for later reference. As for myself, I personally like to exclude redirected folders so that these elements are never part of a profile, even if the redirection fails.

For more information on the official Citrix standpoint, please see `http://support.citrix.com/proddocs/topic/xenapp-xendesktop-75/cds-using-upm.html`.

What about home drives?

I am often asked, "Why not use home drives for folder redirection?" This is a very valid question, and the answer is always "It depends". Do all users have a home drive defined as part of their user account in the active directory? If not, this won't work. Is the home drive location in close proximity to the XenApp session hosts? If not, this can cause latency. You can use home drives, but I generally don't recommend it because in most environments, this is something the Citrix team cannot control and it can greatly impact the user experience.

What about AppData?

You might have noticed that AppData has not been redirected in our sample policy. I have seen too many applications that do not function properly with AppData redirected to a network path. This could be due to the application architecture not functioning with a network path, or it could be due to performance issues with constant writing to a network share. Even though AppData is broken into three categories (Local, LocalLow, and Roaming), some legacy applications might reference Roaming when looking for Local, thus causing errors.

Even if you do not redirect AppData, it is still a part of the profile that is captured and saved using Citrix Profile Management. Most likely, AppData does not need to be shared among multiple operating systems or environments. However, feel free to test in your own environment.

For detailed information on AppData and how it functions, please refer to `http://
www.grouppolicy.biz/2010/08/best-practice-roaming-profiles-and-
folder-redirection-a-k-a-user-virtualization/`.

Configuring Citrix® policies

Citrix policies are defined in Citrix Studio. They are processed through Group Policy
extensions and are applied as part of the Windows policy engine, as noted in the
Policy processing order screenshot. These Citrix policy settings are also available as
Group Policy templates (ADMX files), which can be imported and configured through
Active Directory Group Policy Management Console, if required (we will discuss
more on Group Policies later in this chapter). Within Citrix Studio, you can create
and modify Citrix policies as well as leverage policy templates.

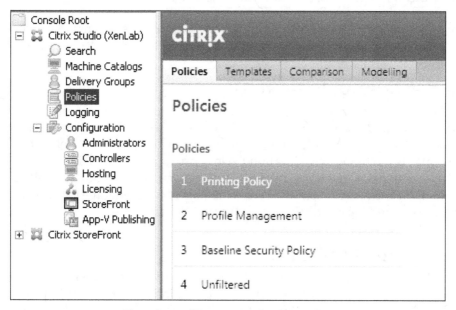

The policy configuration inside Citrix Studio

Understanding the role of the Citrix policy engine

Citrix policies are processed and applied after the local machine policies but before the Active Directory **Group Policy Objects** (GPO) are processed. This means that if there is a conflict between a Citrix-defined policy and a GPO, the GPO will override the Citrix Policy.

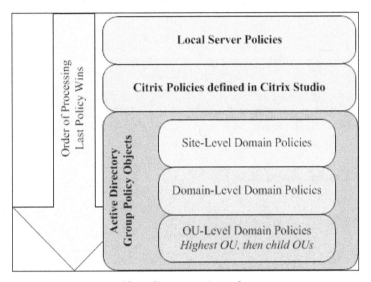

The policy processing order

Since you can define Citrix policies through GPOs, and since GPOs take higher priority, you might be asking yourself why you should use Citrix policies. I prefer to use Citrix policies for several reasons, namely the following:

- Commonly, the Citrix team and the AD team are separate, and the Citrix team might not be able to control the GPOs but it can control the Citrix policies

- Citrix offers some levels of granularity that are not practical or capable within Active Directory. This includes things such as filtering by the client IP address or name, Delivery Groups, and the access control type (such as when are they arriving through the NetScaler Gateway).

In reality, most environments use a mix of Citrix Policies and Active Directory GPOs. We will discuss Active Directory policies later in this chapter.

Using Citrix template policies

When you first access the Policies section of Citrix Studio, you are prompted to either use pre-created templates or create policies manually. The templates are a great place to start in order to understand common settings and optimizations.

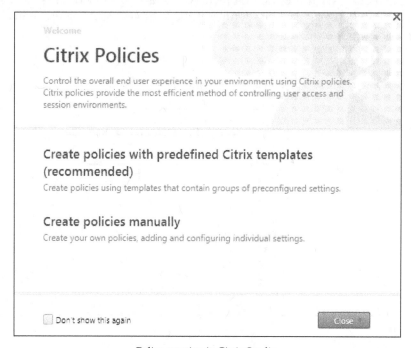

Policy creation in Citrix Studio

The following policy templates are available for use. You can create additional templates as well. Any templates you create can be exported for future use, if required:

- **High Definition User Experience**: These are settings that provide high quality audio, graphics, and video to users. This policy is best for users who need the greatest end-user experience without any concerns about the bandwidth utilization.

- **High Server Scalability**: These are settings that provide an optimized user experience while hosting more users on a single server. This policy is best for a balance of user experience and server scalability.

- **Optimized Bandwidth for WAN**: These are settings that provide optimized experience to users with low bandwidth or high latency connections. This is ideal for users who are working from branch offices over a shared WAN connection or offshore users; the policy focuses on minimizing the bandwidth utilization.

- **Security and Control**: These are settings that disable access to peripheral devices, drive mapping, port redirection, and flash acceleration on user devices. This policy is used to lock down the environment.

I don't use the templates directly, but reviewing these templates can help you understand settings that you might want to use in your own policies. If you want to create a policy from a template, you can select that template in Studio, and then use the **Create Policy from Template** command.

Planning your Citrix policies

When planning your Citrix policies, there are a few key elements that need to be remembered: assignment and priority. Similar to GPOs, Citrix policies have an order of precedence (defined by numerical order — the lowest number wins). Citrix policies can be filtered as well, so the policies will only apply to the appropriate users or Delivery Groups. When a user session connects, all policies are examined. Any applicable policies are merged into a single policy. If the same setting is configured in multiple policies, the policy with the highest precedence wins.

Defining Citrix policy settings

By default, all policy settings are not configured. When configuring settings, they might be **Allowed** or **Prohibited** or possibly **Enabled** or **Disabled**. As mentioned previously, if a setting is applied in multiple policies, the highest ranked policy wins. For example, in the *Policies configuration inside Citrix Studio* screenshot, we have four policies listed. If the baseline security policy (priority 3) and the printing policy (priority 1) have a conflict, the higher ranking policy (**Printing Policy**) will win. To ensure that the policies process in the correct order, you can right-click on a policy and choose to move the policy higher or lower in the priority listing.

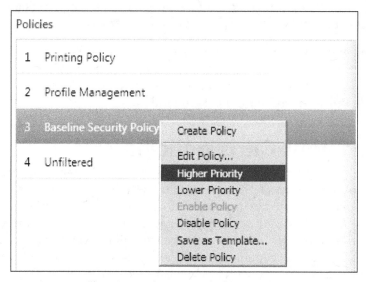

Changing a policy priority in Citrix Studio

When creating or editing a policy, you can filter the settings by an applicable version or by setting the category, and you can enable the **view selected only** checkbox to only see what has been configured. You can also search for settings or keywords if you are not sure where to find the particular settings you need. For a full listing of all policy settings and a description of these settings, please refer to http://support. citrix.com/proddocs/topic/xenapp-xendesktop-75/cds-policies-rules-wrapper-rho.html.

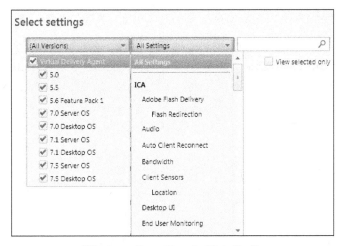

Filtering policy settings in Citrix Studio

After you create policies, you can compare your policies to other policies or templates. This is useful for auditing purposes as well as for design considerations. Also, if you define standards, you can create a template from these standards and then compare the settings at future dates in order to ensure compliance. To compare policies, you can use the **Comparison** tab, and then select your templates or policies for comparison.

In the following screenshot, we compare the baseline security policy that we created (based on the security and control template) with our printing policy. We can see conflicts highlighted, and we can expand these conflicts for more details. Since the printing policy is higher priority, it will win if both are applied within a user session.

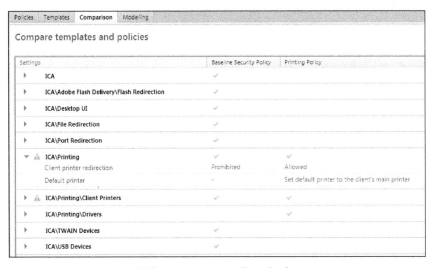

Policy comparison in Citrix Studio

You can also use the modeling wizard to determine which policies will apply, and in what order, to a target user on a target system. Using the wizard, you can select an individual user or an entire OU; it's same with the servers. You can also specify the delivery group, client connection, and access properties in order to simulate the session properties.

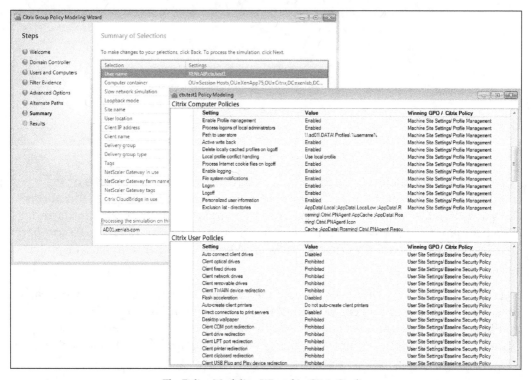

The Policy Modeling Wizard in Citrix Studio

Applying Citrix policy filters

When creating policies, after all settings have been defined, you can then choose the users and machines to which you can apply the policy. You can choose **Assign to all objects in a site** or **Assign to selected user and machine objects**, as shown in the following screenshot. If you choose to assign the policy to all, you are creating an unfiltered policy. This is common for standard or baseline policies and should have lower priority.

Commonly, you will need to create exception or exclusion policies that you want to apply only to certain Delivery Groups, users, security groups, or locations. In these scenarios, you will need to create filters. You can filter a policy by one or more of the following criteria:

- **Access control**: Specify connection types (with NetScaler Gateway or without NetScaler Gateway) to allow or deny a policy. This is useful if you have applications that should only be accessed directly (you could set a NetScaler connection to deny and prevent external access) or from external resources.

- **Citrix CloudBridge**: Specify whether this applies to a CloudBridge connection or not. You can use this to specify bandwidth constraints only for CloudBridge connections. CloudBridge is Citrix's WAN optimization appliance that accelerates traffic to branch offices.

- **Client IP address**: The IP address or network range(s) of addresses of client devices. This is commonly used for location-based or proximity-based settings, such as defining session printers for a certain area.

- **Client name**: This is the device name, including wildcard names, for client devices. It is commonly used for location-based or proximity-based settings, such as defining session printers for a certain area based on endpoint naming conventions. This can also be used for specialty settings based on the device type if a naming convention is standardized (for example, all thin client devices).

- **Delivery Group**: Allow or deny a policy application against specific Delivery Group(s). This is useful if you have a Delivery Group of servers for testing or a different function and you need to isolate policies or test variations.

- **Delivery Group type**: Allow or deny a policy against a Delivery Group types. This is handy if you have a lot of Delivery Groups and need to apply or restrict a policy against a class of groups. The types are private desktop, shared desktop, private application, and shared application.

- **Organization Unit (OU)**: Allow or deny policy application against target organizational unit(s). This can be useful if you segment your machine accounts to different OUs and want to filter settings that way.

- **Tag**: Tags can be defined in Studio for Delivery Groups and Applications (multiple tags separated by a semicolon). You can then filter these tags to allow or deny select policies.

- **User or group**: Specify the name(s) of the user(s) and group(s) in order to allow or deny select policies. This is handy for exclusion policies that need to be applied only to select individuals. This could be limited client drive access for administrators or it could be scanner access for a select group.

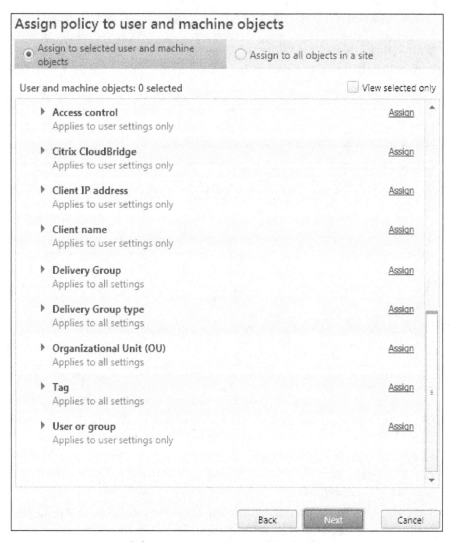

Policy assignment options in Citrix Studio

You can mix and match the filters as required, creating the exact scenario you need. What if you want to allow printing access only for a group of auditors when accessing the system directly from a select IP range? You can do this with a group, client IP address, and the access control filter to enable the policy, allowing client printers.

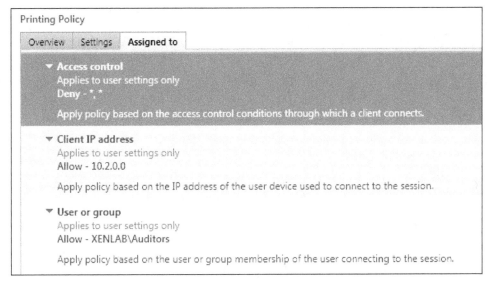

Sample policy filtering using multiple assignment criteria in Citrix Studio

Recommendations for Citrix policies

When defining Citrix policies, I recommend that you create a baseline security policy that disables or restricts most elements, including printer creation, client drive mappings, USB device usage, clipboard access, scanning, and other components that might cause security or bandwidth concerns. You can use the default unfiltered policy for this or your own, but either way, you want this policy to be one of the last policies processed. This is a failsafe policy that is commonly called a *fail closed* policy for security. It ensures that no extra channels or data paths are open unless they are specifically assigned (and filtered).

Other general best practices are to assign polices to groups instead of users and ranges instead of individual IP addresses. You want your filters to be as inclusive as necessary. You also want to make sure that your policies allow any activities that are necessary, but no more than that. All exclusions should have a business reason behind them. Just because users had client drive access previously, it is still worth questioning and investigating whether it is really necessary to grant it now.

Also, be careful with configuring conflicting policies in Citrix and GPOs, as the GPO will win any conflicts and make troubleshooting and modeling difficult. Finally, disable unused policies. Policies with no added settings create unnecessary processing.

For more information on Citrix policies, and a detailed analysis of the policy-planning and application process, please refer to http://blog.citrix24.com/xendesktop-policies-explained/.

Planning Active Directory policies

Like planning your Citrix Policies, you must also plan how and where your Active Directory GPOs will apply. This is done by assignment within the OUs, WMI filters, and inheritance of group policies. Active Directory group policies are stored with the domain controllers and managed using the **Group Policy Management Console**, which can be performed on the domain controllers or another server with the proper roles and features.

Understanding the role of Active Directory group policies

Every Active Directory environment has group policies. With Citrix deployments, there are some necessary settings that are not available through Citrix Policies. When this happens, these settings will need to be applied locally or through Group Policy. Obviously, the Group Policy application is preferred for its reusability and consistency.

Common Group Policy settings for Citrix environments

Each environment is different in standards and necessary settings, but some elements that are applied for Citrix environments are fairly common. This list is not comprehensive, but it should illustrate standard settings:

- **Computer configuration**:
    - Network / offline files / prevent use of offline files
    - System / Group Policy / loopback processing (merge)

- ° Windows components / Internet Explorer / Internet control panel / security page / site-to-zone assignments

- ° Windows components / remote desktop services / remote desktop session host / licensing / configure licensing information

- ° Windows components / remote desktop services / remote desktop session host / session time / define idle and disconnected session time out values

> Loopback processing can have a significant impact on the Group Policy processing, specifically, the speed of machine readiness and user logon processing. When using *Replace,* all GPO settings are replaced. When using *Merge,* all settings are combined, with the higher priority settings taking precedence. If you are experiencing issues with the logon speed or with policies that don't appear to apply properly, check your loopback settings.
>
> For more details on loopback processing, please refer to http://blogs.technet.com/b/askds/archive/2013/05/21/back-to-the-loopback-troubleshooting-group-policy-loopback-processing-part-2.aspx.

- **User configuration**:

    - ° Windows Settings / Folder redirection (if required)

    - ° Control Panel / Personalization / Disable screensaver

    - ° Microsoft Outlook / Account Settings / Exchange / Cached Exchange Mode / Disabled (optional)

    - ° Network / Offline Files / Prevent use and prohibit user configuration

    - ° Start menu and Taskbar / Add logoff to the Start menu and remove most links from the Start menu (optional)

    - ° System / User Profiles / Disable network directories synchronization

    - ° Windows Components / Internet Explorer / disable notifications and prevent wizard

     ° Windows Components / Windows Explorer / Hide drives

     ° Preferences / Windows Settings / Drive Maps (optional, preferred over logon scripts)

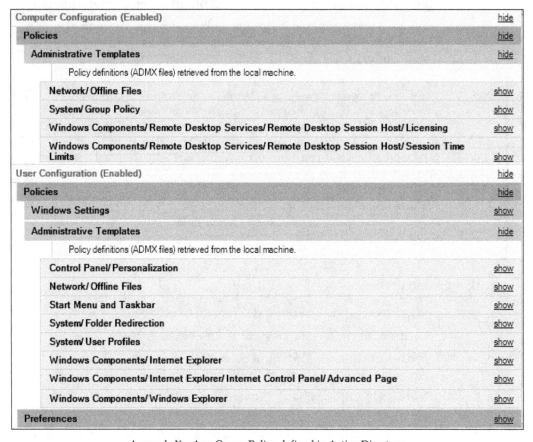

A sample XenApp Group Policy defined in Active Directory

Best practices for Group Policies

The best practices for managing your Group Policy objects are similar to the recommendations for Citrix policies. You want to create functional GPOs (defined for a specific function) as opposed to large monolithic GPOs that do everything. This will provide you with granularity as you apply GPOs. I generally prefer to filter GPOs only by OU assignment and not using WMI filters. Although WMI filters are valid for managing policies, it can cause some logon slowness if your environment is complex.

Another often overlooked element in GPOs is suppressing settings that are not configured. If a GPO does not have user settings defined, you can disable that section of the GPO, as shown in the following screenshot. This avoids unnecessary processing.

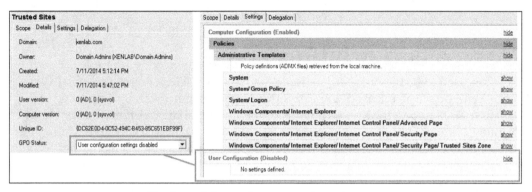

The Group Policy configuration in Active Directory

Finally, when designing a virtualization environment, I prefer to have a dedicated OU for all Citrix components with subOUs for each type of system. You might have an infrastructure container for all of the infrastructure components and a worker container for all of the session hosts. Or you might be more granular and have a container for controllers and a container for each desktop image. Either way, I prefer to block the inheritance at the top level OU for the environment. This ensures that the Citrix team can control which policies are enacted within the environment.

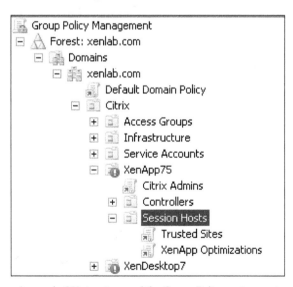

A sample OU structure and the Group Policy assignment

[For more information on Microsoft best practices and optimizing
the performance of group policies, please refer to `http://`
`support.microsoft.com/kb/315418` and `http://technet.`
`microsoft.com/en-us/magazine/2008.01.gpperf.aspx`.]

Controlling printing

Printing used to be the number one issue facing legacy Citrix environments. Ever
since XenApp 6 was released, the Citrix printing system has greatly improved.
This is mainly due to the improvements in the universal print driver and the client
printing system. However, managing printing is important in a Citrix environment.
All printing controls are available through the Citrix policy engine using the
Printing settings.

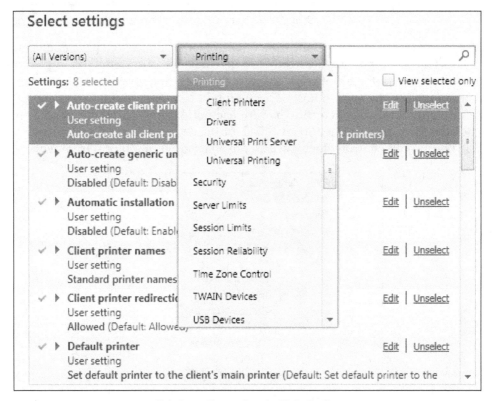

Printing policy settings in Citrix Studio

Understanding the different printing models in a Citrix environment

There are two main types of printers defined in Citrix: client printers and session-assigned printers.

- **Client printers**: These are most common type of printers in XenApp. These are printers attached to the client device; they can be restricted to the default printer only, locally attached printers only, or all printers. When printing to a client printer, if the native print driver is not available on the XenApp server, the universal print driver is used.

- **Session printers**: These are assigned to users and created for each user session through Citrix policy. These printers do not need to exist on the client device. Assigned printers are commonly used for proximity printing, where select client devices (defined by the name or IP) and/or select users require access to network printers. Using session printers requires the native driver be installed on the XenApp server.

Using Citrix Universal Print Server

Citrix Universal Print Server provides printing support for network printers using the same universal print driver used for client printing. This solution enables you to potentially use a single print driver in XenApp in order to manage all client and network printers. This is also helpful in remote printing scenarios, since Universal Print Server transfers the print jobs using an optimized and compressed format that saves on bandwidth and improves the user experience.

Universal Print Server has the following components:

- UPClient, which is the client component, runs on the XenApp servers. This is included in the VDA installation.

- UPServer, which is the server component, runs on the network print server(s). It is supported on Windows Server 2008 and Windows Server 2008 R2 systems.

To configure Universal Print Server, you can create network print queues based on the Citrix universal driver after installing the UPServer software. This enables Citrix VDA to map printers using only the universal driver. The communication is sent from VDA to the network print server using the universal driver. Once it is received on the print server, it is translated to the native driver and spooled to the network printer. For more information on configuring Citrix Universal Print Server, please refer to `http://support.citrix.com/proddocs/topic/xenapp-xendesktop-75/cds-print-univ-print-server.html`.

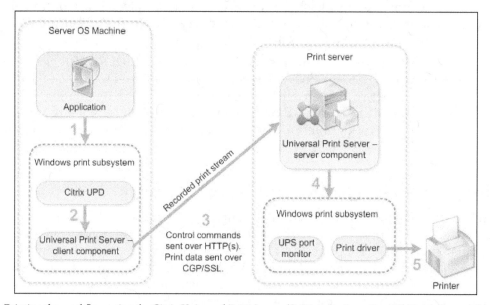

Printing the workflow using the Citrix Universal Print Server (© Citrix Systems, Inc. All Rights Reserved.)

For more information on managing printing in XenApp 7.5, please refer to `http://support.citrix.com/proddocs/topic/xenapp-xendesktop-75/cds-print-intro.html`.

Summary

In this chapter, we looked at optimizing our user experience through the use of profile management, Citrix policies, Active Directory policies, and printing. All of these components are critical to maximizing our user experience, and therefore, the perception of our Citrix Environment. Each of these elements, if configured incorrectly, will negatively impact performance, so it is important to understand the role they play and the steps that optimize our platform.

In the next chapter, we will look at finalizing the implementation of our XenApp solution. This will include building our user workload and fine-tuning our server images. Once we have done this, we can perform our scalability and user acceptance testing. Once all of these steps are completed, we will be ready for our final push to a successful production rollout, including client deployment and extended monitoring.

9

Implementing Your XenApp® Solution

In the previous chapters, we designed and built our XenApp environment to be able to deliver desktops and applications to our users. In this chapter, we will complete the build and deployment of our end user environment and roll out our new production system.

In this chapter, you will learn about:

- Building your production-ready workload server images
- Testing the preproduction environment
- Conducting user acceptance testing
- Planning and deploying your endpoint clients
- Supporting your environment during normal operations

Building your production-ready workload server images

In *Chapter 6, Designing Your Virtual Image Delivery*, we looked at how to capture and deploy server images from an infrastructure standpoint. Now, let's look at some of the guidelines on how to build and optimize a workload server image. These steps are simply recommendations; feel free to modify the processes as best fits your environment.

Initial build

The initial build is pretty straightforward:

1. Create a base virtual machine, complete with the necessary resources (CPU, RAM, network, and hard drive).

2. Install your target operating system, including all patches and updates.

3. Install the virtualization tools.

4. Connect to the domain.

5. Install the VDA software.

6. Save the base image using the following steps:

    ° If using Provisioning Services, install the PVS device software from the PVS media and complete the image capture

    ° If using Machine Creation Services, create a snapshot of the base image

    ° Saving the base image in this state will allow you to have a solid base, which you can use to copy to make alternate images for different use cases, if necessary

7. If using PVS:

    ° Create a target VM complete with Write Cache Drive

    ° Test streaming, in private mode, to the new target VM and format the new drive

    ° Once validated, convert/clone the target VM to a template and set the vDisk to standard mode

Optimizations

Once the base image is created, we can perform the following optimizations:

1. Perform the base operating system optimizations, including turning off unused features and services.

2. Run MSCONFIG to review the startup routines, disabling any items you do not need running in user sessions.

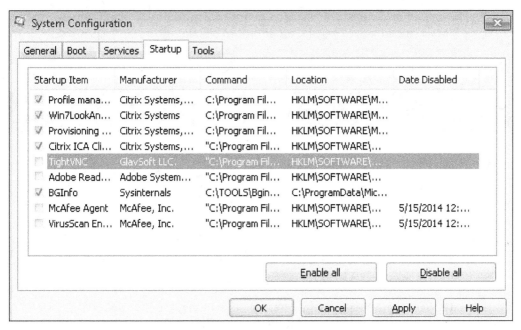

Startup routines displayed in MSCONFIG

3. Review the Citrix Optimization guidelines, and apply the necessary changes:

    °   *How to Optimize XenDesktop Machines*: `http://support.citrix.com/article/CTX125874`

    °   *XenApp Optimization Guide for Windows 2008 R2*: `http://support.citrix.com/article/CTX131577/`

    °   *XenDesktop Optimization Guide for Windows 7*: `http://support.citrix.com/servlet/KbServlet/download/25161-102-648285/XD - Windows 7 Optimization Guide.pdf`

    °   *Citrix Windows 8 and Server 2012 Optimization Guide*: `http://blogs.citrix.com/2014/02/06/windows-8-and-server-2012-optimization-guide/`

4. Download and run the VMware OS optimization tool. Even if you are not on a VMware platform, this is a great tool to check (and apply) optimizations in system and registry settings. The tool is available for free at `https://labs.vmware.com/flings/vmware-os-optimization-tool`.

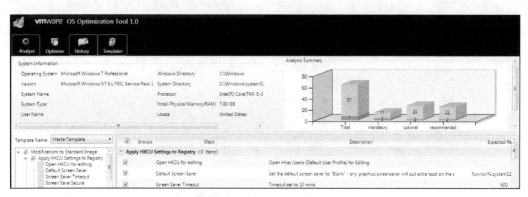

VMware OS optimization tool

Once the standard optimizations are complete, test to ensure the image is fully functional and that the changes you made have not caused any unintended consequences. After the optimized image is validated, I like to copy the image and/or take another snapshot. This provides a good rollback point and a potential starting point for later images, if necessary.

Deploying your server images

Depending on your use cases, you might need multiple images deployed. In our scenario, we deploy two images. Our primary image is a corporate desktop, where users will connect to the shared desktop and run applications locally or remotely. We will have a secondary image used for applications only, hosting specialty line-of-business apps that will not be installed on the primary image. In your environment, you might have just a single image, or you might need different images for different business groups.

If we create two unique images, we will follow this process for *each* image:

1. Make a copy of the Master Golden Image, naming it accordingly.
2. Install the necessary applications for this use case on the duplicate image.
3. Apply the required additional customizations for this use case on the duplicate image.
4. Test and validate functionality.
5. Deploy the image (as defined in *Chapter 6, Designing Your Virtual Image Delivery*) and begin user acceptance testing.
6. Repeat the process for each use case or the new image required.

Testing the preproduction environment

Performance testing the environment is critical before users begin accessing the systems. You can use this time to validate functionality as well as capacity, scalability, and performance of the systems. This gives you the chance to identify and resolve all potential errors or bottlenecks in the design. It is much better for you to find the flaws than for the users to discover them inadvertently.

Reviewing the design plan

Earlier, in *Chapter 3, Designing Your Infrastructure*, we laid out our general architecture plan and resource requirements. Of course, this was a paper exercise based on numerous assumptions. Now that everything is built, we can test and validate the assumptions. Should actual performance vary from our predictions — and it usually will — we can revise the baselines.

We should also take time to review our **reference architecture** against our final as-built architecture. Ideally, this should be the same. However, variations do occur occasionally. Sometimes, our assumptions do not always stay the same, versions change, or other constraints are identified.

Since the reference architecture is a high-level diagram, it might be useful to create a detailed build diagram, such as the one shown in the following figure. During our design phase, we identified the need for storage, but perhaps, we did not have the actual storage volume or **LUNs** (**logical unit numbers**) defined at the time. Now, we can fill in the blanks of design specifics that might have been missing in our earlier diagrams.

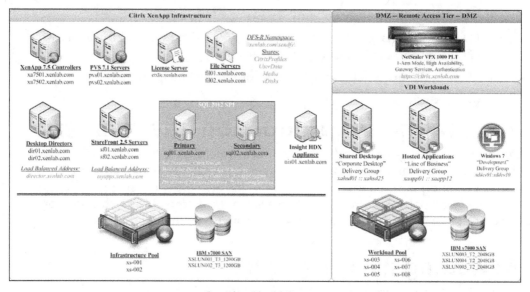

Completed build diagram

Final system validation testing

Once all components are built, functional testing should be performed. This can be done as each component is completed or once all components are finished. This validation should be a functional testing (does the system work as planned) as well as a fault tolerant testing (does the High Availability plan work as designed).

I like to perform much of the validation testing as part of the build process; however, many of these tests also validate interaction between components (for example, database failover testing impacts provisioning services). If you have a self-contained environment, one simple way to test functionality is to shut down all failover partners (such as controller 2, SQL 2, StoreFront 2, and so forth), and then verify that the overall environment is still operational. If the test passes, reverse the test by powering on the failover partners, shutting down the primary systems, and retesting. You might also want to do a hard stop of some of the virtualization hosts to simulate a hardware failure to ensure recovery and continuing operations.

For more information, visit `http://paultechnologies.com/citrix-xenapp-7-5-desktop-virtualization-solutions/validation-testing/`.

Using capacity planning tools

After all of the build activities are completed, but before production begins, capacity planning should be reviewed and confirmed. This testing will create baselines that should be reevaluated daily during the initial go-live phase and periodically once the environment is fully in production usage.

In *Chapter 3, Designing Your Infrastructure*, we based our design on several assumptions. Now that all of the infrastructure and workloads are built, we can reevaluate our design assumptions. To enable this, we have several tools at our disposal:

- **Lakeside Software's SysTrack**, which we discussed in *Chapter 2, Defining Your Desktop Virtualization Environment*, has a feature called **Virtual Machine Planner** (**VMP**). VMP takes the analysis data collected in SysTrack and estimates the necessary resources to support the calculated requirements. In the VMP console, you can specify your virtual machine and host hardware specifications to generate the report.

- The **Liquidware Labs' Stratusphere FIT** product, also discussed in *Chapter 2, Defining Your Desktop Virtualization Environment*, has capacity planning features. Using the collected analysis data in the Stratusphere database, you can estimate the necessary resource requirements to support your design.

- The **VMTurbo's Operations Manager** product includes capacity planning and management, available at `http://vmturbo.com/solutions/use-cases/capacity-planning-management/`, and it can be used to analyze the entire environment (hardware, network, storage, and virtualization layers) to predict capacity and growth modelling.

- **VDI calculator** by Andre Leibovici, available at `http://myvirtualcloud.net/?page_id=1076`, is a Java-based applet used to estimate and calculate capacity and requirements to support your VDI platform.

Performing load testing

When it comes to virtualization solutions, capacity is only part of the equation. Capacity can be useful to help us size the environment accordingly, avoid bottlenecks, and plan for growth. The other aspect is performance. Unfortunately, we never truly know how a system is going to function until we get actual users on board. Luckily, we can conduct load testing to estimate performance and identify any issue before we begin production.

Our monitoring tools and capacity planning tools can help identify bottlenecks. We can also use load testing tools to create artificial, or synthetic, workloads. This is useful to help simulate 500 users at once, using staggered logins, to ensure our environment can meet the anticipated demand.

Load testing typically leverages scripted actions to be repeated over and over again. You can utilize different scripts to simulate different workloads and apply various criteria to simulate production. The following tools are available for load testing; these are not the only ones, but they are the most common ones I have seen in use:

- **LoadRunner**, from HP; available at `http://www8.hp.com/us/en/software-solutions/loadrunner-load-testing`, is designed for application load testing. With LoadRunner, you can record a sample Citrix Session, which captures commands. LoadRunner can then play back these commands hundreds of times to generate an artificial load. The LoadRunner console can then report the performance metrics of the associated loads.

- **Login VSI**, available at `http://www.loginvsi.com/`, is the industry leader for performance and load testing. The Login VSI tools are used in many white papers, including the Virtual Reality Check series available at `http://www.projectvrc.com/`. Login VSI can create and evaluate loads for Citrix products, report on performance, scalability, and bottlenecks, and establish benchmarks for future testing.

- **EdgeSight for Load Testing** (**ESLT**), from Citrix, officially reached end of life on December 31, 2013. Though this product is at the end of its life cycle, it is still widely used in many Citrix environments. Similar to the other load testing products, you can record an ICA session, customize the automation script, and then playback the session. You can define how many sessions you want to run and how frequently the logins occur, allowing you to pace or overload your system as necessary. Documentation for ESLT is available at `http://support.citrix.com/proddocs/topic/edgesight-loadtest-38/es-loadtest38-landing-page.html`.

When using load testing, you cannot anticipate every user action or combination of actions. For this reason, the results should be taken with a grain of salt. Understand that synthetic transactions are merely another tool, which should not be a replacement for actual user testing.

For additional Citrix approved load testing and/or capacity planning utilities, check out `http://www.citrix.com/ready`.

Conducting User Acceptance Testing

User Acceptance Testing (UAT) is the process of having target users test and validate your XenApp solution. This is to ensure that you are meeting all of their business needs and objectives. The outcome of UAT is to ensure you can support day-to-day business operations.

Defining your criteria

Clearly defining the acceptance criteria is necessary when performing UAT. This allows you to ensure the environment meets design requirements and user expectations. If your business requirements specify a login time of 30 seconds or less, you can monitor and validate whether the test users' performances meet the requirement. Other common criteria include smooth roaming between devices, connection speed, profile and personalization settings being saved, application transaction times, and graphical quality. Some criteria might be measurable, other criteria might be subjective. Even subjective criteria should be measured through the feedback process.

UAT process

The first part of the UAT process is identifying the users for testing. Test users might be identified during use case development (*Chapter 2*, *Defining Your Desktop Virtualization Environment*) or later during the build phase. These users should be a cross-section of your typical users; some will be standard users while others might be power users. Regardless of the user types or how/when they are identified, you need to make sure these are users who will actively test the new system and provide detailed feedback.

Once you have identified the users for testing, you will need to allocate them rights in the new system. For XenApp, this includes adding them to a security group, which is in turn assigned to Delivery Group. You might use existing security groups for this, or make specialty groups only for the testing phase.

After users are assigned rights, you will want to spend some time with them, instructing them on the new system. This includes basic elements such as what website to use for login and how to launch applications. You will also want to set baseline expectations, including the performance to expect, how profiles will work, and so on. This might be as simple as a one-page primer that instructs users on the website to use, the fact that the first login might take 60 seconds and future logins should take 20 seconds, which applications are available, and how/where documents and settings are saved. I find explaining expectations up front greatly eases the transition to the new environment.

During the early part of UAT, you will want to actively monitor usage and user performance to ensure it meets your expectations. This should include the use of Director as well as in-person monitoring or shadowing, where possible.

UAT feedback

Soliciting feedback is critical to UAT. It is not good enough to have an open door policy where users can provide feedback; you must actively seek the feedback. During UAT periods, whether you are testing a single use case or an entire environment, you should conduct regular meetings. Feedback can also be solicited through surveys and online feedback forms, but nothing beats speaking with the users themselves. User feedback meetings tend to work best in a round-robin format, where each user can discuss whether they have been using the system, what they perceive the performance to be, and if there are any issues that need to be addressed. These issues might be software functionality, policy-based, the need for additional software or configuration, or overall performance.

This feedback is critical to success. In most cases, the team building the Citrix environment is not generally the consumer of the same environment. We build the Citrix platform to support the business units; only those business units will really be able to tell us whether everything is working properly. In the end, it is all about the applications, business processes, and user experience.

As part of the feedback process, there should be a formal acceptance or approval agreement. This will generally be from the business unit manager or the technical liaison defined for the various use cases. This ensures you have met all of their requirements and have the green light to begin production rollout. This acceptance might also be part of a services agreement when using an outside consultant or hosted solutions.

Production rollout

Once UAT is complete, you can commence with your rollout plan. UAT might lead to changes and modifications, and it is typically the final phase of testing and validation. This is in line with what we discussed about managing your project in *Chapter 1, Planning Desktop Virtualization*. These modifications are critical as they help identify and resolve potential issues before the full implementation occurs. Once validation is finalized, you are ready to deploy.

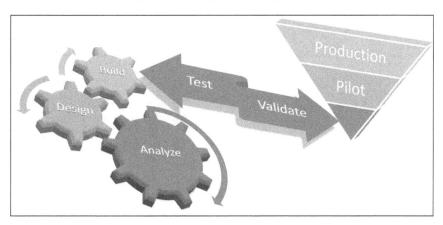

Project methodology

Communication plan

As previously mentioned, a communication plan is critical to success. This communication ensures the user population knows what to expect, what they need to do, when the changes occur, and who to contact with problems. This will ease their anxiety and help smooth any transition. This communication should include the following elements:

- **About the project**: What is being built, and the business drivers and benefits behind it

- **What is going to happen**: Provide dates for when the project/site/business unit is going live

- **What will be different**: Changes the users can expect from their current state to the new environment

- **What the users need to do**: Things such as installing a client, going to a website, validating access, and so on

- **How to get help**: Links to frequently asked questions and the help desk e-mail or ticketing system

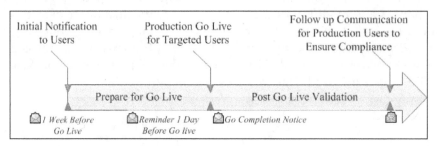

Sample communication plan timeline

Pilot rollout

Defining a pilot phase is very similar to selecting a population for use case development: select as many as necessary but not too many. In most environments, the Pilot deployment targets 500 users or 10 percent of the user population, whichever is less. This should provide an ample size of early adopters. You might want to selectively target users who are willing to assist and promote the initiative. This will provide good will and help in the overall adoption of the environment. These early adopters can be used to help in the training and support of additional users within their business units as well.

In some smaller environments, Pilot and UAT are the same process. In other environments, UAT is part of the development life cycle, and Pilot is part of the production life cycle. If you treat Pilot separately from UAT, you should adhere to a similar feedback solicitation plan.

The Pilot phase should not take longer than 1 month for a small environment, and it should not take longer than 3 months for a large environment. It should be long enough to identify and resolve any problem and gain a broad acceptance that the environment is production-ready.

The Pilot phase is also an ideal time to validate your capacity planning and performance under load. Since a Pilot program is based on only a fraction of users, this may require generating artificial loads or reducing the total capacity to simulate a full load (such as shutting down all but one or two virtualization hosts and limiting the number of available XenApp virtual machines). This will provide you with a controlled environment to confirm any design assumptions or identify any bottlenecks within the infrastructure. It will allow you to gauge the performance under load.

I have found that in the early rollout phase it's often a good idea to artificially load your production servers to simulate a full load. This will allow you to see if your capacity estimates are correct, and give some early warning of any potential bottlenecks which may crop up at full workload. It will also set user expectations as you won't end up with early adopters getting "a server to themselves" and get blisteringly fast performance which is not sustainable once all users get deployed.

– Neil Spellings, Citrix Infrastructure Architect/Owner, XenCentric

Phased production rollout

A phased rollout is ideal as it allows you to closely monitor performance and capacity. If any issues or problems arise, they will generally manifest during the earlier phases and not impact the larger part of a population. The actual number of phases in a deployment will vary for each project. A phase might be indicative of a business unit, a location, an application set, or simply a segment of your user population. The important takeaway is that you want to ramp up to full production over time, not all at once. The more variables you can control, the higher the likelihood of success.

Each phase of rollout should include a communication plan and close monitoring to ensure that you are not overloading your infrastructure and that your user experience is a positive one. When each phase deploys, you should review your target baselines to make sure all scalability assumptions are valid. You might find that the scale is not linear; so, as more users access the systems, the density might change.

In the following figure, we have a sample phased rollout for 1,000 users, based on the following guidelines:

- Pilot: 100 users (this 10 percent population will also serve as our UAT audience)
- Phase 1: 100 users, keeping growth limited to an additional 10 percent
- Phase 2: 200 users, doubling our current workload
- Phase 3: 300 users, scaling up to 700 total users
- Phase 4: 300 users, representing a full production workload

Of course, your phased deployment plan should be more precise and focused on your specific environment.

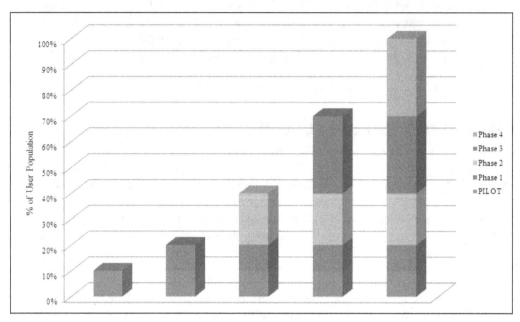

Phased production rollout approach

Supporting your environment during normal operations

As previously mentioned, you need to actively monitor your environment during the validation, user acceptance testing, and rollout phases. Of course, monitoring does not end once production rollout is complete. Day-to-day monitoring and reporting is a critical function of any Citrix environment.

Delegated administration

Delegated administration allows you to provide role-based access to users and groups within your organization. Ideally, all security should be applied to groups as opposed to individual accounts. However, you may find it necessary to add individuals for select purposes.

Delegated administration is most commonly used to differentiate between a full administrator role and a help desk role. Delegation can also be used to create administrators for select Delivery Groups only, or with restricted rights to only certain functions.

Administrators are defined under **Configuration** in Citrix Studio. Typically, you will have your Citrix administration team in a group (in our case, **XENLAB\ CTXADMIN**) as well as a Help Desk Group (**XENLAB\CitrixHelpDesk**). You might also find the need for read-only administrators for users who need access to view, but not change, settings such as auditors or outside consultants.

XenApp site delegated administrators, as shown in Citrix Studio

The following are three components to delegate administration within Citrix Studio:

- **Administrators**: Users and groups have access
- **Roles**: Roles (collections of rights) the users are assigned
- **Scopes**: Where the rights apply

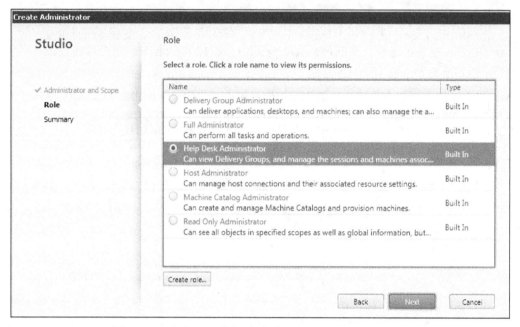

Selecting a role for new delegated administrators in Citrix Studio

The following roles are predefined within Citrix Studio:

- **Delivery Group Administrator**: This manages all aspects of a Delivery Group, including machines, desktops, applications, policies, and associated sessions.
- **Full Administrator**: This can perform all tasks and operations without restriction.
- **Help Desk Administrator**: This views Delivery Groups, Machine Catalogs, and Host Information. It can also manage sessions and view performance data for associated Delivery Groups.
- **Host Administrator**: This manages host connections and resources and has no rights to machines, applications, desktops, or user sessions.

- **Machine Catalog Administrator**: This creates and manages Machine Catalogs and provisions new machines into existing catalogs. It can leverage host connections, Machine Creation Services, and Provisioning Services. It can manage base images, but cannot assign users.

- **Read Only Administrator**: This only reads rights to all global information and specified scopes, but cannot make any changes.

The predefined roles encompass most activities. However, customized roles can be created for more granular access control. Perhaps you want to have a help desk member that also has rights to add users to published applications; in this case, you can define a custom role.

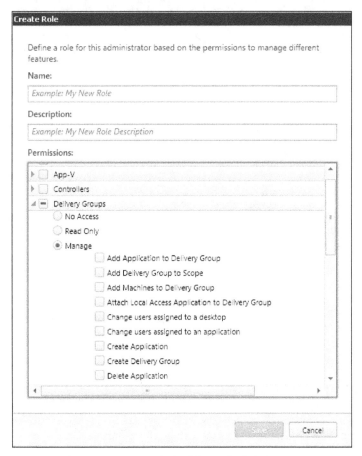

Creating a custom role for delegated administrators

The only predefined scope is **All**, which encompasses all of the XenApp site elements. In smaller environments, this might be sufficient to define administrators. In larger environments, or organizations that require more detailed control, you can create custom scope definitions. These custom scopes are generally filtered by Delivery Groups, but they might also be filtered by Machine Catalogs and hosting connections. Typically, they are used to delegate administration to members of other departments to manage their own Delivery Groups or catalogs, when necessary. So, Jane Smith, a senior software developer, might need to manage only the legacy applications since she is in charge of their development and maintenance. In this case, we can create a custom scope just for the legacy apps Delivery Group.

Creating a custom scope for delegated administrators

For more information on delegated administration, check out `http://support.citrix.com/proddocs/topic/xenapp-xendesktop-75/cds-manage-delegatedadmin-intro.html`.

Using Director

In *Chapter 7, Designing Your Supporting Infrastructure Components*, we looked at using Director as part of our monitoring solution. Director can help make sense of current performance and environment health on the **Dashboard** view. For our purposes of monitoring during the testing and go-live phases, however, the **Trends** view provides the context we want to examine.

The following trend reports are available:

- **Sessions**: View the concurrent session counts and analyze use patterns

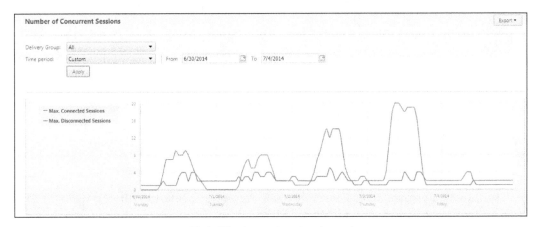

Citrix Director sessions trend report

- **Connection Failures**: View any connection failure in the environment, filtered by **Delivery Group**, **Machine Type**, and/or **Failure Type**; hover on data points for more details

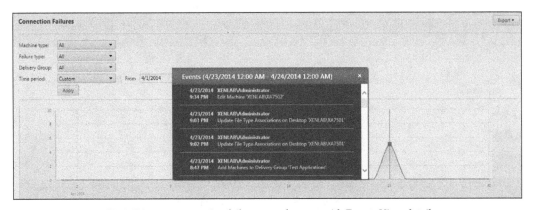

Citrix Director connection failures trend report with Events View detail

- **Failed Desktop OS Machines**: View any machine failures in the environment, filtered by **Delivery Group** and/or **Failure Type**; hover on data points for more details

- **Failed Server OS Machines**: View all machine failures in the environment, filtered by **Delivery Group** and/or **Failure Type**; hover on data points for more details

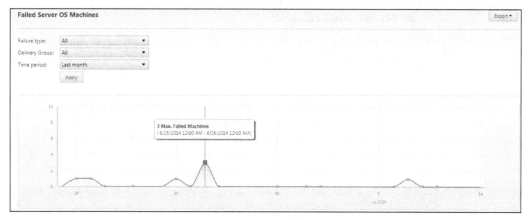

Citrix Director Failed Server OS machines trend report with highlighted details

- **Logon Performance**: This is the user logon performance, filtered by **Delivery Group** and **Time period**; details include a breakdown of the logon component time (see the *Concurrent usage report from Director* and the *Logon performance report from Director* screenshots in *Chapter 7, Designing Your Supporting Infrastructure Components*, for more details)

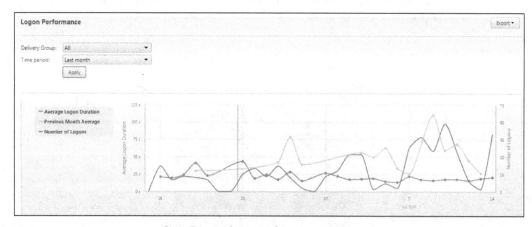

Citrix Director logon performance trend report

- **Load Evaluator Index**: Shows load distribution performance and number of sessions, filtered by **Delivery Group**, **Server OS machine**, and **Time period**
- **Network**: This is only available when used with HDX Insight Appliance; you can filter your view by user, application, or desktop for a detailed look at the ICA traffic

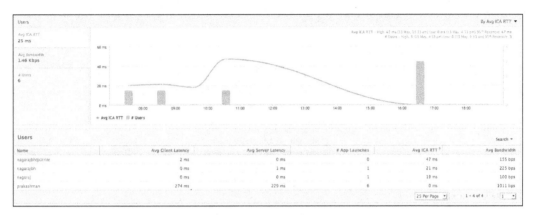

Citrix Director network user trend report

All of the trend reports allow various filters, specific to the report, as well as date filters. Time period filters are preset for the past day, week, month, and year, or a custom (user-defined) range. Hovering over data points in any graph will show the data point's detailed information. Clicking on a data point will open an events window, showing recorded events from the monitoring database (as shown in the *Citrix Director Connection Failures trend report with Events View detail* screenshot.)

The data in the reports can also be exported using the **Export** button. You can choose to export the graph in PDF format, or export the graph data in CSV format. This allows you to share the graphs or further analyze the data outside of Director.

For more information on trend reports in Director, check out `http://support.citrix.com/proddocs/topic/xenapp-xendesktop-75/cds-use-view-historical-trends-site.html`. You can also create custom reports for Director using the steps outlined in `http://blogs.citrix.com/2014/01/14/creating-director-custom-reports-for-monitoring-xendesktop/`.

SQL queries for monitoring/reporting

As discussed in *Chapter 7*, *Designing Your Supporting Infrastructure Components*, we separated the Monitoring database from the Site database. All monitoring data is stored in this database.

The following screenshot shows the basic tables available in the Monitoring database. A full database schema is available at `http://blogs.citrix.com/2013/08/27/xendesktop-7-monitor-service-what-data-is-available/monitordataschema/`.

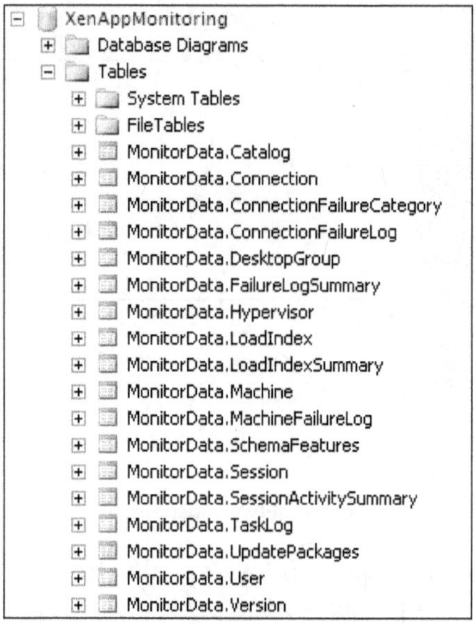

Citrix Monitoring database tables

If you want to find someone's logon activity, you can use the following SQL query statements. These are written in SQL Management Studio, but any query utility will work. First, find their User ID value from the `user` table. You can search by `UserName`, UPN, or Full Name, if necessary:

```
Select id, UserName from [MonitorData].[user]
where UserName = 'jane.smith'
```

Once you have the user ID value, you can search the `Session` table. Assuming the user ID value was 2, we can use the following query:

```
select UserID, StartDate, MachineID from [MonitorData].[Session]
where userID = 2
order by StartDate DESC
```

This will return a list of machine connections ordered by the most recent start date. This will tell us how often a user connects, ordered by their most recent connection time, and where they are connecting. This is useful to find out whether a target user is actually using the system.

Using the `MachineID` form from the previous query, we can look up the actual server name from the `Machine` table:

```
select DnsName from [MonitorData].[Machine]
where ID = 'ECC5B1A7-E884-4ACF-91DF-664A0E3B3FF8'
```

Of course, we can also combine all of these elements together into one consolidated lookup, using `join` statements, as shown:

```
Select [MonitorData].[user].UserName as 'User',
[MonitorData].[Session].StartDate as 'Login Time',
[MonitorData].[Machine].DnsName as 'Server Name'
from [MonitorData].[Session]
join [MonitorData].[user]
on [MonitorData].[user].ID = [MonitorData].[Session].UserID
join [MonitorData].[Machine]
on [MonitorData].[Session].Machineid = [MonitorData].[Machine].ID
Where [MonitorData].[user].UserName = 'jane.smith'
Order by [MonitorData].[Session].StartDate DESC
```

This will yield results similar to what is shown in the following screenshot:

SQL Management Studio query and results to find user sessions

Additional troubleshooting tips and tricks

The following items are common troubleshooting tips and tricks you might need to use when managing your XenApp 7.5 sites. These might come in handy during your rollout as well as normal operations.

Troubleshooting the VDA registration

Inside Citrix Studio, you can view the registration status of your VDAs. Servers (or desktops) showing as **registered** indicate they have checked in and are ready to receive connections. Items showing as **unregistered** will be unavailable for user connections.

Sometimes, it can be frustrating when servers seem to randomly report as unregistered. When this happens, I like to modify my display columns so that I can see *why* they are unregistered. In the following screenshot, you can see where we clicked on **Select Columns** and added **Last Deregistration Reason**. We can add **Last Deregistration Time** as well, which I might do if there is a widespread problem, so I can understand when the issues occurred.

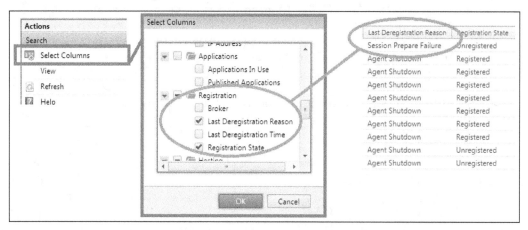

Adding display columns in Citrix Studio used for troubleshooting registration states

In this instance, we can see the server in question has an error noted as **Session Prepare Failure**. To view the various fault codes, refer to `http://support.citrix.com/article/CTX137378`. For a detailed VDA registration troubleshooting flowchart, refer to `http://support.citrix.com/article/CTX136668`.

Troubleshooting Active Directory

Within Active Directory, you need to verify that your OU structure is correct. This includes ensuring the proper OU permissions are granted for PVS machine account management. You also need to verify that all policies are successfully applied, and all policies that should be blocked are properly blocked. As previously mentioned, you will also need to monitor the impact of group policies on the login speed.

Other elements of Active Directory, which can cause issues, are making sure DNS names are being updated and DHCP addresses are being assigned and released as planned. If you have issues with Active Directory replication or latency, you need to verify that the Active Directory sites are properly defined and your servers are assigned to the correct site.

Troubleshooting PVS performance

When deploying Provisioning Services, you can configure each PVS server to write events to the Windows event log instead of a text-based logfile. This greatly eases troubleshooting when validating PVS functionality as well as when tracking down potential issues.

All the PVS events will be marked in **Application Event Log** with the **StreamProcess** source. Some of the import events are listed as follows:

- **Information: Login initiated for device [TargetDeviceName]**: This indicates a target device is requesting a vDisk. This is indicative that PXE is functioning properly.

- **Information: Device [TargetDeviceName] moved to [IP Address:Port Number] for IO**: This indicates a device has been found in the database, and the streaming process is being directed to the PVS server and port listed. This is indicative of a successful connection and proper load balancing.

- **Information: Service granted for device [TargetDeviceName], [TargetIP Address:StreamingPort]**: This indicates that a target device is successfully streaming the assigned vDisk and is using the assigned port from the port range. This is indicative of a successful stream process.

- **Information: Device [TargetDeviceName] boot time: X minutes XX seconds**: This indicates the total boot time for the target device. It represents the completion of the boot process and when the delivered operating system is ready for the user.

- **Error: Unable to contact Citrix license server [License Server Name]**: This indicates whether the license server is unavailable or unreachable. When this happens, the system will enter a grace period. This might occur on a PVS server reboot and is not an issue, unless it remains in the grace period for a prolonged state.

- **Warning: Currently in grace period, PVS has 720 hour(s) remaining**: This indicates the PVS server operates in a grace period and how much time remains before operations stop.

- **Information: Successfully contacted Citrix license server [License Server Name]**: This indicates licenses were properly acquired.

- **Error: AcquireLock failed for vdisk id = 3, device id = 1, status = -32745 <VdiskHasExclusiveLock>**: This indicates why a vDisk stream failed; in this case, it was due to an exclusive lock.

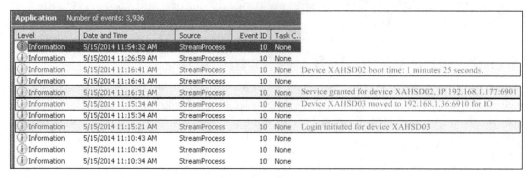

PVS events in Application Event Log

Within the PVS console, you can monitor the usage of the vDisks. This includes which target devices are connected and to which version of the vDisks. The vDisk usage screen also includes the number of retries. An excessive number of retries might indicate networking issues. You can monitor the packet retransmit rates on the network switches. Since PVS relies on the overall health of the network, it is important to monitor these elements for potential issues.

Troubleshooting storage performance

When troubleshooting potential storage issues, you will want to look at the switch fabric and storage controllers to monitor bandwidth utilization and latency. High levels of latency (generally more than 10 ms) can be indicative of potential bottlenecks or problems. With storage, you also want to keep an eye on your amount of data allocation compared to the amount of data space consumed (especially when using thin-provisioned storage).

As mentioned in *Chapter 3, Defining Your Infrastructure*, you can use IOMeter to provide reports on IOPS per system, which can be used to help identify throughput bottlenecks on the defined storage. This can help answer the question, "Is the storage performing as planned?"

Troubleshooting Windows system performance

Monitoring the overall health and performance of the Windows servers used for XenApp connections can be another daunting task. Luckily, there are some ready-to-use toolsets available to ease this process.

uberAgent, developed by Helge Klein (`http://helgeklein.com/uberagent-for-splunk/`), is a **Splunk** (`http://www.splunk.com/`) add-in. uberAgent does not rely on Windows performance counters, so it can provide an independent view of system performance. uberAgent can monitor and report on process startup, system boot performance, logon durations, application performance, and general user experience. Splunk is available for onsite enterprise or cloud-hosted deployments. Splunk also offers a free sandbox edition for testing and development, which you can use to analyze your environment even if you are not a current customer.

Sample uberAgent report

Windows Performance Toolkit (WPT) can be used to monitor system activity and performance, including CPU usage, disk activity, file activity, networking activity, memory usage, and audio/video quality. The toolkit includes two utilities: Windows Performance Recorder to collect data and Windows Performance Analyzer to graphically analyze and parse the collected data. For more detailed information on using WPT to analyze your environment, check out `http://blogs.technet.com/b/yongrhee/archive/2012/11/23/wpr-xperf-capture-high-cpu-disk-i-o-file-registry-networking-private-bytes-virtual-bytes-paged-pool-nonpaged-pool-and-or-application-slowness.aspx`.

Troubleshooting application performance

The SysInternal tools are great utilities to monitor application and server performances. These tools can help track down application access issues, conflicts, and memory leaks. All of these tools, and more, are available at http://technet.microsoft.com/en-us/sysinternals/bb795533.

Process Explorer (ProcExp) is a graphical utility used to identify what files, registry keys, and other object processes have open, which DLLs they have loaded, and more. You can filter select processes as well, narrowing the focus to determine what a program is accessing and how it impacts your system.

Monitoring performance using SysInternal's Process Explorer

Process Monitor (ProcMon) is used to monitor filesystem, registry, process, thread, and DLL activity in real time. This can be used to show elements in use by an application or process and is useful for troubleshooting.

System Monitor (SysMon) is used to monitor and log system activity to the Windows event log. It provides detailed information about process creations, network connections, and changes to file creation time. This can be used to detect malicious activity as well as to monitor process utilization via event logs.

Using Citrix troubleshooting tools

XenApp 7.5 includes a utility called Scout. This utility can be used to create **Citrix Diagnostic Facility (CDF)** traces as well as collect any available logs from the XenApp environment. Running Scout, you can select from which servers you wish to collect data. Scout will collect data from the following elements:

- Hardware
- Software
- Registry
- Event logs
- Site settings
- Database information
- Hypervisor status
- CDF traces
- VDA information
- Site logs

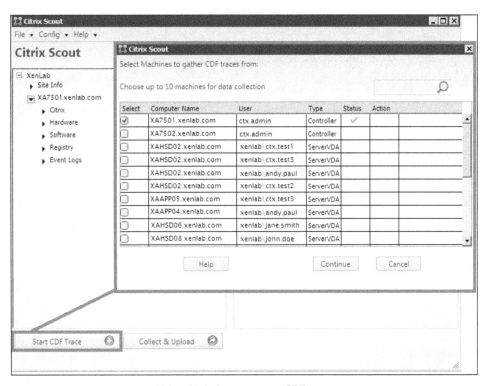

Using Citrix Scout to create CDF traces

All CDF traces and collected reports are saved as a ZIP file. These can be automatically uploaded to the AutoSupport site, or they can be saved and manually uploaded later. You can connect to `https://taas.citrix.com/AutoSupport/` to either upload your ZIP files generated by Scout or to review previous cases. You need a valid MyCitrix account, but you do not need an existing support case. Once your files are uploaded, they will automatically be analyzed by Citrix's automated support services. You can view the analysis results as well as any recommendations or health check concerns.

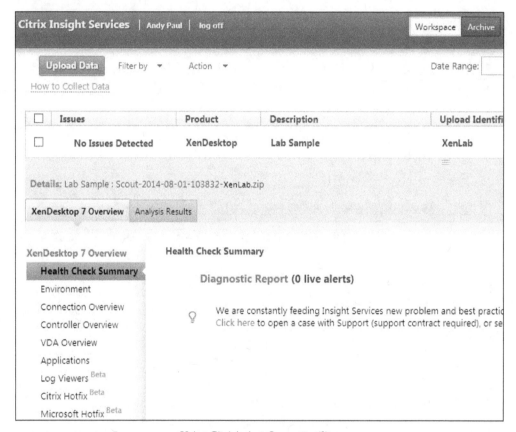

Using Citrix's AutoSupport utility

For more information on Scout, check out `http://support.citrix.com/article/ CTX130147`. For more information on CDF traces, check out `http://support. citrix.com/article/CTX111961`.

Soliciting user feedback

Finally, as part of managing your environment, you need to continue to solicit feedback from your users. We discussed this as part of user-acceptance testing and production rollouts. We also talked about the criticality of clear communication. This communication does not end once the environment is in full production. Being proactive in collecting user feedback can garner a good relationship with users and help detect issues and improvements.

Having an open forum meeting is not always feasible in a large production environment. However, there are several methods you can use to ensure you get the necessary feedback. The following are a few suggestions, but it is not a proscriptive listing:

- **Online surveys**: This can be an internal survey hosted on SharePoint or a web server, or it can be a private survey hosted on a service such as Survey Monkey (`http://www.surveymonkey.com`). Ideally, these surveys will rank user experience around components such as ease of use, functionality, performance, and so on. The results can then be compiled and reviewed to ensure you are meeting the customer needs.

- **Quarterly user forums**: These are open forums, either in person, online, or teleconference. The idea is to give users an open forum to express feedback, positive or negative. It is also a chance to explain any initiative or upcoming change for the environment.

- **Ongoing user training**: Something as simple as a monthly or quarterly lunch-and-learn training event or webinar can go a long way in educating the user population. This can be technically focused on how the environment works, it can be an overview of operations, or it can be a reminder of how to use some of the features and how to request help.

- **Ticketing system reviews**: Whatever system you use for help desk requests, whether it is a ticket-tracking system, a community mailbox, or just a whiteboard, you will want to review issues and complaints. Look for patterns or repeated problems that can be focused on, recreated, and resolved. Publishing resolutions to the users as well as a frequently asked questions listing, where appropriate, can ensure the fix is truly a fix.

- **Performance tracking reports**: Making performance and tracking reports, such as those from Director, readily available for all users, greatly helps in transparency. This can be combined into a regular (weekly, monthly, or quarterly) report as part of a greater communication plan.

Summary

In this chapter, we finalized our XenApp environment and put forth a plan to move from design to implementation and full production. We looked at building and optimizing our workload images that will host our user sessions. Then, we focused on finalizing our environment through validation testing and ensuring all components work as designed. This includes interoperability and high availability testing, reviewing capacity planning, and performance load testing.

Once everything is validated, and the Citrix design team believes the environment is production-ready, we can move forward with user acceptance testing. This process is the final step before we move into production. This ensures the target users approve of the application functionality and performance. Once this hurdle is passed, we move into finalizing a deployment plan.

As part of the production rollout, we discussed managing the endpoint devices and deploying Citrix Receiver. We also looked at tips and tricks to manage your environment during production rollout and normal operations. We looked deeper at delegated administration, trend reports, custom monitoring searches, and additional PowerShell commands for daily administration of applications.

Of course, deploying our XenApp virtualization solution is only one step. We still need to maintain, monitor, and revise as we go. Maintaining communication with the end users is critical to ensure we are meeting the business needs of our users.

Now that you have all the steps and decisions laid out, good luck!

Index

K

Keywords 168

L

Lakeside Software SysTrack
  about 47, 271
  benefits 47
  implementing 47
  URL 48
license server
  design decisions 213
  High Availability, considerations 212, 213
  planning 209
  requisites, for installing 211
  role 210
license server VPX appliance
  URL 211
linked clone technology 176
Liquidware Labs' Stratusphere FIT 271
load balancer, NetScaler Gateway
  configuring 105, 106
load balance virtual servers
  configuring, on NetScaler 111, 112
LoadRunner
  about 272
  URL 272
load testing
  performing 271, 273
local profile 234
Login VSI
  about 272
  URL 272
LOK 186
loopback processing
  about 257
  URL 257
LUNs (logical unit numbers) 270

M

Machine Catalog
  about 118, 151-156
  creating, with PVS deployment wizard 194-199
  machines, moving between catalogs 165

managing 163
  planning 163
Machine Catalog, options
  desktop OS and applications 151
  remote PC access machines 152
  server OS and applications 151
Machine Creation Services. See MCS
mandatory profile 234
master image
  about 176
  preparing, for MCS 178, 179
  preparing, for PVS 191-194
MCS
  about 153, 173-176
  catalog, creating with Citrix Studio 179-182
  catalog, updating 182-184
  master image, preparing for 178, 179
  references 176
  storage impact 177, 178
Microsoft Azure 68, 78
Microsoft DFS-R 220
Microsoft folder redirection
  AppData 245
  folder exclusion 245
  home drives 245
  planning 243, 244
Microsoft Hyper-V Server
  about 68, 72-74
  benefits 72, 73
  URL 72
Microsoft Key Management Service (KMS) server 211
Microsoft Remote Desktop Services (RDS) license server 211
monitoring
  design decisions 226
  Director, using 226-230
  High Availability, considerations for Director 226
  implementing 223
  requisites, for installing Director 224, 225
  requisites, for installing Insight Center 225
  role 223
Monitoring tier
  about 62
  diagrammatic representation 62

Thank you for buying
Citrix XenApp® 7.5 Desktop Virtualization Solutions

About Packt Publishing

Packt, pronounced 'packed', published its first book "*Mastering phpMyAdmin for Effective MySQL Management*" in April 2004 and subsequently continued to specialize in publishing highly focused books on specific technologies and solutions.

Our books and publications share the experiences of your fellow IT professionals in adapting and customizing today's systems, applications, and frameworks. Our solution based books give you the knowledge and power to customize the software and technologies you're using to get the job done. Packt books are more specific and less general than the IT books you have seen in the past. Our unique business model allows us to bring you more focused information, giving you more of what you need to know, and less of what you don't.

Packt is a modern, yet unique publishing company, which focuses on producing quality, cutting-edge books for communities of developers, administrators, and newbies alike. For more information, please visit our website: www.packtpub.com.

About Packt Enterprise

In 2010, Packt launched two new brands, Packt Enterprise and Packt Open Source, in order to continue its focus on specialization. This book is part of the Packt Enterprise brand, home to books published on enterprise software – software created by major vendors, including (but not limited to) IBM, Microsoft and Oracle, often for use in other corporations. Its titles will offer information relevant to a range of users of this software, including administrators, developers, architects, and end users.

Writing for Packt

We welcome all inquiries from people who are interested in authoring. Book proposals should be sent to author@packtpub.com. If your book idea is still at an early stage and you would like to discuss it first before writing a formal book proposal, contact us; one of our commissioning editors will get in touch with you.

We're not just looking for published authors; if you have strong technical skills but no writing experience, our experienced editors can help you develop a writing career, or simply get some additional reward for your expertise.

Getting Started with Citrix® CloudPortal™

ISBN: 978-1-78217-682-4   Paperback: 128 pages

Get acquainted with Citrix Systems®' CPSM and CPBM in order to administer cloud services smoothly and comprehensively

1. Overview of CPSM and CPBM architectures, and planning CPSM and CPBM.

2. Become efficient in product management, workflow management, and billing and pricing management.

3. Provision services efficiently to cloud consumers and clients.

Getting Started with Citrix® Provisioning Services 7.0

ISBN: 978-1-78217-670-1   Paperback: 134 pages

An example-packed guide to help you successfully administer Citrix® Provisioning Services

1. Install and configure Citrix Provisioning Services quickly and efficiently.

2. Master the architecture of Citrix Provisioning Services.

3. Successfully manage and operate Citrix Provisioning Services.

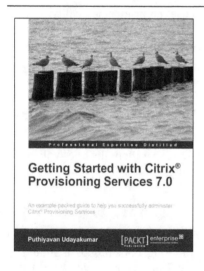

Please check **www.PacktPub.com** for information on our titles

Citrix® XenApp® 6.5 Expert Cookbook

ISBN: 978-1-84968-522-1   Paperback: 420 pages

Over 125 recipes that enable you to configure, administer, and troubleshoot a XenApp® infrastructure for effective application virtualization

1. Create installation scripts for Citrix XenApp, License Servers, Web Interface, and StoreFront.

2. Use PowerShell scripts to configure and administer the XenApp's infrastructure components.

3. Discover Citrix and community written tools to maintain a Citrix XenApp infrastructure.

Getting Started with Citrix VDI-in-a-Box

ISBN: 978-1-78217-104-1   Paperback: 86 pages

Design and deploy virtual desktops using Citrix VDI-in-a-Box

1. Design a Citrix VDI-in-a-Box solution.

2. Get the budget for Citrix VDI-in-a-Box by building a case.

3. Implement a Citrix VDI-in-a-Box proof of concept and Citrix VDI-in-a-Box solution.

www.ingramcontent.com/pod-product-compliance
Lightning Source LLC
LaVergne TN
LVHW062306060326
832902LV00013B/2069